THE
TEARDROP
ISLAND

THE TEARDROP ISLAND

Summersdale Publishers Ltd
46 West Street
Chichester
West Sussex
PO19 1RP
UK

www.summersdale.com

Printed and bound by CPI Group (UK) Ltd, Croydon, CR0 4YY

ISBN: 978-1-84953-414-7

Substantial discounts on bulk quantities of Summersdale books are available to corporations, professional associations and other organisations. For details contact Nicky Douglas by telephone: +44 (0) 1243 756902, fax: +44 (0) 1243 786300 or email: nicky@summersdale.com.

For my parents in England
For A.S. in Sri Lanka

THE TEARDROP ISLAND

FOLLOWING VICTORIAN FOOTSTEPS ACROSS SRI LANKA

CHERRY BRIGGS

summersdale

AUTHOR'S NOTE

In writing this book I hoped to give a faithful portrayal of Sri Lanka, based not only on my travels in the footsteps of Sir James Emerson Tennent, but also on my two years in Colombo. Whilst the descriptions of the journeys and places that follow are accurate and unembellished, a small number of the characters have had their identities and locations disguised to protect their privacy. Wherever I have taken creative liberties with the descriptions of these characters or deviated from strict non-fiction, I have tried to replace or merge any details with those of other people I met on the island, and the stories they were kind enough to share with me have remained unchanged.

SRI LANKA

CONTENTS

INTRODUCTION

As dawn was breaking on 29 November 1845, a British steamship landed at a fortified harbour town on the western coast of a teardrop-shaped island in the Indian Ocean. Standing on the deck in the early morning light, an Irish traveller looked out over the still waters of the bay towards the headland shaded by slender palm trees, gently inclining their crowns towards the sea. Inland, beyond the fortified town, lay a ridge of mauve hills and far in the distance towered the island's sacred peak, still shrouded by the morning clouds.

The traveller had been at sea for many weeks, whilst the leaves had turned to the colours of autumn and fallen from the trees in the country he had left far behind. The ship's slow passage through the latitudes of the ocean had allowed him to become gradually accustomed to the rhythm of the climate in the tropics: the clear, muted mornings, the oppressive humidity of the early afternoon that drained the life from even the most animated of the ship's passengers, and the close warmth of the evenings that hung like a haze, masked by the darkness and never quite cleared. The clothes that had been stitched by his tailor in Belfast had become uncomfortable and stifling, and he looked wistfully at the bare-backed fishermen, whose little vessels were darting between the large ships in the harbour. Their fishing boats were graceful canoes, built from two hollowed-out tree trunks, lashed together and balanced by a log of buoyant wood that floated alongside. The rising sun was chasing them back to the shore, their hulls full of slippery piles of fish with cold, metallic scales.

The ship landed at an old pier that jutted out into the bay and the traveller stepped into line behind the other passengers who were filing gingerly along the pier onto the land. The morning clouds had lifted and the sky above was hard and blue. Sweat began to trickle down his back and he took a handkerchief from his pocket to wipe away the salty drops that were collecting on his brow. A few Europeans who already lived on the island were hanging around the landing stage, wearing flimsy white cotton clothes and standing in the shade of Japanese umbrellas. Everything else that greeted his eyes was foreign. The local chiefs had come out to meet the ship, dressed in billowing trousers and heavily embroidered belts, fingering their ceremonial swords. A couple of Buddhist monks wrapped in coarse, yellow robes stood amongst traders from China and chetties from South India who wore headdresses and ornate earrings. They look like women, he thought, as he pushed his way through a group of local men who had neatly coiled up their long, black hair and fixed it to the tops of their heads with tortoiseshell combs. They also seemed to be wearing petticoats. He squatted down in the perfumed shade of a twisted tree, whose waxy leaves were studded with star-shaped white flowers, and began to undo the buttons of his tight boots.

The traveller had spent many hours in the dim light of his cabin, poring over descriptions of the small island in the leather-bound volumes he had been sold in London. It had attracted the attention of great men, from Ptolemy to Marco Polo – men whose names were remembered and words were revered years after their death. When he had been chosen to sail to the island at Her Majesty's pleasure, there were mutterings in London that he was not great enough, too inexperienced, not up to the job. His departure had left grey men in the corridors of Parliament shaking their heads and whispering hopefully of his failure.

Two naked children, their hair wavy and shining, joined him under the tree and began to fight playfully with each other on the dusty ground. The heat was exhausting. It's probably snowing in Belfast, he thought.

The island had been known, from ancient times, by many different names to a succession of invaders and explorers who had landed on its shores. In Sanskrit it was named Lanka by its large and often troublesome neighbour, India. Early visitors to the island discovered sapphires and rubies deposited in its hillsides and riverbeds, and named it Ratnadvipa or 'Island of Gems'. A recalcitrant Bengali prince, banished to the island with 700 followers, found a strange land ruled by a demon queen and named it Tambapanni, after the rich, red soil he encountered on its northern shores. The Sinhalese inhabitants of the island first spoke of their homeland in their mother tongue, by the name of Simhaladvipa, meaning 'Island of the Lion Race'. To the Tamils it was simply known as Eelam. Its Portuguese colonisers called it Ceilão, under the Dutch it was renamed Zeilan and on the clear November morning in 1845, after almost half a century of British colonial rule, the island was known as Ceylon.

To the outside world, Sri Lanka – the name the island finally chose for itself following independence from Britain – has two very different faces: a tropical paradise of palm-fringed beaches where European couples spend their honeymoons, and a tsunami-dashed warzone that was home to one of the most ruthless terrorist organisations of recent history. In 2010, a year after the civil war ended, I was trying to inspire teenage boys to take an interest in enzymes and photosynthesis in the gloomy laboratories of a boys' boarding school outside Oxford. I had cycled to the southern tip of India several years earlier and looked out across the Indian Ocean towards the small, war-torn island on a clear, December evening. I couldn't see it, but on the map it looked tantalisingly close, as if a fragment of the subcontinent had fallen away and not managed to drift very far. When a school in the island's capital needed a biology teacher, I decided to go.

I landed on the island on a humid afternoon, the air heavy with the tension of an impending deluge and warm winds whipping the palm trees. 'Our roads are very bad, madam,' said the taxi driver, as we crawled along the potholed road into the capital, breathing the exhaust fumes of a lopsided bus. 'You can't get decent wine or cheese here,' complained an expat who was desperate to leave. 'I hope you weren't expecting air conditioning,' said the school's headmaster.

I was already well travelled – or so I thought. I had drifted along the backwaters of Kerala, cycled along the Ho Chi Minh Trail, climbed up some volcanoes in Indonesia and shivered in the foothills of the Himalayas. I had travelled with Asian families, I had eaten Asian food, I had read Asian newspapers, cycled in Asian traffic and slept on Asian trains. Living in Sri Lanka should therefore have been an easy transition for me.

It was not.

Impatient by nature, I struggled with the slower pace of life. I couldn't suppress my sense of urgency; I wanted immediacy. My wonderful Sri Lankan students smiled good-naturedly as I perspired in front of the whiteboard and stumbled over their polysyllabic surnames. I was amazed by how often things could malfunction and couldn't comprehend the smiles and shrugs of my colleagues in reprographics when the photocopier juddered to a halt for the third time in the same week. 'What to do?' they said with cheery fatalism. They had a sense of perspective, I did not. But I didn't realise that until later.

Almost a year after I had arrived on the island I met Mr Fernando, an eccentric Sri Lankan Anglophile and one of my neighbours in Colombo. He could remember the last days of colonial rule, had run a tea plantation in the hill country and maintained an unwavering belief in the predictions of his horoscope. Although he was nearing his seventieth year, his hair was still thick and dark, and a small blue sapphire – a charm recommended by an astrologer for his protection – twinkled from centre of a gold ring on his little finger. He lived in a whitewashed colonial bungalow in the heart of the city, which he shared with an enormous collection of books that he had amassed over his lifetime. 'You must come and visit my library,' he said to me one afternoon, when I met him in the lane as he was inspecting the pink blooms of the hibiscus that tumbled over his front wall. 'As someone from Britain, you would find some of the colonial books in my collection particularly interesting.'

He led me between the cylindrical columns of the bungalow's terracotta-tiled veranda and into a dark room that was lined with bookcases and smelled of leather and damp. It was July, the month when the rains of the Yala monsoon drench the capital city, and the polished, concrete floor of the library was covered with white jasmine flowers that had blown through the shuttered windows during the afternoon's storm. An old, yellowing astrological chart that had been drawn up on the day of his birth was rolled up in a small wooden chest in the corner of a Victorian writing desk, behind which Mr Fernando gestured to me to take a seat; and he began to select from the shelves disintegrating books with embossed, leather covers, and pages that had crinkled and hardened from years in the tropical humidity.

The books were works about Sri Lanka written by a collection of British adventurers, soldiers, politicians and anthropologists, who had visited the island in previous centuries and recorded their impressions. They had travelled across the island on horseback, cutting paths through the unmapped jungle, with trails of porters and elephants carrying their loads. They counted and recorded the species of birds and insects, investigated the island's botany and geology, made sketches of the 'natives' in their traditional costumes, and tried to comprehend the local customs and beliefs.

An English sea captain named Robert Knox was shipwrecked off Sri Lanka in 1659 and held captive by the kings of the hill country for nineteen years. He made sketches of the island's tribesmen, discovered a city of women who took many husbands, and showed a curious interest in how the islanders dealt with the bodies of their dead. When he finally escaped with the help of the Dutch and returned to Britain, the account of his experiences that was published in London brought him widespread fame and became an inspiration for Daniel Defoe's *Robinson Crusoe*. William Skeen, an English adventurer, arrived in Ceylon in 1860 and wrote an account of the wet, miserable pilgrimage he made, fuelled by beer and brandy, to the shrine on the island's sacred mountain during the monsoon, during which he almost fell to his death. A businessman named Henry W. Cave established a printing firm in Colombo in 1876 and wrote about his journey deep into the jungle to the lost, ancient cities, as well as his travels around the island, chugging along the railways in the new British steam trains.

'If you are going to read any of them, it should really be this one,' said Mr Fernando, as he passed me two thick volumes embossed with gold lettering and spotted with damp.

The work was simply called *Ceylon* and was written by a newly knighted Irishman named Sir James Emerson Tennent, who had been sent to the island in 1845 by Her Majesty's Government as the colonial secretary in Ceylon. Although his name has since disappeared into obscurity, he was a well-known figure in Victorian Britain and his full-length portrait still hangs in Belfast City Hall. Tennent was something of a Renaissance man; he was a politician, an explorer, a writer and a renowned historian. He had a controversial career in

British politics, jumping from the Whigs to the Conservatives as a young man, and he went on to become the MP for Belfast for thirteen years. He was a passionate supporter of Greece's struggle for independence from the Ottoman Empire and travelled through the country during the Greek War of Independence, to research a book about the country's history and culture. He published a series of letters from a trip through the Aegean, wrote a book about Belgium, and travelled up the Nile and through the Holy Land. His writing was not just confined to travel and he seemed to produce books on any subject that took his fancy, from firearms to the taxation of wine. In London, as part of the Victorian intelligentsia, he mingled in erudite and literary circles with the likes of Robert Browning, Anthony Trollope and Michael Faraday. He was a close friend of Charles Dickens, with whom he spent many happy days travelling through Italy, discussing politics, and Dickens dedicated his final completed novel, *Our Mutual Friend*, to Tennent in 1865, a few years before his death.

Tennent lived on Ceylon for four years with the pet baby elephant he rescued from an elephant corral in the hill country. Like many of the Brits before him, he obsessively collected facts on any topics relating to the island, from the behaviour of the local crocodiles to the islanders' experiments with early lightning conductors. But unlike many of the other writers, who had simply catalogued the island, his book had an additional section – a personal narrative of the trips he had made to the four corners of the island. Like any good travel writer, he made his journeys as much of a focus as his destinations, and he had an eye for the unusual and absurd. He recorded the difficulties and frustrations of finding food and transport, the disasters of lost luggage and disappearing pathways, and gave candid impressions of the people and communities he encountered along the way. His route took him through the busy colonial cities, along the pilgrimage trails to the island's sacred monuments, deep into the unmapped jungle to its ruined cities, and over the scorching plains and lagoons to the islands of the arid north.

In the introduction to his enormous two-volume work, which numbered over 1,000 pages, Tennent explained in 1845:

> There is no island in the world, Great Britain itself not excepted, that has attracted the attention of authors in so many distant ages and so many different countries as Ceylon. There is no nation in ancient or modern times possessed of a language and a literature, the writers of which have not at some time made it their theme. Its aspect, its religion, its antiquities and its productions have been described as well by the classic Greeks, as by the members of the Lower Empire; by the Romans; by the writers of China, Burma, India and Kashmir; by the Geographers of Arabia and Persia; by the mediaeval voyagers of Italy and France; by the annalists of Portugal and Spain; by the merchant adventurers of Holland and by the travellers and topographers of Great Britain. But amidst this wealth of materials as to the island... there is an absolute dearth of information regarding its state and progress in the more recent periods, and its actual condition in the present day...

One hundred and sixty-six years later, when I read this in Mr Fernando's library, the same was more or less true. Although the civil war had been over for a year, many of the areas that Tennent passed through had been out of bounds to travellers for so long that it was still difficult to find any recent accounts of these areas, leaving them shrouded in mystery. The north and the east of the island, an arid plain dotted with palmyra palms, was the Tamil Tigers' coveted land of Eelam and had been a warzone for twenty-six years. It was rumoured that the ground was still littered with landmines and many people were still living in refugee camps, whilst the victorious soldiers of the Sri Lankan army ruled the region from behind the razor wire of their army barracks. Foreigners who had tried to travel through the region had been stopped at military checkpoints, had their vehicles searched and were nearly always turned away. The north of the island had been notorious amongst international journalists during the civil war for being one of the hardest warzones to penetrate. Their visas were denied, reporters were obstructed or terrorised and, even today, Sri Lanka is still known as a very dangerous place to operate as a journalist. But it was not only foreigners and journalists who hadn't travelled to these regions; a whole generation of Sri Lankans who live in the south of the island had never visited the north or the east, as during their lifetime it had never been safe to do so.

Outside Mr Fernando's library the sky was beginning to darken, as slate-grey clouds gathered above the city and the first rumblings of thunder began in the west. As I studied the map in the front of Tennent's book, which had been sketched by a Victorian cartographer in London over a century ago, I realised how much of the island lay in the region that I might never visit before I returned to England. 'You had better wait until the storm passes,' said Mr Fernando, as he began to close the wooden shutters of the library against the first, heavy drops of rain. He turned one of the volumes over in his hands and fingered the gold lettering on the spine fondly. 'I won this book as a prize when I was at school,' he explained, 'and I really don't believe that anyone has written anything about our island in such depth since.' He smiled sadly. 'We were once called "the Pearl of the Indian Ocean", but what do they say about us now?' He looked at the map and began to trace the route Tennent had taken across the island. 'It would be interesting to follow his route now and see how much has changed,' he said thoughtfully, moving his finger along the coastline and deep into the jungle interior. 'We think we have changed so much, but I expect in many ways we have not changed at all.'

The idea appealed. I had lived in Sri Lanka for a year and, in spite of my good intentions to immerse myself in the local culture and learn about the island's complex history, I was falling slowly into the expat habit of spending the weekdays working in the capital, whingeing about the traffic, humidity and inefficiency, and the weekends lounging around in tourist resorts by the coast, whingeing about the service. If something didn't change, I would return to England in another year understanding little more about the country than I had when I arrived. As Mr Fernando outlined James Emerson Tennent's route on the map, it looked both feasible and the perfect antidote to my predicament. The route would take me from the south-west corner of the island to the summit of its sacred mountain, north to the capital and inland to the tea plantations of the hill country. From there, the route descended through the central forests that are still home to Sri Lanka's indigenous people, down to the barren, eastern plain, up the east coast to the island's northernmost tip, ending in the crumbling, ancient cities at the island's centre. The journey would be just over 1,600 km, perfectly achievable in a year and, as many of the roads I would be following had not changed course since they had been built by the Victorians, keeping to Tennent's route would not be difficult.

'But what about the old warzone?' I asked Mr Fernando, looking at the east coast and the narrow, northern peninsula. 'Isn't it still impossible to go through this region?'

'It would be difficult, I'm sure,' he agreed, stroking his chin. 'But if the planets are in an auspicious alignment, anything can happen.'

Chapter One

GALLE

It was unusually cool under the corrugated iron roof of Colombo's bus station, which stands in the oldest part of the city, surrounded by bazaars of the Pettah or the 'Black Town'. I had arrived early in the morning, before the sun had brought colour to the pale sky and the usually chaotic bus stand was slowly coming to life. The fruit and vegetable sellers were spreading their mats on the ground, and wheeling crates of bananas and beans in-between the buses on small, flat-bottomed barrows. Scrawny, barefooted men with cigarettes pinched into the corners of their mouths were opening up the backs of their trucks and climbing around on the mounds of hairy coconuts inside, which they began to roll down to their helpers on the ground. A couple of men dressed in cotton shirts and sarongs were sitting on the edge of the road next to their three-wheeled tuk-tuks, waiting for their first passengers of the day, whilst a few unhealthy stray dogs crawled around under the empty buses.

I had come to the Pettah to catch a bus to Galle, a fortified harbour town in the south of Sri Lanka that overlooks the Indian Ocean from the island's west coast. In 1845 Galle was the point of arrival for most Europeans and Tennent was one of the many colonial visitors who started their tours of the island from its harbour. In the bottom of my rucksack I had a cheap edition of James Emerson Tennent's *Ceylon* that I had found in one of the bookshops in Colombo. Unlike the leather-bound copy, lovingly pressed and embossed in London, the pages of my paperback looked as if they had been hurriedly photocopied in a back room somewhere in the city, and were bound carelessly together with so much glue that the paper spine was lumpy and wrinkled.

The buses that ply the Sri Lankan roads have old, battered, steel frames and small, smeared windows, which are permanently wedged open to allow the breeze to cool their dark interiors. Most of the seats on the Galle bus were already taken, so I was forced to take the front seat 'reserved for the clergy' and hoped that I wouldn't be evicted by one of the island's many orange-robed Buddhist monks. The driver lit an incense stick, which he wedged into a small hole in the centre of the steering wheel, before he jumped down from the bus and disappeared into one of the dark stalls that lined the bus stand.

Whereas the dashboard and windscreen of the public buses in Europe are usually littered with various stickers and documents certifying the safety of the bus and the legitimacy of the driver, there are no such pretentions in Sri Lanka. Instead, the drivers and the passengers freely acknowledge a bus ride is a potentially lethal experience and appeal to the gods for protection. The driver of this particular bus had decided to spread his luck evenly amongst the island's deities, and had hung a plastic icon of the Buddha flanked by four Hindu gods above the windscreen. An elderly man pulled himself up the steps of the bus, and shuffled up and down the aisle with a large basket of lentil patties and dried chillies, followed by a teenage boy carrying plastic bags of chopped mangos sprinkled with chilli seeds. Most of the passengers had slid down their seats into sleep and the ones who were awake were sitting in vacant silence, staring out of the windows.

A middle-aged man in a sarong, who was carrying a wooden crate of small, green citrus fruit, sat down on the seat next to me. After he had balanced the crate precariously on his lap, he produced a small plastic comb from the pocket of his shirt, which he ran first over the streaks of sparse, well-oiled hair on his head and then through the black bristles of his thick moustache. He gently patted the sides of his head with his hands and, satisfied he was in a respectable state, selected a handful of the citrus fruit, which were the colour of limes but more spherical, and dropped two into my lap.

'These are organic oranges, madam,' he explained, as he started to tear the thin peel from one himself, 'they are from my own plantation and have been contaminated by no unnatural chemicals.'

This was not the first time I had been fed by a complete stranger on a Sri Lankan bus, and I always accepted with a twinge of guilt, as it would never occur to me to share my food with anyone I did not already know. The flesh was a pale orange colour and had the kind of unripe, acidic taste that makes you wince spontaneously. I asked the man where he was going and he said that he too was on the way to Galle.

'I tried to take the train, but when I arrived at the station this morning, first and second class were already full,' he said. shaking his head, as he looked despondently out of the window. 'I do not like to take the bus.'

If you mention to most people that you are going to take the Galle Road that runs along the coastline between Galle and Colombo, their usual response is to flinch, shake their heads with pity and suggest you take the train instead. Although the Galle Road is one of island's main arteries and conveys vast numbers of cars, buses and heavy goods vehicles every day, it is still only a very narrow, single-carriage road and is shared with a large number of villagers on bicycles, who sometimes choose, intriguingly, to cycle in the opposite direction to the traffic. As a result, progress is always very slow and the average speed rarely exceeds 50 km per hour. Ever since I arrived in Sri Lanka I had heard rumours that an 'express highway' was being built somewhere further inland, which would apparently transform the journey to Galle into a smooth and luxurious experience. Nobody seemed to know exactly where this mysterious highway was, but every couple of months someone would declare the new road was to be unveiled any day now and people claimed with reverence to have seen sections of the highway hidden in the jungle. There were even rumours that the local tuk-tuk drivers were sneaking onto the sleek tarmac in the night to joyride their little three-wheelers up and down over its smooth surface.

Gradually the bus began to fill up – first the seats, then the aisles, followed by the doorways and, finally, with a few people perched in the driver's booth, the bus began to lumber its way out of the station and through the city towards the sea.

The buildings and monuments that line the Galle Road tell the story of the island's past. The signs that hang above the small stalls selling king coconuts and powdered milk, Dayananda Stores, Café Gunasekara, bear the traditional Sinhalese names from a time before the island was colonised. The white dagobas and statues of the seated Buddha that smile placidly from the temple courtyards were brought by Indians, in one of their more well-meaning visits to their small neighbour. The island's first colonisers, the Portuguese, left their mark on the island with the pastel-coloured facades of the catholic churches, and the garlanded shrines of the Virgin Mary and the infant Christ that sit in glass cases by the side of the road. The Dutch left the bungalows with their tiled roofs and sloping, column-supported verandas, under which the elderly Sinhalese slumber away the humid afternoons. When the British arrived as the island's third and final colonisers, they built the road and the broad-gauge railway line that runs along the coast, so close to the sea that on a stormy day the carriages are sprayed by rolling waves from the Indian Ocean, from the Jaffna Peninsula in the arid north, down into the humid wetlands of the deep south.

After a couple of hours, the villages and stalls had almost disappeared, and the road ran alongside the shoreline, separated by only a few metres of sand from the brightly coloured fishing boats that rose and fell on the currents. We were now deep in the heartland of the Sinhalese. Whereas many other regions of the island have gradually assimilated large communities of Christians, Muslims and Tamil-speaking Hindus, this region has remained predominantly Sinhalese in language and Buddhist in faith. The more cosmopolitan areas of Sri

Lanka have the reputation of being parochial and somewhat backward – 'like the American Midwest', a Sri Lankan friend had helpfully explained.

The driver's mate, a gangly teenage boy with slicked-back, curly hair, had been busy tearing up strips of betel leaf, which he folded around pieces of areca nut and slaked lime crystals, and fed into the mouth of the driver, who chewed it into paan, the red psycho-stimulant that dribbles from the lips of bus drivers all over South Asia. When the bus screeched to a halt beneath the enormous white dagoba of the Buddhist temple in Kalutara, the driver handed his mate a few coins and sent him off the bus to deliver the money to a small offering box by the side of the road. Crowds of Buddhist devotees dressed in white were making their way into the temple with offerings of purple lotus flowers, and as they surrounded the driver's mate he put his palms together and quickly raised his hands to his head in prayer, before scrambling back onto the bus. The gentleman who had shared his organic oranges with me also raised his hands to his head and then turned to me and whispered, 'Are you Catholic?'

I shook my head and he frowned. 'Whoever your god is you should say a small prayer. We need his protection on our dangerous roads.'

Galle is now Sri Lanka's fourth-largest town, and its modern buildings sprawl well beyond the walls of the fort in both directions up and down the coast. The modern part of Galle is in many ways typical of towns that are rapidly expanding all over the island. The streets are glutted with three-wheeled tuk-tuks and Japanese motorbikes, convolutions of electrical cables sag across the shopfronts, there is an enthusiasm for anything wrapped in fluorescent plastic and sun-bleached photographs of a young David Beckham advertise the local hair salons. Even the beggars sitting by the roadside seem to be playing with cheap Nokia mobiles and the small tea shacks are dwarfed by enormous billboards above the doorways, showing unconvincing photographs of gourmet banquets.

I walked away from the noise and traffic of the new town, following the road past Galle's international cricket stadium, along a short stretch of seafront and past the ramshackle fish market just outside high walls of the town's old European fort. The brightly coloured fishing boats had already landed after their early morning trips and were now moored to the palm trees that separated the fishing harbour from the narrow road. Barefooted fishermen, with sarongs pulled high above their knees, were carrying large, silver fish by their tails, up from the shore to the crowded stalls – simple shacks made from planks of wood clumsily nailed together, with woven palm fronds forming awnings over the day's catch on display. Old-fashioned pairs of weighing scales hung from the awnings and the stallholders were splashing cool water over the rows of silver scales in an attempt to keep them fresh in the morning's mounting heat.

When you walk through the walls of the fort you leave Asia behind and enter the cobbled streets the Europeans built to remind them of home. The Dutch lined the Portuguese streets with low, shuttered bungalows topped with sloping terracotta-tiled roofs, supported by cylindrical columns that formed shady verandas to protect the delicate Europeans from the tropical climate. Their plastered walls are painted in shades of green and ochre, and twisted frangipani trees and pots of deep red cannas frame the doorways. Time in the fort has the rhythm of a Mediterranean afternoon just awaking from the siesta. Elderly men meander through the streets on rusting upright bicycles or slump in the shade of their verandas, chewing the cud with their neighbours. Their toothless wives twitch the net curtains and sweep the doorways with twiggy brooms, whilst their grandchildren kick footballs against the walls. When the island saw off the last of its colonisers in 1948 and started to destroy its colonial buildings to erase the evidence of foreign rule, UNESCO stepped in to protect the buildings in the fort for the steady trickle of tourists returning after the civil war.

It had been several hours since I had breakfast in Colombo, and I was starting to feel the dry throat and dull headache of dehydration. I sat down on the veranda of a small cafe that looked up to a large Victorian lighthouse on the fort wall, and asked the waiter for a lime juice and soda water. He wrote down the order and then gently waggled his head from side to side as if he was subtly trying to check whether his brain had come loose from his skull. The gesture always flummoxes Europeans when they first arrive on the island and, although they are used to it by the time they leave, they never really work out exactly what it means. In this case it meant 'sure, no problem' and a glass of bitter effervescence arrived a few minutes later.

I was joined on the veranda by a middle-aged Sri Lankan couple, who sank down into the chairs next to me and started fanning themselves limply with the little cardboard menus.

Judging by the gentleman's baseball cap and sunglasses, and the lady's octagonal pagoda-shaped hat that was covered with reflective silver foil, they were tourists. When they had removed their hats and mopped their streaming brows with the little flannels they produced from their pockets, the gentleman turned to me and pointed up to the lighthouse.

'Did you know they used to release carrier pigeons up there, to send the letters to Colombo that arrived on the ships from Europe and the Americas? The fastest pigeons could fly to Colombo in forty-five minutes. We drove here in our car this morning and it took us four hours to cover the same distance. Sometimes I think this country is moving backwards, not forwards.' He folded up his damp flannel and put it back in his pocket. 'Are you Australian?'

I explained I was from England but I was working as a teacher in Colombo, and the gentleman removed his sunglasses in excitement.

'I was in England from 1989 to1991,' he declared. 'It was for my diploma in education. I had to visit schools all over the north of England, but I don't think I really saw the best parts. They sent me to Doncaster, Hull and Hartlepool. All the English people I knew kept saying, "Sarath, why do you only go to these awful places? You should go to Cambridge or the Lake District." Apparently the north has some very beautiful, old schools run by monks, but I didn't get to see those ones.'

He turned to the lady and patted her on the shoulder. 'This is my sister Chandani. She has never been anywhere, have you? Out of Sri Lanka, I mean.'

Chandani had very thin, spindly legs that were carrying what seemed to be a disproportionately wide waist and big soft arms with no discernible elbows. She confirmed that she had not left Sri Lanka thus far, but that she and Sarath would be travelling to Delhi the following month to visit family.

'When you visit India, you realise what a paradise Sri Lanka is,' said Sarath with a wrinkled nose. 'I couldn't live there, all the beggars, the cows, the filth. But I hear that Delhi has a very luxurious airport these days.'

I said I had been through Delhi airport about seven years earlier and that my only memory of it was the monkeys that jumped about in the rafters. But maybe it had been refurbished in the meantime.

'Monkeys?' screeched Chandani. 'You must have been most disgusted!'

I told Chandani, with slight embarrassment, that having never seen wild monkeys before, I had actually found it most delightful. It felt like I was admitting to a fondness for rats.

She frowned at me. 'You do not have monkeys in England?' she asked with surprise.

'Um, no.'

'Not even in the jungle?'

Sarath jumped in with embarrassed exasperation. 'They don't have jungles in England,' he snapped at her, rolling his eyes to me. 'They have the New Forest, but it isn't really a jungle.'

I asked Sarath and Chandani why they were visiting Galle, and their faces clouded over. Their family originally came from Galle and, although Sarath and Chandani had settled in Colombo, they used to make frequent trips back down the coast to visit their extended family. Since the Tsunami had hit Sri Lanka, however, they had been reluctant to return and this was one of their first visits to the area in recent years.

The tsunami took place on Boxing Day morning in 2004, when the Indian tectonic plate pushed itself beneath the Eurasian plate off the coast of Sumatra, causing a massive underwater earthquake. The coastlines of Thailand, Malaysia, Myanmar, Sumatra, the Bay of Bengal and various small islands in the Indian Ocean, including Sri Lanka, were dashed by high-speed walls of seawater which swept away the buildings and communities in their path.

'If you go inside the cafe, the owner has an album of photographs that he took in the days after the tsunami,' Sarath said. 'You will probably find it very interesting. Chandani didn't want to look at it, she finds these things too upsetting, but I think we should face up to these things.'

The owner showed me the photographs he had taken, which showed the streets of Galle several feet deep in water, with overturned buses and fishing boats lying in the roads. I commented to Sarath that you couldn't see a trace of the devastation in Galle anymore and he laughed drily. 'That's because they had to get Galle and the west coast back on its feet, so it wouldn't upset the tourist industry. Go over to the east of the island and you'll hear that it was a different story,' he said.

When Sarath and Chandani had left, I leafed through the first chapter of Tennent's book to read through records that he had made about the history of Galle and his impressions of the town in 1845.

Tennent was forty-one years old when he arrived in Ceylon, having been recently knighted in London, and although he had already travelled extensively in Europe, this was his first encounter with tropical Asia. From the moment he looked out from the deck of his ship, over palm-fringed coastlines and hillsides shrouded in jungle, he was captivated by the natural beauty of the island and many of the pages of his book were devoted to mesmerising descriptions of Ceylon's natural landscape. He also developed a fascination with the dress and behaviour of the 'natives' he encountered and made detailed sketches of the local people in their national costume. Not surprisingly, Tennent displayed a number of the prejudices of his time but although he was repulsed by some of the local customs he encountered, he was generally respectful of the people and intrigued by their way of life. Although Tennent made no mention of the rest of his family in his book, and the only companion he mentioned was his beloved pet elephant, his letters suggest that his wife and daughter spent several years in Ceylon with him, whilst his son, William, was left behind in England. Tennent would probably have spent many weeks at a time away from his family whilst he toured the island and would have spent most of his time in the company of the other British men running the colony.

Galle had been one of the ancient trade emporiums of the Indian Ocean and Tennent's inspection of its bazaars convinced him that Galle was in fact the biblical port of Tarshish, the land ruled by kings, where King Solomon sent his ships to procure peacocks, ivory and apes. The historian and traveller Al-Masudi, the Herodotus of the Arabs, came to Galle in the tenth century and found that the town was the resting place for sea-faring traders, who dropped anchor in its harbour as they plied the eastern trade route between India and China.

The Europeans first set their sights on Galle in 1505 when Don Lourenço de Almeida, a member of the ruling family in the Portuguese colony of Goa, was blown by a storm from the Maldives into the protection of the Galle harbour. The event was interpreted by the ship's resident Franciscan friar as a divine signal that the Portuguese should expand their empire to include Sri Lanka. The Portuguese made a series of looting expeditions to Sri Lanka in the following years. When they arrived in Galle and took control of the town in 1587, they celebrated in a style typical of Portuguese imperialism, by spending three days raiding its warehouses and setting the boats in the harbour ablaze.

Meanwhile, back in Europe, the naval supremacy of the Portuguese was being challenged by the British and the Dutch, and by the end of the start of the seventeenth century, the Portuguese became paranoid about an attack from Holland. As the Dutch began to make deals with the island's kings in other regions of the country, the Portuguese became increasingly panicked as fleets of Dutch ships were spotted, loitering in the sea around Galle. Eventually their fears were realised when the Dutch stormed Galle and took possession of the region in 1640, after a bloody, eighteen-day siege. The Dutch chose Galle as their seat of government, expanded the small Portuguese fortifications and began to dispatch ships laden with elephants, cinnamon, pepper, areca and coir to Europe. The transfer of Galle into the hands of the British in 1796 was a very calm and civilised event in comparison with the violent clashes of previous centuries, and on the day of the handover the keys to the gates of the fort were neatly placed on a silver tray and solemnly handed from the Dutch commandant to a British officer.

Galle was still an important trading hub when Tennent walked the lanes of the fort in 1845. He found a colourful and cosmopolitan community of Europeans strolling under the shade of Japanese parasols, and traders from Arabia, China, Malaysia and India mixing with the local Buddhist monks and village headmen. He was somewhat disconcerted by the dress, physique and long hair of the local Sinhalese men:

> With their delicate features and slender limbs, their frequent want of beards, their use of earrings and their practice of wearing a cloth round the waist called a comboy, which has all the appearance of a petticoat, the men have an air of effeminacy very striking to the eye of a stranger.

Although Galle is no longer a trading centre for jewels and spices, a new breed of merchants has arrived in the fort over the past ten years. Real estate is now the precious commodity in Galle, and the crumbling colonial villas are being sold to foreign investors to be converted into boutique hotels and luxury second homes. Many have already changed hands and it is easy to identify which. Tiles slip from the roofs of the villas still inhabited by the Sri Lankan families that have lived in the fort for generations. Their doors and shutters are open to the world, and passers-by can see into the simple dark interiors furnished with plastic chairs and sagging mattresses. Next door, the freshly painted and retouched villas, named by brass plates on the wall and guarded by young boys in uniform, have their shutters and doors firmly closed, whilst they wait for their foreign owners to return from their snorkelling trips.

Later that afternoon I got into a tuk-tuk and asked the driver to take me to a small village called Seenigama, which lies to the north of Galle. Seenigama was one of hundreds of villages around the island's coastline that was completely destroyed in the tsunami seven years earlier, and I was on my way to meet a survivor. Kushil Gunasekera, agent to the famous bowler of the Sri Lankan cricket team Muttiah Muralitharan, was the man who was responsible for rebuilding Seenigama and fifty more of the destroyed villages in the south-west region of the island.

The road to Seenigama runs along the palm-fringed coastal road. Many of today's fishing boats are still built according to the traditional and elegant Sinhalese design known as an *oruwa* – a narrow canoe with a single out-rigger attached to one side, which acts as a stabiliser. Groups of men were on the sand by their boats, mending their fishing nets and tinkering with the engines, or simply sitting under the palm trees watching the gentle afternoon waves. Although most of the buildings destroyed by the tsunami were hurriedly rebuilt afterwards, there were still some remnants of the dashed shells of houses, with no windows or roofs, looking out over the sea that destroyed them.

The tuk-tuk driver was a short, tubby man with a small pot belly that jiggled about on his lap whilst he was driving. He asked me with surprise why I wanted to go to Seenigama, which he claimed was home to a large number of alcoholics and heroin addicts. I had not felt comfortable asking questions about the tsunami in Galle; so many people had lost family, homes and businesses in the area that it seemed insensitive to probe. The tuk-tuk driver, however, seemed very cheerful at the mention of the tsunami, in spite of the fact his family's coastal house had been completely destroyed. He was one of the lucky few who had not lost any close family in the disaster and, in addition, he had received a brand new house – which he claimed to know for a fact was built using money donated by people from Liverpool. All in all, he said, he had come out of the whole thing rather well.

Kushil Gunasekera was a small, slender man in his fifties, with a round, boyish face, incongruously silver hair, twinkling eyes and a crushing handshake. I met him in his family's ancestral villa in the middle of the village, which was now an administration centre for the charity he had set up following the tsunami. He led me into a glacially air-conditioned office and seated himself in a leather swivel chair, under a plastic Buddha that was studded with multi-coloured flashing LEDs. His charity, The Foundation of Goodness, which sounded more like a Christian cult than a development foundation, had been set up by Kushil as a fairly small project five years before the tsunami. Although Kushil had been born in Seenigama, where his family had lived for generations, his father was a wealthy lawyer and had paid for his son to be educated in one of the private schools in the capital. 'Whenever I returned to the village, I noticed that my childhood friends, many of whom had been much smarter and more talented than me, had stagnated and were achieving nothing, purely because of the lack of opportunities in our rural communities,' he explained, as he leaned back in his chair. 'By 1999 I was doing well and had made a name for myself in the business world, so I started a small project in Seenigama to try to provide computer and language training for the young people in my ancestral village.'

The morning of the tsunami was one of the island's Poya days – the day of the full moon, which is a Buddhist public holiday every month – and many of the families from the village had gone down to the beach early. Kushil had travelled down from Colombo to spend the Poya running a scholarship programme for local children.

'It was about nine a.m. and I was sitting in a building in the middle of the village with thirty of the scholarship children, waiting for the last few people to arrive so we could begin the meeting,' explained Kushil, as he sat forward and began to rub his temples. 'At about 9.25 a.m. some of the villagers who had been down on the beach that morning came running back into the village screaming that we must start to run, because they had seen the sea beginning to race inland. I had heard of tidal waves before but none of us had ever heard of a tsunami and nobody in the village had any idea what was happening. All we could do was gather the children and run along the back roads of the village to the temple, which was up on the higher ground. As we were running, the first small three-foot wave passed us. Twenty minutes later, as we looked down towards the sea from the temple, a thirty-foot wall of water rolled through the village, demolishing everything in its path.' Kushil sighed and sat back heavily in his seat.

'As I stood in the temple watching the waves roll towards us, I thought the world was coming to an end. The villagers just looked on in disbelief as they saw the little they had being destroyed in front of their eyes. We must have stayed there watching and waiting for about five hours until the mid afternoon, when some of us made our way along the back roads to look at the devastation. Even five hours after the waves had subsided, the roads 2 km from the shore were still 2-ft deep in water. There was debris everywhere and the dead bodies of the villagers who hadn't managed to escape were floating in the water.'

I asked Kushil what had happened in the days immediately after the tsunami, before any of the relief work could be coordinated. Kushil had managed to hitch-hike his way back to Colombo that night and collected two lorry loads of donated supplies, which he drove down the ravaged coastline back to Seenigama several days later.

'When we got back to the village, most of the people whose houses had been destroyed were gathered in the temples, which were acting as shelters for displaced families all over the island. In the meantime, the foreign donations had started rolling in and we turned this villa, my ancestral home, into the coordination centre to distribute the emergency supplies. For almost six months there was a constant queue outside the door of up to a hundred people, just waiting for basic supplies to allow them to survive.'

Very quickly, however, Kushil's charity had to stop simply dealing with the present and start planning for the long-term future, too. Most families no longer had a house to live in and many of the men in the area had lost their livelihoods.

Seenigama had been a village of coral miners but the tsunami had destroyed kilometres of coral reef all along the coast. Over the next two years, The Foundation of Goodness built over 1,000 houses, and gave the men tuk-tuks, fishing boats, grocery stores and farming equipment – anything that they could use to make a living.

I had already had a chance to look around the village, which had a modern medical centre, an ICT suite, and a wide range of sports facilities, including a large swimming pool sponsored by Bryan Adams, and a cricket pitch, gym and netball court that had been possible due to donations by a charitable sports foundation. I presumed that none of this had been present before the tsunami and would probably not have come into existence had it not been for the massive foreign donations. I put this to Kushil and he laughed. 'Do you know, many of the villagers actually refer to the tsunami as "the Golden Wave" these days. You are quite right. In material terms, many of these people now have far more than they did before the tsunami. Of course, it was a tragedy; many families lost four or five people to the wave, but the opportunities that are now available to the younger generations are beyond anything they could have ever imagined.'

Whilst Kushil's project in his village seemed a huge success, many people criticised the way foreign donations had been handled in other parts of the island. There were even rumours that large sums of foreign aid money had made their way into the funds of the Tamil Tiger separatists and fuelled the civil war. Three-quarters of the coastline, from the northernmost point in Jaffna, all the way down the east coast, and from the southernmost point up the west coast to the capital, was dashed by the high-speed waves. What had been the story in these areas?

'Our project was a success because my charity had started planning the development of the area long before the tsunami. But, even more importantly, we are still here to maintain the work that was carried out at the time. What is difficult to comprehend is the level of sheer chaos that there was after the tsunami. Enormous sums of money were flooding into the island, but there was no real plan as to what to do with it. Many large building projects took place very quickly, but then, when the charities disappeared the next year, there were no relevant skills or knowledge about how to maintain the projects, so many have now fallen into disrepair. Also, a large number of people became very greedy when they saw the money rushing in and saw this as a chance to exploit it. Some families had seen everything they owned washed away and decided this was their one opportunity to gain something, so they squeezed it for all it was worth. A number of families lied to the charities and got two or three new houses instead of one, and some of the money is simply unaccounted for and nobody has any idea where it went.'

Kushil continued to talk about his work in the village and his ambitions to try to replicate his successful project in the war-torn regions in the north of the island. He smiled at the flashing statue of the Buddha and spoke about the 'divine forces' that he was convinced had helped him along the way. It seemed that, seven years on, some now viewed the tsunami as a natural event rather than a natural disaster – a strange twist of fate that had improved the lives of as many as it had taken.

The sun was falling from the sky when I returned to the fort and I climbed a set of stone steps to a path that ran around the top of the rampart walls. It was a Friday evening and many of the inhabitants of the fort had gathered on the southern wall to watch the sun set over the ocean. Three Buddhist monks, their orange robes whipping about them in the evening breeze, were looking out across the Indian Ocean, their hands clasped above their shaven heads in prayer. Groups of teenagers sat on the wall, their legs dangling high above the waves breaking on the rocks beneath. Several Muslim families – the men dressed in pale robes and crocheted caps, and the women in head scarves and long black gowns – were sitting on the walls with rolled-up prayer mats on their knees, waiting for the call to prayer from the fort's white, latticed mosque. As dusk began to descend, the wailing call reverberated around the fort and the families began to slowly climb down from the walls, moving together towards the prayer halls. Further along the walls, groups of men of all ages were playing games of cricket in the dwindling twilight. Cricket is the unrivalled religion on the island and every evening the tuk-tuk drivers, schoolboys, shopkeepers and cafe owners of the fort leave their work, and congregate at the ramparts with their worn willow bats and frayed leather balls. As the sun finally dipped over the horizon, a swift event seven degrees from the equator, the families of the fort seemed suddenly to disappear, leaving the dark walls empty and the streets silent.

Chapter Two

ADAM'S PEAK

On a clear day, if you look inland north-east from Galle across the lowlands of the jungle, you can just make out the wooded slopes of the hill country and the sharp, distinctive summit of the island's sacred mountain Samanalakanda. For centuries, this has been a pilgrimage site for the followers of Sri Lanka's major religions, who climb the mountain between January and May to worship at a small shrine on the summit. The shrine covers a vaguely foot-shaped impression in a slab of rock, known as Sri Pada, or 'the sacred footprint'. Millennia ago the aboriginal inhabitants of the island worshipped nature on the peak long before a footprint existed, but over the centuries each of the island's religions has composed a different legend about how the mysterious footmark came into existence.

The Buddhists claim that the footprint was left by the Lord Buddha himself, on one of his alleged trips to the island from India. According to the ancient Sri Lankan chronicle, 'The Mahavamsa', the mountain was the home of the god Saman, the lord of the heavenly beings the Devas and the protector of the island. When the Buddha came to Sri Lanka to purify it from the mystical and demonic beings the Yakkhas, who were wreaking terror on the island, he preached to many of the island's gods, including Saman. On his third and final visit to Sri Lanka, he rose to the top of Saman's mountain and made an impression of his footprint on its summit, before continuing to roam the island.

The Sri Pada is also a place of pilgrimage for the Hindus of the island; they believe that the footprint is that of the god Shiva, who spent a period of isolated austerity on the mountain and to commemorate his time there stamped his foot into a rock on the summit. For the Muslims of Sri Lanka, the footprint is believed to be that of Adam and this belief gave the mountain its other, widely used name of 'Adam's Peak'. Although there is nothing in the Quran that associates Adam with the sacred mountain, the Arab traders returning to their dusty, barren lands from the lush beauty of Serendib probably spoke of the small island as some kind of Eden, and from there it became associated with the first man. The Islamic legends that link Adam with the footprint vary in their details; some say that when Adam was cast out of paradise he stood for many years on one foot at the top of the mountain as an act of penitence and hence a single footprint remains. A different legend claims that Eve fell from Paradise in Saudi Arabia and was separated from Adam for 200 years; when they were finally reunited by the angel Gabriel, they retired to Sri Lanka to continue to propagate the human race.

When the Portuguese arrived in Ceylon in the sixteenth century, aside from systematically burning and pillaging the island's towns, converting the natives to Roman Catholicism was one of their primary aims. The Portuguese displayed little respect for the local religions and, after they had torn down their temples, they turned their attention to Adam's Peak. Tearing down a mountain was beyond even the violent capabilities of the Portuguese, so instead they dismissed any local legends about the footprint and grafted their own story onto its presence. Not wishing to agree with the Muslims, they rejected any association with Adam and instead opted for St Thomas, who presumably visited Sri Lanka after his alleged trip to spread the gospel in Kerala and stamped his print onto the mountain top.

Tennent, like many others who approached the island's western coast by sea, had immediately noticed the distinctively shaped peak from the deck of his ship. After spending one night in Galle, he set off north the next morning in one of the government's horse-drawn mail coaches along the coastal road to the town of Kalutara, from where a river runs inland to the base of the mountain.

Early the next morning, I made my way out of the gates of the fort to pick up a bus that was heading north along the Galle road. The bus station was not yet busy and I was able to get a seat on one of the small, modern minibuses, which are generally considered to be luxurious in comparison with the bigger, older, overcrowded, government-run buses. There is, however, a problem with these minibuses: their speed. Whereas the speed of the older buses is restricted by their dimensions, and the unfavourable relationship between the weight they are carrying and their horsepower, the little nippy minibuses can shriek up and down the roads, trying to squeeze through impossibly small gaps between other vehicles and occasionally mounting the pavements. In countries where the Highway Code is obeyed, or even acknowledged, speed is a distinct advantage. But on the chaotic roads of Sri Lanka – where everyone has right of way (including animals and limping beggars), the rearview mirror and indicators are rarely used and drink-driving is still considered by some to be a skill – a little acceleration can be terrifying. The website of the British Foreign & Commonwealth Office gives a fairly accurate description of the hazards you may experience on Sri Lanka's roads:

> Erratic driving is common and as a result, road accidents are frequent. Pedestrians and animals often appear in the road without warning. Vehicles do not stop at pedestrian crossings. Always wear a seatbelt… If you drive, make sure you are comprehensively insured.

The road to Ratnapura followed the palm-fringed coast for several hours as far the bustling town of Panadura, where it turned inland and continued into the jungle. Strategically placed at various points along each road were large billboards of President Mahinda Rajapaksa, whose image appears on roadsides all over the island to remind the islanders of his power. Some billboards simply show his squinting, moustachioed face grinning down at the cars, whilst on other billboards he is illuminated in a halo of light, much like icons of Christ, or surrounded by flocks of fawning children.

Mahinda Rajapaksa and his three brothers, Gotabaya, Basil and Chamal Rajapaksa, have dominated Sri Lankan politics since 2005 when Mahinda was first elected president. At the time of writing, Mahinda is the president, minister of defence, minister of finance and planning, and minister of ports and aviation. Basil is the minister for economic development, Gotabaya is the defence secretary and Chamal is speaker of the parliament. Various cousins have also been given ambassadorial positions around the globe. In spite of the fact that some government ministers have violent and abusive histories, there are mutterings of election fraud, dissenting journalists disappear and the UN is currently investigating human rights abuses by the government, Mahinda Rajapaksa is genuinely popular with many Sri Lankans, who regard him and his brother Gotabaya as heroes for finally ending the island's civil war.

Sitting next to me on the bus was a Sri Lankan lady in her late thirties who had boarded shortly after me in Galle. From the moment she stepped onto the bus, she had looked rather uneasy and slightly repulsed by the dirty floor and frayed seats. From her carefully manicured hands and the expensive sunglasses that were perched on her head, I guessed she was unaccustomed to public transport. She caught me staring up at one of the billboards of the president as we were nearing Panadura and said to me in almost accentless English, 'And what do you think about our president?' I looked at her in surprise; I had never been asked this question quite so directly since I had lived on the island. People were usually reluctant to broach the subject, or were just keen to expound their woes or praise of the government. 'Do speak freely,' she said encouragingly. 'It is always interesting to hear a foreign perspective on these matters.'

I edged cautiously around the observations I had made and asked her how she felt about the powerful Rajapaksa family. 'The situation in this country worries me very much,' she said. 'We are living under a virtual dictatorship, with a president who is determined to found some kind of dynasty that will rule the island forever. Even those in the government who are not directly related to the president are thugs with blood on their hands.'

The lady was a doctor from Galle, who had been educated in London and had come back to practice in her home country and to be with her family. She was married to a wealthy businessman and, had it not been for the car refusing to start that morning, she would never have contemplated taking public transport to visit her pregnant sister-in-law in Ratnapura. She spoke about the comparative comfort of a National Express bus she had once taken from London to Cambridge, and how she still 'made a pilgrimage' to Sainsbury's whenever she went back to England to visit members of her family in Surrey. She asked me how old I was and, when I told her, she asked whether I had any intention of getting married and having children. As she was a full-time career woman with a husband and several children, I asked her whether she would recommend it. She put her hand on my arm and smiled as she looked out of the window. 'I think it is good for women to work,' she said, 'but it is my children that are my life, not my job.' As she got down from the bus just outside Ratnapura, she turned back to me as I waved goodbye. 'Cherry, you must get married and have many children!' she called through the window with a laugh, as the bus revved its engine and left her standing on the road.

The bus pulled in to the dismal bus station in Ratnapura in the mid afternoon. The bus stands were lined with concrete benches, on which lines of despondent-looking Sri Lankans were slumped, staring vacantly at the overcrowded buses belching clouds of asphyxiating black matter from their exhaust pipes. Packs of wretched-looking stray dogs were dodging in between the vehicles, whimpering softly, and breaking into scraps of snarling and biting. Men and women sitting in the waiting buses hung their heads and limbs out of the windows, like prisoners, in a desperate attempt to feel some air that was cooler than the sweaty, claustrophobic interior.

I hurried out of the bus station as quickly as possible and was immediately accosted by a moustachioed tuk-tuk driver.

'You want a taxi, madam?'

'Do you know Hotel Ratnaloka?'

'I know the place. Come.'

We crossed the road and I threw my rucksack into the back of his green three-wheeler that was parked on the side of the road. The name Ratnapura means 'city of gems' and conjures up an image of a wealthy, sparkling metropolis. The reality is, as usual, very different. The main street was lined with small open-fronted shops selling coconuts, selections of withered vegetables, and a variety of packaged biscuits and lurid, carbonated drinks. The walls of the buildings had once been painted in bright shades of green, orange and yellow, but with the increasing number of polluting vehicles that pass along the road, they had become covered by a permanent film of black grime. Sinewy men in sarongs and sagging shirts trudged barefoot up and down the streets carrying sacks of rice or lentils on their backs, whilst wizened old ladies with waist-length, greasy hair stood on the pavement, sucking their empty gums and staring with glazed eyes at the activity.

As a result of the civil war and the absence of many international firms on the island, few foreign visitors had ventured to the more remote parts in recent years, and anyone with fair skin outside the major towns or resorts is regarded with curiosity. As I looked ahead through the front windscreen I caught the driver's eye in the mirror as he was looking back at me, which he took as a cue to begin the predictable string of questions:

'What is your country, madam?'

'I'm from England.'

'For how long are you on holiday in Sri Lanka?'

'I live here.'

'No!'

'Yes.'

'You are working here?'

'Yes, I'm a teacher.'

'You like Sri Lanka?'

'Yes, very much.'

'You know Kevin Pietersen?'

'I'm not particularly interested in cricket.'

A look of disgust and incomprehension was sent in my direction via the rear-view mirror.

Then came the inevitable:

'You have a husband?'

From the repertoire of tuk-tuk drivers' questions, this one is the most irritating, as whatever you say subjects you to further questions of an increasingly personal nature. If you say 'yes' then you are interrogated about the number of children or lack of children you have and the reason for your husband's current absence. If you say 'no', then the exact nature of your inadequacy and misfortune is probed, to be occasionally followed by some kind of indecent proposal.

I must have made my irritation evident as the driver grinned at me again in the mirror and said with glee, 'This question is making you very angry, madam! You have no husband!' and proceeded to giggle to himself all the way to the hotel.

During the pilgrimage season, Ratnapura swells with devotees stocking up on provisions, or recovering from journeys from distant parts of the island before they start their ascent to the shrine on the summit. When I arrived, the pilgrimage season had finished several months earlier and I was one of only a handful of guests in the large hotel. The others were three Japanese ornithologists, who spent all of their time peering through binoculars into the surrounding jungle, and running up and down the veranda, assembling and dismantling their enormous camera and tripod.

When I had mentioned to my Sri Lankan colleagues in Colombo that I was intending to climb Adam's Peak out of the pilgrimage season, I was told, bluntly that this was a stupid idea. When the pilgrims flock to the mountain, the pathway to the summit is lit by a string of electric lamps, and tea shacks and food stalls line the path to provide sustenance and rest for the climbers. Out of season none of this exists, and I was told that I would almost certainly get lost and pass out from hunger and exhaustion. Radica, an elderly colleague at my school in Colombo, was particularly worried about another aspect of my plan, and drew me to one side in the corridor one morning to express her concerns. In hushed tones she explained that with the tea shacks closed, there would be no toilets. 'For us, it is not a problem,' she said uncomfortably, 'we can use the bushes. But for you Britishers of course... That's not possible is it?' When I told her it was not unheard of for the British to relieve themselves in the undergrowth – and that during country rambles on the North Yorkshire moors as a child I had gained significant experience of this – her jaw dropped as the illusion of British 'civilisation', carefully woven over the many years of the British Empire, evaporated. Finally, I was told by another colleague that the path up the mountain was isolated and 'dangerous', although the exact nature of the danger remained a mystery. All in all, everyone agreed that under no circumstances should I attempt the climb on my own.

I had rung ahead to the hotel several weeks before to book a room and to find out whether the hotel knew of any local guides who could accompany me on the path to the summit. Traditionally, the pilgrims climb along the lamp-lit paths through the night and watch the sun rise from the peak, but out of season the darkness of the trail makes this much more risky. I therefore arranged to be met by a local guide the next morning as soon as it was light, in order to try to make it up to the summit and back down before nightfall.

I spent the evening in the empty hotel; the Japanese ornithologists had disappeared into the jungle without their large camera, but with a large amount of infrared night-vision equipment and an iPod of recorded bird calls. Sitting on the veranda in the muggy night air, I began reading a collection of accounts from other travellers who had encountered the sacred mountain in centuries gone by. The great Venetian traveller Marco Polo learnt of Adam's Peak during his homeward voyage from the empire of Kublai Khan in the thirteenth century. According to his somewhat confused account of the legends associated with the mountain, Adam's Peak was the site of Adam's tomb rather than his footprint, and within the tomb lay samples of Adam's hair, his teeth and a basin of which he made use. On hearing of these relics, Polo records that Kublai Khan became so desperate to acquire them that in 1281 he sent an envoy to the island, who somehow persuaded the islanders to hand them over.

Another account of Adam's Peak was compiled in the fourteenth century by a traveller who went by the name of Sir John Mandeville, who claimed to be a knight and a native of St Albans. The validity of his work *The Travels of Sir John Mandeville*, and even his identity have been a matter of historical debate, and many of his accounts of regions of Asia seem to be pure fantasy. Whether he made it to Sri Lanka is uncertain, but his account of Adam's Peak echoes many aspects of the legends that would have been circulating at the time.

And there ben also many wylde Bestes, and namelych Olifauntes. In that yle is a great Mountayne; and in mydd place of the Mount, is a gret lake in a fulle fair Pleyne, and there is gret plentee of Watre. And thei of the Contree seyn, that Adam and Eve wepten upon that Mount an 100 Zeer, whan thei weren dryvn out of Paradys. And that Watre, thei seyn, is of here Teres: for so much Watre thei wepten, that made the forseyde Lake. And in the botme of that Lake, men fynden many precious Stones and grete Perles. In that Lake growen many Reedes and grete Cannes: and there with inne ben many Cocodrilles and Serpentes and grete water Leches.

Like me, Tennent had started his ascent to the peak from Ratnapura and recorded a trek through a 'laberiynthe of hills which cluster around the base of the sacred mountain... covered with forests frequented by elephants, wild boars and leopards... across brawling rivers; through ravines so deep that nothing but the sky is seen above'. But what struck him most was not the climb or the shrine at the summit, but the amicable relationship that existed between the devotees of the different religions, who each laid claim to the footprint. 'At the present day, the Buddhists are the guardians of the Sri Pada, but around the object of common adoration the devotees of all races meet, not in furious contention like the Latins and the Greeks at the Holy Sepulchre in Jerusalem, but in pious appreciation of the one solitary object on which they can unite in peaceful worship,' he wrote.

I had been told that I would be met by my 'trekker' guide at 6 a.m. the next morning and that a tuk-tuk had also been arranged to drive us to the small village of Palabaddala, where a temple marks the starting point of the pilgrimage route. The term 'trekker' evoked an image of the Gorkha-like figures that lead treks in the Himalayas; small, lean and ferociously fit. When I met Shivanta, my trekker, the next morning, I was therefore surprised to see a podgy man in his early twenties, with short, stumpy legs, wearing a pair of tight jeans, a skin-tight spandex button-down shirt (popular with young Sri Lankan men in the Colombo nightclubs) and a pair of backless, slip-on leather shoes. He looked at my hiking boots and rucksack uncomfortably and asked the receptionist if they could spare him a bottle of water, as he had not thought to bring anything to drink on the day-long climb. Standing next to him was his lanky friend Santush the tuk-tuk driver who, it became clear, was also going to do the climb with us. He had brought a pale-pink fleecy baby hat with him and nothing else. Feeling unconvinced and slightly concerned, I climbed into the tuk-tuk and we set off.

The road from Ratnapura to Palabaddala is built into the hillsides of the Central Highlands and winds its way through the thick jungle that clings to the slopes. The air was already warm and damp, and the ground was oozing with the festering smell of the tropical undergrowth. The combination of the rich red soil, the heat and the rainfall makes the wetlands and hill country of Sri Lanka extremely fertile, and the vegetation grows hungrily and greedily, with no apparent discrimination. Climbing vines wrap themselves around the telegraph poles, grasses sprout from the roofs of the houses, and lilies and lotus flowers sprawl over the surfaces of ponds and clog the waterways. As the tuk-tuk climbed higher up the mountain road, I saw that great sections of the hillside had been cleared and turned into neat, well-ordered rubber plantations. Each of the tall, slender trees had a number engraved on its trunk and the dribbles of white latex ran along gently scored lines in the bark that directed the rubber from its tapping point into a cup formed from a coconut shell, which was tied round the trunk.

Shivanta and Santush chattered continuously in Sinhala, not seeming to pay much attention to the small villages along the way which, in the absence of any road signs, usually act as navigation points. After an hour Santush stopped the tuk-tuk and crossed the road to ask another driver, who was slumbering behind the wheel of his vehicle, how far it was to Palabaddala. From the driver's laughter and gestures to the road behind us, and from the worried exchange of glances that passed between Shivanta and Santush, it was clear we had been going in the wrong direction for some time. With a nervous laugh and an embarrassed smile, and much to the amusement of the other villagers who were standing by the roadside listening, Santush turned his vehicle around.

Half an hour later we finally arrived at Palabaddala. The village is elevated on a plateau at 335 m above sea level and initially looked no different from the other small settlements we had passed on the road from Ratnapura. A few small, one-storey houses, and the odd banana and powdered milk shop lurked in the jungle foliage, and other than the shrill calls of the jungle birds the village sounded deserted.

The three of us set off along a narrow cobbled lane that forked upwards, away from the village's main road. Shivanta had slipped his leather shoes off, replacing them with a flimsy pair of rubber flip-flops, and Santush had opted to walk the route in bare feet. The haze of the morning was clearing and the sharp, angular peaks of the surrounding mountain ranges rose into the sky above the jungle. The cobbled street was lined by low, barn-like buildings with firmly closed doors. A few old men in sarongs, with bare, splay-toed feet, crouched by the walls of the barns, chewing pieces of grass and barely registering our presence. I asked Shivanta whether these buildings were tea stalls and rest places during the pilgrimage season and he confirmed that they were. I had read that the pathway up to the peak was now an almost continuous staircase formed from tens of thousands of stone steps, and after we crossed a small stream by a rickety bridge the first section of the flight came into view.

The sand-coloured steps were built into the mountainside many years ago, in order to make the steep ascent more manageable. As the pilgrimage season had finished almost five months earlier, the grasses and wild flowers of the hillside had already started to sprawl over the steps and the branches of the ancient, moss-entwined trees met overhead, forming a canopy over the path. After we had climbed a few hundred steps, Shivanta, breathing deeply and streaming with sweat, insisted we stop.

'Is he OK?' I asked Santush, who was still wearing his woolly jumper and had been handling the steps far more easily, springing up them on the toes of his bare feet.

'Shivanta has very bad asthma, madam,' he replied, looking sorrowfully at his wheezing friend. 'Sometimes, it is very difficult for Shivanta to breathe.'

'Does he have an inhaler?' I asked, miming an inhaler action by pointing my fingers into my mouth. Shivanta and Santush watched my mime with confusion and came to the conclusion that I wanted to be fed. Santush looked at the one packet of biscuits he had brought along with protective concern.

Shivanta did not have an inhaler and so the three of us sat down on one of the steps and waited for him to recover. No one spoke. The birds continued to sing. If we continued to stop every ten minutes we would not reach the peak until nightfall. I decided the best strategy would be to take the lead at a brisk pace and that, if Shivanta's asthma was as bad as it seemed, it would be best to discover this early on rather than halfway up the mountain. After a brisk ten-minute march and several hundred stone steps later, Shivanta sank weakly to his haunches at the base of a tree and had an emergency cigarette to aid his breathlessness. Santush, on the other hand, seemed to be doing well and started bouncing up and down, swinging his arms energetically to demonstrate his superior level of fitness. Shivanta gazed at the flight of steps ahead, looking utterly miserable, and after a brief discussion it was decided Santush and I would carry on and Shivanta would somehow catch us up later, at his own pace.

The steps soon led deep into the jungle and the surrounding hillside disappeared from view. We had been climbing steadily upwards for some time, and the combination of the shade and elevation introduced a welcome chill after the stifling humidity lower down. Other than the occasional, cheerful villager – mostly young barefooted boys carrying sacks on their shoulders – we saw no one. Santush was very quiet and seldom spoke, but I did learn that he was twenty-nine years old and, being a devout Buddhist, this was his eleventh trip to the peak.

After another half an hour of continuous climbing we came to a clearing and saw the first signs of habitation since Palabaddala. A collection of small brick buildings and a small shrine of a seated Buddha were surrounded by a low wall, on which three pairs of black army boots were drying in the sunshine. Santush explained that this was an army base, although what the role of the army on a deserted mountainside could possibly be remained unclear. A few young soldiers wearing T-shirts and shorts rather than the usual camouflage jumpsuits wandered in and out of the various buildings, not really appearing to be engaged in anything much, and huddled in a corner to have a good look at the white female. As we crossed the small base and continued up more steps back into the jungle, Santush said with reverence, 'The Sri Lankan army are number one! They kill all the LTTE. We have a very great, very strong army.' Whilst the end of the Sri Lankan civil war is now considered by the international community to have been little short of ethnic cleansing of the LTTE (Liberation Tigers of Tamil Eelam) by the Sri Lankan army, still many Sri Lankans outside of Colombo are very proud of the army's victory and feel that the Tamils in the north generally got what they deserved.

The steps continued up and up through the jungle with markings on the edge every hundred steps to mark the pilgrim's progress. After we had climbed 2,500 steps, we came to a tree with a small wooden sign nailed to the trunk with the word 'Nilihela' painted in neat script. Through the trees was a steep precipice and the face of a neighbouring mountain that descended sharply to the plain below. Santush walked to the edge of the steps, cupped his hands and shouted '*Nilihela-akke!*' loudly at the curved mountainside. The words reverberated through the mountains and were echoed directly back to us. Another of the many legends of the mountain says the echo is caused by the spirit of Nilihela, a young girl who fell from the path and died in the abyss below, and when she hears the pilgrims shouting '*Nilihela-akke!*', which means 'Sister Nilihela', she replies.

As we climbed for a few more hours, the tropical plants, with their bottle-green waxy foliage and ostentatious flowers, were replaced by more delicate alpine plants with smaller, pale leaves and fragile blossoms. We passed through several more army bases, each manned by a small group of very bored young men, lolling in the shade of the trees or running through the buildings, chasing each other and yelping like schoolboys. I wandered into one of these bases alone, whilst Santush stopped to take a leak in the undergrowth, and immediately felt uncomfortable as a group of young men made their way towards me, making lewd gestures in my direction, and calling to anyone left in the buildings to come and have a look. I was relieved when Santush appeared, muttered some words to the soldiers in Sinhala and, taking my arm, marched me quickly through the base and onto the steps on the other side.

All the way the summit of the mountain had been flashing tantalisingly in and out of view, distinguishable from the surrounding mountain tops not only by its sharp peak but also by the sprawling white monastery buildings that teeter on the top and spill over onto the upper slopes. When we had been walking for over three hours the peak appeared again, but now the monastery was shrouded by the afternoon rain clouds. The peak did not seem any closer than it had earlier that morning and I asked Santush how much longer it would take to reach the summit. He looked uncertain and estimated another three hours at least. It was already midday and I calculated that, even if we made our descent in half the time it took to reach the summit, we would be walking through the unlit jungle after the sun had set. Suddenly, I looked at Santush's bag and realised the torch we had brought for this reason was still with Shivanta, who was probably still sitting on the steps, wheezing, further down the mountain.

'What are we going to do about the torch, Santush?' I asked in a panic. 'It will be dark by the time we come down, won't it?' Santush frowned, pulled his mobile phone out of his pocket and tried to call Shivanta, who was several kilometres behind us by now.

'No signal,' said Santush, looking at his phone forlornly.

He suddenly started rummaging in his pockets and drew out his cigarette lighter. We both looked at the lighter for a few moments and then looked uncertainly at each other. We both knew it was a pretty hopeless solution, but we had no alternatives.

'With this and the mobile phone light, we will be safe!' said Santush decisively, as he leapt to his feet, indicating that we were off again.

We climbed for several more hours, crossing shallow streams and passing in and out of the forest canopy. The peak came into and out of view, sometimes shrouded in cloud and sometimes glimmering in the sunshine. The air became cooler and the trees more sparse and willowy. Finally, we stepped into a large clearing and up ahead, across a level path, was the neck of the peak – a short but very sharp ascent up to the summit. The steps were now so steep and shallow that metal handrails had been built alongside them for climbers to hang on to and pull their weight upwards. After the warm claustrophobia of the jungle, the final pathway felt coldly exposed and views of the jagged peaks of the surrounding mountain range, swathed in jungle, rolled out towards the horizon. The afternoon clouds that build up in the rainy season had been gathering as we climbed and their misty wisps whipped about us, obscuring the view and giving the air a sharp chill. Whether it had been a particularly gusty day when Tennent climbed the mountain or whether he suffered from vertigo, I wasn't sure, but when he stood on the same set of steps leading up to the summit, he seemed to fear for his life.

As the pillar-like crag rounds away at either side, the eye, if turned downwards, peers into a chasm of unseen depth; and so dizzy is the elevation that the guides discourage a pause, lest a sudden gust of wind should sweep the adventurous climber from his giddy footing, into the unfathomable gulf below. An iron ladder, let into the face of a perpendicular cliff, upwards of 12 m in height, lands the pilgrim on the tiny terrace which forms the apex of the mountain; and in the centre of this, on the crown of a mass of gneiss and hornblende, the sacred footstep is discovered under a pagoda-like canopy, supported on slender columns and open on all sides to the wind.

There had also been no sign of the lurking elephants or leopards Tennent wrote of and, whilst the scenery was definitely dramatic, I didn't find it as wild or threatening as the descriptions I had read on the hotel veranda the previous evening.

When I pulled myself up the last few steps, the cloud had descended so heavily that the surrounding landscape had completely disappeared in a thick grey mist. The steps ended at the bottom of the monastery walls, which up close were not the gleaming white they had seemed from the slopes, but a murky grey. The doors and windows of the monastery looked as if they had not been opened for months and the whole place had an air of abandonment. Opposite the monastery stood a couple of closed-up refreshment shacks and a small building with the words 'Donation Centre' above a metal grill. The pagoda-shaped buildings were still standing in the middle of the stone terrace, but they had now been fitted with embossed, gold doors which were tightly shut. Although one of these housed the footprint, it was impossible to get into any of them. I stood and watched as four unhappy dogs huddled together for warmth on the steps of the platform. Obeying the instructions on the small gate to the shrine, I removed my walking boots and watched as steam rose from my warm feet as they touched the chilly stone slabs. The only sound was coming from several large silver bells being rung by three elderly men with cotton scarves wrapped around their bald heads, whose thick socks peeped out from under their sarongs. They, too, were huddling together in the shelter of the shrine to protect themselves from the biting wind.

I was joined a few moments later by Santush, who climbed the steps of one of the pagodas and knelt with his head to the ground before a small plaster cast of a seated Buddha surrounded by plastic flowers. He put his palms together and touched his thumbs to his head. The three old men picked up their shoes, filed down the steps of the terrace and disappeared off down the opposite side of the mountain. From the steps of the pagodas it was possible to see in all directions around the mountain – a panorama that Tennent described as the grandest in the world. In the mist, however, it seemed as if we were suspended in a lonely, cold, grey vacuum. Santush produced the pink fleecy baby hat from his pocket that I had seen him carrying at the start of the day, pulled it over his head, and went off to try to find a toilet. A startled monk, bearing the cold in only his orange robe, emerged from one of the decrepit buildings and blinked at me, seeming surprised to have any company. He was followed by a fat, scowling man in the similarly nonchalant attire of a sarong and no shoes or shirt. Whilst I waited for Santush, the man in the sarong leant against the steps, chewing a mouthful of paan. Every few minutes he would stop chewing to spit jets of blood-coloured spittle into what looked like a blood-stained bucket on the concrete slabs, whilst he eyed me with suspicion. The four dogs, who had been contentedly sharing their body heat on the steps, suddenly awoke in a frenzy when an interloper canine arrived on the scene, having dragged its scrawny body up the mountain. They chased the newcomer up and down the steps of the shrine, their claws skidding over the paved surface as they howled and tore at its fur. I sat on the stone steps, feeling depressed; I was freezing, it was lonely and dreary in the mist, and I could not see the sacred footprint. I was tired, it was a long way back down, it would be getting dark soon and we had no torch.

With gravity in our favour, getting down the steps was much quicker than the journey up, but the strain it put on my knees and calves soon reduced my legs to jelly. Santush, too, was suffering from the raw skin that was developing on the soles of his feet after his long ascent on the rough stone steps without shoes. We trotted down side by side, having to stop every few hundred steps for me to shake the lactate from my legs, whilst Santush sat on the stone steps and poked at the red patches of skin on his soles. It was now 5 p.m. and the daylight was beginning to fade. The peak behind us had disappeared under the clouds and, as we descended back into the darkness of the tropical jungle, I began to wonder what we would do in an hour when the sun finally set. As we returned to the clearing of the highest of the army bases we had passed through a few hours earlier, we saw the soldiers gathered around a Humpty Dumpty-like figure seated on the wall. As the figure started to wave to us, Santush recognised it as Shivanta, who had been following us all along, realising we would need the torch. Shivanta and Santush fell on each other and began hugging boisterously. The three of us grinned at each other with relief and set off down the steps together. As we neared the foot of the mountain, the evening air started to regain its humid warmth and the sky turned to violet as the last rays of the day bathed the clouds in a pale glow, silhouetting the darkening peaks of the surrounding mountains. Soon the sun disappeared altogether and we climbed the last few kilometres of the staircase in darkness, the light of the torch barely illuminating the steps ahead.

When I returned to the hotel that evening, the manager asked me what I had thought about the famous footprint. When I told him it had not been possible to see it, he looked confused. 'I think it is always possible to see the footprint, madam,' he said, frowning. 'I think that maybe your guide was mistaken.' As nobody else I spoke to had ever tried to climb the mountain out of the pilgrimage season, I never found out. Tennent had, however, managed to see the footprint and had been unimpressed. 'The indentation in the rock is a natural hollow, artificially enlarged exhibiting the rude outline of a foot about 1.5 m long, and of proportionate breadth; but it is a test of credulity too gross even for fanaticism to believe that the footstep is either human or divine,' he wrote.

The next morning, I made a visit to the town's famous temple complex, the Maha Saman Devale, which is dedicated to one of the island's protector gods, Saman. Buddhists and Hindus both make offerings to these deities, whose legends have become intertwined with both religions. The road that ran up to the temple was lined with stalls selling baskets of fruit, bundles of incense sticks, pots of coconut oil and large bunches of purple lotus flowers for the devotees to offer to the gods in the Devale. Outside the gates fragile old ladies, bent double in their baggy saris, were shuffling through the crowds at the entrance, wafting smoking incense sticks and trying to sell handfuls of white jasmine flowers.

The main temple to Saman looked from the outside like one of the many colonial buildings, with whitewashed walls and a terracotta-tiled roof supported by four wooden pillars. This imposing building was at the top of a flight of stone steps in the centre of a large open courtyard, flanked by long, low, cloister-like buildings. Piles of sandals had been left at the gates and families clutched their offerings as they made their way barefoot up the steps, before standing in silence in the large room at the top, praying with their palms together in front of their chests. Groups of worshippers were seated in front of a large image of the god Saman standing in a halo of light, riding an elephant and holding a lotus flower. I stood and listened to their soft chanting and then followed a family who were leaving via a side door. This led out into another courtyard with a smaller stone temple and some large urns filled with sand, into which people were sticking bundles of billowing incense sticks. The breeze wafted the clouds of sickly smoke around the courtyard, where families sat on the ground in the shade of the walls or queued to get into the smaller temple with their offerings.

I squeezed into the smaller temple with a uniformed army officer who was carrying a bunch of purple lotus flowers. Inside the warm, dark chamber was a statue of the Buddha, which had almost disappeared behind a pile of flower petals that the stream of devotees continued to add to, quietly pinching the flower heads from their long stems. The air was warm and smelled of clammy bodies and petals that were starting to rot. Three old ladies with sharp elbows jabbed their way through the crowd to get their few minutes in front of the Buddha. I began to feel sick. I pushed my way out to the courtyard and sat down in the shade of a tree to watch the streams of worshippers passing between the temples. In spite of the number of people, the whole Devale had an almost soporific aura of tranquillity; a haven from the noise and grime of the town outside. Groups of young girls were sitting on the outer walls, softly whispering to each other, and old men and women slumped under the branches of the bo tree watching the activity around the temple.

I was sitting next to an elderly gentleman who was wearing a white shirt and sarong, and surreptitiously peering through his wire-rimmed glasses at a copy of the day's newspaper in his lap. On the front page was the headline 'Monks murdered in temple', with a photograph of a clutch of orange-robed monks congregating on the street outside some temple walls. I asked one of my colleagues whether he had heard about this over lunch when I got back to Colombo.

'Do you know, one of the monks actually was beheaded,' he replied, as he looked up from his Tupperware box of rice and curry. 'I heard on the radio that his head was completely severed from his body.'

'Do they know who did it?' I asked.

'Well, the newspapers are saying that it was thieves, trying to steal a valuable jewelled sword that was owned by the temple and the two monks who were killed caught them at it. But there is a second theory I have heard mentioned. It is thought that the killer was a disrobed monk who had been a former disciple of one of the elderly monks that was murdered. Maybe he had come back to settle some old score from the time before he left the temple. It's not unheard of you know – monks killing each other over disputes in temple leadership,' he finished, with a dismissive wave of his hand. Evidently these places weren't quite as peaceful as they seemed.

When Tennent returned to Colombo after climbing Adam's Peak in 1845, he didn't follow the jungle road, but instead took one of the boats that ferried rice and areca nuts along the Kalu Ganga River from Ratnapura to the town of Kalutara on the west coast. The torpid, murky river still flows through Ratnapura, lined by tall clusters of yellow bamboo. A few dugout canoes drifted slowly downstream and several families stood in the shallows washing their clothes, but any commercial traffic along the Kalu Ganga had all but disappeared. I found a tuk-tuk to take me back to the bus station, where I boarded the afternoon bus that was heading back to Colombo.

Chapter Three

COLOMBO

Colombo is not a city you remember entering or leaving, for it is hard to know where it begins and where it ends. It has no real centre and is composed of a jigsaw of intriguingly named districts and suburbs – such as Slave Island, Cinnamon Gardens, Bambalapitiya – which straggle and merge into the neighbouring coastal towns that differ only in name. Whether you approach the city from the north or the south, the suburbs of Colombo are always a miserable welcome back to the capital. Whereas the beaches that line the island's coasts and the jungles of the interior embody the best of Sri Lanka, the suburbs of Colombo embody the worst. The small towns of Panadura and Moratuwa, which once formed continuous gardens of cinnamon and coconut palms, are now lined with cracked-facade shops, crammed along the pavement, built over and in-between each other – selling hubcaps, pirate DVDs and cheap PVC handbags – as well as greasy 'curry dens'. The traffic crawls along at little more than a standstill, whilst exhaust pipes choke the air. Children stare vacantly out through grille windows above the shops and tired laundry sags on ropes. Here and there, beggars kneel limply on the pavement with their arms outstretched or simply sleep in the dust and fumes by the side of the road. Towering overhead, large billboards show fair-complexioned women advertising 'Lakshmi's Gold Jewellery', the latest laptops and plasma-screen televisions, all seeming ludicrously inappropriate for the poor audience below.

Given that most visitors to Sri Lanka simply regard Colombo as a headache that must be endured between the airport to its north and the beach resorts to its south, grim suburbs are all that many people see. According to the Lonely Planet, 'Colombo doesn't quite embody the paradisiacal island image of Sri Lanka', and its arch rival, the Rough Guide, says that its 'lack of obvious charms means that it is unlikely to win any immediate friends'. Even Tennent wrote that 'Colombo, as a town, presents little to attract a stranger', and spent a large number of words describing how its location on the island was most ill-suited to that of a capital city, arguing that the town of Trincomalee on the east coast would be a far better choice.

If Bangkok is Asia's city of sex and drugs, Calcutta the city of death and poetry, and Tokyo the technotropolis of innovation, then Colombo is their immature sibling, still trying to find and assert its identity. Over the past few years the city's identity crisis has become a cause of insecurity to some people, causing various brash and sometimes ridiculous statements to be issued about Colombo's future on the world stage. An enormous and ugly Chinese-funded theatre complex was thrown up in a few months, in the hope that Colombo would attract enough world-class performers to become an Asian centre of the performing arts. I heard rumours that Colombo was hoping to become a major shopping destination in South Asia and the plan to build a shopping mall 'so big that it can be seen from Bangladesh' was an optical impossibility bandied about for a while.

To refer to Colombo as a city is also rather misleading; in many ways it bears far more resemblance to a village. The community is close and slightly incestuous – it is impossible to go anywhere without meeting someone you know and you very soon get the impression that many of your acquaintances share not too distant relatives.

'So you two must be some sort of cousins then,' I said to the two men I was sitting with at a dinner party in Colombo one evening, after they had both explained their relationship to our host.

'Yeah, I guess we must be,' they agreed, without much interest.

Then there is the pace of life. Whereas the other capitals of Asia throb twenty-four hours a day with the noise of trade and traffic, by 10 p.m. many of the roads in Colombo are empty, the traffic lights have been switched off, and many of the streets are silent and dark. During the day, Buddhist devotees sit peacefully in the shade of the bodhi trees in the temples around the city and the tuk-tuk drivers need to be roused from sleep if you want to go anywhere. Even the packs of mongrel dogs stretched out on the pavements seem drugged and can rarely be bothered to chase the meandering bicycles down the road.

When the bus had pulled into the central bus station, I flagged down a tuk-tuk to take me through the old part of the city, where many of the red-and-white-brick colonial

British buildings remain, past the city's small lake with its floating temple, to my house in Cinnamon Gardens. This part of the city was named after the gardens of cinnamon laurel the Dutch planted in the area, which have long-since gone and were replaced by the British with large, white, colonial mansions surrounded by walled, tropical gardens. As the tuk-tuk drove down the quiet, tree-lined roads, flocks of fruit bats flew overhead, their large, sinister forms silhouetted against the violet evening sky. Most of the roads in Colombo still have an army presence and, even though the war has ended, young khaki-clad soldiers wearing green berets, with rifles strapped across their shoulders, stand on most street corners during the day. As the day was drawing to a close, many of the young soldiers were on their way home, riding a single bicycle as a pair, one sitting on the saddle pedalling whilst their friend sat sideways on the frame in front, casually balancing their firearms in his lap.

As we passed the Sinhalese Sports Club, which houses one of the city's cricket stadiums, I saw a group of teenage schoolboys draping enormous blue and yellow silk flags over the walls. 'It's for the Royal–Thomian cricket match tomorrow, madam,' said the tuk-tuk driver. 'Very old match madam, very famous match. Will you be watching?'

The Royal–Thomian Cricket Encounter is Sri Lanka's equivalent of the Oxford–Cambridge Boat Race and is the annual sports fixture between the country's oldest, rival academic institutions that has taken place for the past 133 years. Royal

College and St Thomas' College were both founded in the mid-nineteenth century by middle-aged British Etonians, to provide a combination of academic tuition and religious instruction for an elite, emerging class of westernised Sri Lankans in the colony's capital. Being able to speak English was necessary for even minor posts in the British administration of the island at that time and so an education from one of the capital's 'English medium schools' was seen as a way of attaining social mobility. Both Royal College and St Thomas' College were run by a series of British headmasters, who had all followed the same path from the boarding houses of Eton and Wellington, through the quadrangles of Oxford and Cambridge and on to a teaching post at an English public school. Eventually they made their way to Colombo, where they continued to operate in exactly the same way as they had in England, but in a warmer climate.

Not surprisingly, 'Royal' and 'St Thomas', as they are simply referred to nowadays, still bear many similarities to the public schools of England. The lessons were taught in English and the curriculum was the same as that being taught in Victorian England, with the history and geography of Ceylon being ignored in favour of that of Britain. Each school still has a Latin motto, a school crest and a school song that describes education as some kind of epic journey. The traditional British school sports of cricket, rugby and rowing were also introduced and even today both schools still use quaint, public-school phrases, referring to their 'house captains' and the sportsmen who have earned 'colours'.

In the good old-fashioned spirit of public schoolboy rivalry encouraged by the English schoolmasters, the Royal–Thomian

Cricket Encounter was first played in 1880. The match was devised by a Mr Falkner of St Thomas' College and a Mr Walker of Royal College, who had played cricket together at Cambridge before they ended up teaching in the island's rival schools – and presumably liked the idea of reliving their youth on foreign soil. The three-day cricket match, which has taken place every year since 1880, undeterred by World Wars One and Two, is now a huge event which grinds parts of the capital to a halt and is followed closely by the national press.

I had first heard about the Royal–Thomian from Preneetha, the wife of one of my colleagues. She told me proudly that her brother had captained the Royal College eleven in the 1970s and had returned to Colombo for the weekend, with his Royal College tie and blazer, to watch the match with his old team-mates. When I mentioned to a colleague that I was thinking of trying to get hold of a ticket for the match, he rolled his eyes and sighed.

'Why do you want to have anything to do with those schools?' he asked. 'They are outdated time warps, stuck in the nineteenth century. They are obsessed with maintaining all these silly British traditions that don't even exist in England anymore.' He shook his head in frustration. 'They need to come into the twenty-first century and realise that we are no longer a British colony,' he said.

Intrigued, I went down to St Thomas in the seafront suburb Mount Lavinia to try to track down any remaining tickets for the famous 'Battle of the Blues'. I arrived just as school had finished and the whole scene reminded me of the minor public boys' boarding school in which I had taught for three years in Oxfordshire. The school was housed in a number of pale, neoclassical, stone buildings and a large chapel, dotted around extensive grounds overlooking the sea. Streaming out of the school gates and lolling around by the side of the road were the St Thomas boys in their blue and black sports kits, toting badminton rackets, swimming towels and cricket bats. Sri Lankan mothers wearing sunglasses, platform heels and brightly coloured, manicured nails were leaning out of the windows of their Land Rovers, yapping on mobile phones and waiting to pick up their children. I walked through the grounds and bought my ticket from a young man in a small office in one of the old stone buildings. Most people, he informed me, had bought their tickets weeks in advance and I was extremely lucky that I had managed to get one of the last remaining few.

The cricket ground of the Sinhalese Sports Club was only a stone's throw from my house and I could already hear the match taking place as I walked out of the front door. Cricket matches in Sri Lanka take place against a background of beating drums and snarling trombones, played by troops of excitable boys who jump up and down, dancing with their instruments on the sidelines. Hanging around outside the stadium, boys from both of the schools were dressed in their school uniform of starched, white trousers and white shirts, with the addition of large, straw hats, with flowers in the school colours pinned to the upturned brims. Families carrying picnic hampers and the schools' silk flags were queuing up to get through the gates and hordes of middle-aged men wearing old school blazers or polo shirts, with the year they graduated emblazoned on the back, all jostled for space.

When I finally managed to push my way through one of the gates, I found an empty seat next to a couple of schoolboys dressed in the white uniform and yellow-and-blue-striped ties. I asked which of the schools they were from and they said Royal College. They were both eighteen years old and in their last year of school. I asked how difficult it was to be selected for the team and they both shook their heads. 'It's so hard, like you wouldn't believe,' said one of the boys with reverence. 'We have been coming to the match since we were small boys and everyone who plays cricket at school wants to play in this match when they are in the sixth form. If you play in the match, there is a whole network of old boys around the island who are just waiting to offer you a job. If you captain one of the teams you can take your pick.'

Even these students had something strangely reminiscent of the British public schoolboy about them. They spoke English eloquently, with the body language of a relaxed, good-natured confidence that the world was at their feet; they had been educated in an establishment that had been tried and tested by generations before them, and once they uttered its name they had nothing more to prove. The boys were also noticeably taller and more powerfully built than the average scrawny Sri Lankan teenage boys who walk the streets of Colombo, which presumably added to their sense of ease. They told me that St Thomas had been the favourites to win that year; their team was stronger and had won more of the friendly matches throughout the season. The match had started to turn in Royal's favour the day before, however, and they said (with a wink) that they were sure they could turn the game around.

Down on the pitch, under the relentless mid-morning sun, the schoolboy cricketers seemed to be flagging, and looked limp and tired in their cricket whites and floppy sunhats. Luckily, it was the end of the first innings and, as the players disappeared off the pitch into the shade, the crowds of spectators jumped out of their seats, climbed over the barriers and descended onto the field. Fifty boys from each of the schools ran around the pitch carrying a 10-m-long silk flag in their school colours, whilst the bands of trombones and drummers hurled themselves around the sidelines to the baton of a conductor who threw his arms in the air and jived with them under the midday sun. Crowds of boys from each school gathered in crowds to bellow chants at each other across the pitch, whilst the frail old boys in their gaping blazers and polo shirts watched limply in slight bewilderment, sucking ice lollies in the shade.

Sitting on the seats behind me was a row of five men who looked to be in their sixties, and had been growing more and more merry as the morning wore on. This was largely due to the bottle of Johnnie Walker Red Label they had been passing along and liberally sloshing into their polystyrene cups. I turned round and asked them which team they were supporting. 'We are all from St Thomas' College,' said the slender, clean-shaven man who was sitting directly behind me wearing a baseball cap. 'We all left in 1959 and we have watched the game from these five seats every year since then. Some of us don't even live in Sri Lanka anymore,' he said, grinning at a short tubby man sitting at the end of the row. 'He has lived in England since 1964, but still he comes back for the match every year.'

The other four men still lived in Colombo and I asked them how they had spent their lives since they left St Thomas over half a century before. 'Well, this is a very powerful man,' said the clean-shaven man with a wink, gesturing to the small, tidy man to his right, who had a neatly trimmed moustache, a carefully pressed shirt and thinning, black hair, slicked back across his head. The man looked rather sheepish and offered me his hand to shake. 'He was a commander in the Sri Lankan army for many years, but every year when we are back here together, we cut him down to size!' he said gleefully, slapping his old friend on the back. 'My friend and I are both retired lawyers,' he continued, gesturing to the friend to his right, 'and this chap,' motioning to a broad, soporific man with shoulder-length, grey hair and a long, wispy beard that straggled down his torso, 'is a celebrated surgeon.' The men had all brought Tupperware boxes of white-bread sandwiches with the crusts cut off, which they shared with each other and with me. I asked if they had made the sandwiches themselves and they began to giggle. 'This is the one time of year when our wives let us out,' said one of the lawyers, 'but they still insist that we take their sandwiches with us.'

As the morning turned into afternoon and the match resumed, the men behind me became more and more giggly, and I could hear them reminiscing about the past as they gripped each other's knees and slapped each other on the back. From time to time they recognised more old friends, who they jumped up to greet with hugs and handshakes, before sinking back into their seats to talk about the old days, whilst keeping half an eye on the cricket. It was clear that, much like the Oxford–Cambridge Boat Race, the match was really only an excuse for a day out. The girls from the local convent schools, wearing big plastic earrings and tight jeans, came to proudly hang off the arms of their boyfriends; the children came for the ice-cream, their fathers for the beer and the mothers to gossip with the other women; but, mainly, the match was for the old boys of Royal and St Thomas, who occupied most of the seats in the stadium. For them it was a chance to escape from imperfections of the present, from their wives and responsibilities and to revisit their schooldays, through the rosy, blurred focus of alcohol and nostalgia.

Soon after Tennent arrived in Colombo he was sworn in as a member of the Executive Council, the governing body that ruled Britain's crown colony of Ceylon. Over the following months he started to familiarise himself with the administration of the colony, in particular with the ways in which the colonial government used Ceylon as a source of income. For a member of the colonial government, Tennent was surprisingly critical of many of the liberties that were being taken to extort money from the islanders, including the tax imposed on rice cultivation, and the tolls charged on bridges and ferries. Queen Victoria, thousands of miles away in England, was the only person who could grant permission for anyone on the island to collect salt or distil arrack from the juice of the coconut palm – and she also controlled a monopoly of the island's pearl fisheries.

Tennent spent several months in the capital before he embarked on the next stage of his trip and I, too, had an enforced break from travelling as the school term had started again and I had to return to the classroom. Like Tennent's, my journey was not a continuous one – both of us being tied to Colombo for months at a time by the jobs that had initially brought us to the island. One weekend, soon after term had resumed, I went along to a large book fair that was being held in one of the assembly halls in the centre of the city. Most books in Sri Lanka have to be imported from branches of the big publishing houses in India and finding books in the city can be difficult. The book fair is a massive event every year that lasts for a week, and people from Colombo and its suburbs rush to stock up on enough books to last them until the fair returns the next year.

As I was squeezing my way through the crowds crammed between the shelves, I came across a small, leather-bound volume called *On Demonology and Witchcraft in Ceylon* by a Sri Lankan named Dandris de Silva Gooneratne. The book had first been published in 1865 and was an extraordinary account of the many superstitious practices the author had witnessed taking place all over the island at the time. Intrigued, I elbowed my way out of the crowd and sat down at a table in the shade to read more. The book spoke about the worship of various demons who were thought to be the cause and cure of disease, and the charms and ceremonies the islanders used to protect themselves from their malevolent influence. It talked about the worship of the planets and the stars, whose movements the islanders believed dictated the future, as well as the horoscopes they lived their lives by. Dandris de Silva Gooneratne had also come across Tennent's work on Ceylon, which would have only been published a few years before his own. Whilst he regarded Tennent's book as 'the last and greatest' work that had been written about the island, he criticised Tennent for having failed to notice the massive influence superstitious beliefs had on the lives of its inhabitants. This seemed a little unfair as Tennent pointed out that beneath the daily rituals of Buddhism lurked 'the unextinguished fires of another and a darker superstition, whose flames overtopped the icy summits of the Buddhist philosophy and excited a deeper and more reverential awe in the imagination of the Sinhalese'. He wrote about the island's devil priests and the ceremonies they performed, which he regarded as so barbarous as to be revolting, and the devil dancers who were summoned to cure the sick and the dying.

I had been amazed when I first arrived by the number of superstitions that still shape the lives of even the most highly educated, rational Sri Lankans on a daily basis. I first heard about them even before I started work, from a British architect who had been living in Sri Lanka for fifteen years. He told me: 'Even when we are planning large-scale, commercial buildings, if we are working for a Sri Lankan company, they will often consult the local Buddhist priest about our plans. The priest then names an "auspicious time" determined by the alignment of the planets, which dictates the date and the exact time at which the foundations must start to be laid. It's not unusual for us to end up starting the building work at 3.46 a.m. in the pouring rain, just because a priest has said so. It makes no sense to me, but that is what everyone believes, so we have to respect it.'

Marriages, too, are determined partially by the advice of an astrologer. Many marriages in the country are still arranged and, as part of the process, the horoscopes of the prospective bride and groom must be compared by an astrologer to determine whether it is an auspicious match. 'I decided not to have our horoscopes compared,' a Sri Lankan friend told me a few days before her second wedding. 'My first husband and I went through the whole process and apparently the horoscopes were a perfect match, but that marriage only lasted a year. It's odd though,' she said pursing her lips, 'although I know it's all rubbish, I'm still a little uneasy that we haven't checked.'

But most bizarre and worrying of all are the attempts of the island's astrologers to stick their oar into national politics. The Sri Lankan newspaper *The Sunday Times* ran a story about the potentially disastrous effects that the entry of Saturn into Virgo and the entry of Jupiter into Taurus were predicted to have on the president. As one astrologer explained, if the head of state was entering a malefic period of his life, this meant a bad period for the country as well. In such situations, a handful of the capital's celebrated astrologers said they had no choice but to advise the president to leave the country for a while. When the president announced his plans to travel to Cuba and Brazil, many people believed this was why. The president's personal astrologer, however, denied these claims. Having seen the president's birth chart, he said he could confidently say that transitions of Jupiter were in fact a good thing for the president and he would be far better off staying at home.

I showed my new book on demonology and witchcraft in Ceylon to Mr Perera, my erudite and well-travelled school librarian, who had left Sri Lanka in his early twenties to see the world. Mr Perera was a Roman Catholic and, although he was proudly dismissive of most of the island's superstitious practices, his mother's superstitious beliefs had shaped his early years. I asked him whether he thought demon worship still went on in Sri Lanka, as it was something I had heard nothing about and I assumed had died out. 'Ah, you mean the bali ceremonies,' he said with a smile, as he pushed away a pile of books and leant back in his chair. 'My mother took me to one when I was about twelve years old, in our town of Badulla in the hill country. They used to happen a lot in those days and I wouldn't be surprised if those things still go on in our rural communities in the south. The towns have moved on, but some of the rural areas really have not changed that much.'

'Can you remember much about the ceremony?' I asked him. Mr Perera crossed his hands behind his head and smiled at me. He had a talent for telling vivid, descriptive tales and I knew this was going to be good.

'They always took place at night, at around eleven p.m., and you could tell when a ceremony was taking place because you could hear the drumming and see the flames a long way off. When I was at boarding school in Kandy, my boarding house looked out over the river and the bali ceremonies would take place on the banks. Some nights the drumming was so loud that I could not sleep. The purpose of the ceremonies was to summon the demon spirits to cure someone who was unwell. In those days, the villagers believed that all illness was caused by these evil spirits. The person who was sick would be covered in a white shroud, and they would be surrounded by masked drummers and people holding burning torches. The drummers would beat a furious rhythm and the villagers would dance, shaking their bodies violently until they were all in a trance. Then the priest would throw a kind of resin on the torches, which would explode into flames and light up the night sky. Next a chicken would be brought into the ring and the neck would be broken to spill the creature's blood. Everyone was hot and sweating, and a lot of the young village girls would work themselves into such a frenzy that they would have to be carried off into the cool jungle to recover. My mother claimed that when she had been at one of these ceremonies, the branches of the trees overhead all fell to the ground simultaneously. She was convinced that it was caused by the spirits moving in the trees.'

When Tennent had travelled through the south of the island, along the road from Galle to Colombo a century earlier, he described an almost identical ceremony involving the sacrifice of a cockerel and a frenzy of masked men dancing in the dark jungle. He also observed another occult practice in which the locals would fasten a fan of leaves to the stems of the fruit trees. 'This is to denote that the tree has been devoted to a demon. This ceremony is called Gok-handecma, "the tying of the tender leaf", and its operation is to protect the fruit from pillage until it is ripe enough to be plucked as an offering to the divinity to whom it is consecrated.'

Mr Perera took his glasses off and rubbed his eyes. 'You could always go down south and try to find a ceremony you know, but you would be getting into some very murky areas. I'm not sure it would be wise for a European,' he said.

I asked him whether his superstitious mother had a horoscope drawn up for him at his birth. 'She did, but I burned the damn thing,' he said with a sniff. 'It's all mumbo-jumbo if you ask me, but many people still believe it all. There's the horoscopes, the palm reading, the evil eye and then of course there are the Hindus with their ola leaves. Now they are very strange, those ola leaves – very strange indeed. You should really look into them.'

I had first heard of the ola leaves from Rajiv, a gentle Tamil man with a thick, dark moustache, who was a lecturer of mathematics at a local university. Although he had lived in Jaffna as a child, like many young people from wealthy, educated families in the north, he had been sent to university abroad during the civil war. When he returned to Sri Lanka the war was in its final, bloody stages, so rather than returning to the north he moved south and tried to find a job in the capital. 'But I was having so much trouble finding employment,' Rajiv told me indignantly, 'me, with my bachelors and masters in mathematics from a very, very prestigious Indian university! I could not believe it. I became very depressed and I did not know what to do.' It was then that a Tamil friend of Rajiv's, who was also living in Colombo, had directed him to a group of astrologers who operated in a small, dilapidated apartment by the seafront on the edge of the city.

According to southern Indian mystics, there lived 2,000 years ago a group of seven sages or *rishis* in India, who were able to predict the futures of every single person on earth, both in their present incarnations and in their future reincarnations. Helpfully, they inscribed a number of these predictions, firstly on animal skins, then on copper and finally on ola leaves – the narrow leaves of the talipot palm. The inscriptions were scored onto the leaves using a sharp, nail-like device and were written in Vatta Ezhuthu, an ancient, poetic Tamil script. Many of these ola leaves were discovered by the British during their period of rule in India. Whilst many were sold to communities of astrologers in South India, others were scattered throughout the world. A number of bundles of these ola leaves apparently fell into the hands of a group of Tamil men in Colombo who will, for a fee, search through the leaves to find the details of your future. Large numbers of people in both India and Sri Lanka go along to have their ola leaves read to them, not only to find out specific details of their future, but also to search through the information in the leaves that may explain current problems in their lives and offer guidance as to what to do.

Rajiv's friend had taken him along to the ola readers in Colombo in order to find out why he was having such unexpected difficulty finding a job. 'At first I did not believe in any of this stuff,' said Rajiv in a low voice, 'but everything they said was right! First they told me my mother's and my father's names, which were completely accurate. It could not have been a lucky guess though, as my mother and father both have very unusual Tamil names. And then they told me that I would become a lecturer. But I was so angry when I heard this. Lecturers do not earn high salaries. It is not a well-respected job and I really wanted to work as a software engineer.' Here, Rajiv lowered his voice even further and spoke gravely. 'But then I saw an advertisement for a lecturing job. Before I had spoken to these men I would never have applied, but I had not earned money for so long that I made the application. And in the end, they offered me the job. Never would I have thought I would end up as a lecturer, but here I am.' Straightening himself up again Rajiv looked at me triumphantly. 'So, you see, what is written in the ola leaves must be true. Now, whenever I have an important decision to make I go to them first and they tell me what I should do. I think they will do readings for foreign people too if you want, but it will probably cost more money.'

I considered asking Rajiv whether he would have even applied for a lecturing job if he had not been more or less instructed to do so, but instead, I decided to go along to these intriguing men by the sea and see whether they had anything helpful to tell me.

The ola leaf readers were not easy to find. I searched the Internet, I trawled through the telephone directories and street maps of Colombo in vain. Although many people were aware of their existence, they seemed to have the status of a notorious secret organisation and nobody could tell me where exactly in the city they could be found. I also searched through Tennent's book to see whether he had come across the ola readers, but although he mentioned there was a professor in every village to construct horoscopes and cast the nativities of the peasantry, he did not seem aware of their existence. Eventually, a colleague at my school admitted she had visited the ola readers and the next morning she slipped a small piece of paper into my hand, on which an address was scrawled in pencil and the instruction 'Be there before 8 a.m.'

The next morning I got up early and set off through the unusually quiet streets of Colombo on the old, steel bicycle I had recently purchased to simultaneously avoid feelings of environmental guilt every time I got into a carbon monoxide-belching tuk-tuk and the protracted arguments with the tuk-tuk drivers about the price of every journey. Although the sun had risen, it was still low in the sky and the streets of the city were bathed in pale, early morning light. The roads were pleasantly free of traffic and I was able to cycle slowly through the shady streets of Cinnamon Gardens and watch the maids and 'boys' opening up the gates of the large, white colonial residences. Behind the gates the gardeners were already at work, watering the hibiscus and bougainvillea that spilled their brightly coloured flowers over the whitewashed walls.

I made my way down the recently reopened Bauddhaloka Mawatha, one of the central roads in the city which is home to various army and government buildings. On the pavement outside, young skinny boys wearing camouflage uniforms and green berets leant out of corrugated-iron watchtowers with rifles over their shoulders, monitoring the passing traffic. The trees that lined the road were so large that the branches met overhead, giving the impression of driving through a dark tunnel. I turned my bicycle onto the only four-lane road in the country, which runs through the city's main shopping district, and then down a narrow lane and onto the coastal road known as Marine Drive.

Cycling from Cinnamon Gardens onto the parched, dusty tarmac of Marine Drive is like entering a different and less-developed country. There are no trees to provide either shade from the equatorial sun or shelter from the strong sea breeze, which blows in from the blue expanse of the Indian Ocean that stretches to the horizon. The only thing separating the road from the sea is the train track. Groups of small Muslim boys wearing white, crocheted caps and *salwar kameez* (a thin tunic worn over light cotton trousers) were walking along the road with their mothers, who were dressed from head to toe in black, as they headed towards the mosque. A few creased old men, bare-chested and wearing sarongs, were shuffling slowly along the road by the side of the railway lines, leaning on walking sticks and occasionally holding out a begging bowl to passers-by. As I was cycling along, licking the sea salt on my lips, I heard a rumbling in the distance; suddenly a flock of seagulls that were pecking at rubbish along the railway ascended into the sky as the morning commuter train roared by.

The scrawled address on the scrap of paper led me to a shabby apartment block, set back from the sea along a narrow, unpaved lane. Although there was no sign anywhere to indicate which flat was home to the ola readers, I could see a large pile of about thirty pairs of shoes at the bottom of one of the staircases, below a gaudy poster of Ganesh, the elephant-headed Hindu god. Assuming that this must be the place, I climbed up a winding flight of stairs and came out onto a narrow balcony overlooking the lane, off which two small flats had their doors wide open. Seated on plastic chairs that ran the length of the balcony, a row of Sri Lankan men and women of all ages sat in reverential silence, peering through the open doors of the two flats. An elderly gentleman, dressed in a white sarong and a white shirt, padded up and down the balcony in bare feet and silently motioned to me that I should enter one of the flats. Inside, more men and women were sitting on velour armchairs and settees in silence, evidently waiting for something to happen. More colourful pictures of Ganesh hung on the walls in gilded frames, and large statues of Ganesh and Shiva, the multi-armed Hindu God, were arranged in the corner of the room, strung with garlands of marigolds.

I sat down on the only unoccupied seat in the corner of the room and tried to ignore the many pairs of eyes staring at me, clearly intrigued as to what a European was doing there. Seated with me in the room was a pair of young men absorbed by their mobile phones, and three elderly Hindu women wearing polyester saris and various pieces of dented gold jewellery. Several middle-aged married couples stared vacantly at the wall and a pair of teenage girls in skinny jeans whispered to each other. The air was muggy with the sickly, smoky smell of incense and stacked underneath all of the pieces of furniture were hundreds of blank TDK cassettes, still in their plastic wrapping.

We all sat in silence for a further half an hour, until a group of four portly, middle-aged men, all wearing white sarongs, swept through the flat and unlocked the door to a back room. This was clearly what we had all been waiting for and, within seconds, everyone in the room had jumped to their feet and raced to the opened door. Everyone on the balcony was also trying to crowd into the room and the two groups of people, who had been sitting so placidly in silence, were now pushing and elbowing their way past each other with a newly fired aggression. I hovered gingerly at the back of the queue and, when I finally entered the room, I was ushered to a large desk, behind which stood one of the men dressed in white, with the others hovering around him. The man sitting at the desk had a thick black moustache and smears of grey ash on his forehead. A small piece of paper was pushed in front of me and one of the hovering men snapped, 'Left thumb!' I looked at my left thumb in confusion, before it was taken from me, rolled along a strip of ink and printed onto the piece of paper. 'And what is the day of your birth?' asked another hovering man, who quickly transcribed my reply onto the same piece of paper. 'Finished!' declared a third man and I was ushered back out of the room.

The four men in white locked the door again and we all returned to our seats, to resume our waiting in silence. I was now sitting next to the two teenage girls, who smiled at me shyly whilst they licked and rubbed their purple thumbs to try to remove the ink. One of them whispered to me, 'What is your country?' I explained that I was English but that I lived in

Colombo and they smiled with interest. I asked them if they had been to the ola readers before and if they knew what we were waiting for now. 'The men are now reading our thumb prints to see if they have our ola leaves,' one of the girls explained. 'They don't have ola leaves for everyone, only for some people. If they have the ola leaf for your thumb print, they will give you the time when you must return this afternoon.' The girls were both first-year medical students at the University of Colombo and they had come to the ola readers to find out whether they would pass their next set of exams. 'We have to pay for every exam we sit, so if we don't pass it, it's a big waste of money. If they tell us that we will not pass, then we will not enter ourselves for the exam. We will revise for several more weeks and come again to have another reading. Only when they tell us we will pass will we sit the exam.'

After about twenty minutes, the men in white emerged from the room and, one at a time, our dates of birth were read out. One by one we each received our thumbprint, with the time and date at which we should return scrawled across the bottom in ballpoint pen. We were also handed what looked like a menu, from which we could select a 'chapter' – of what seemed to be a selection of randomly assorted details about our lives – to be read to us from the ola leaf on our return. I sat back down with my menu and tried to decide.

- 1st chapter: General introductory chapter to establish genealogy, etc. Central to correct reading of other particulars

- 2nd chapter: Particulars relating to education, family life, eye vision, etc.

- 3rd chapter: Particulars relating to brothers and sisters, and beneficial effects they have on you

- 4th chapter: Particulars relating to mother, housing, lands, buying and selling, vehicles, etc.

- 5th chapter: Particulars relating to birth of children, childlessness, and children's education and future

- 6th chapter: Particulars relating to enemies and adversaries, illness, lawsuits and the effects of the actions of enemies

- 7th chapter: Auspicious periods for marriage, causes of the delay of marriage, characteristics of prospective life partner

- 8th chapter: Life span, malefic periods, accidents, etc.

- 9th chapter: Father, father's assets, pilgrimages and blessings by holy persons

- 10th chapter: Employment, business, trade, profession and what is most suitable for you

- 11th chapter: Sources of income, wealth and the benefits of a second marriage

- 12th chapter: Place/country of rebirth and travel overseas

- 13th chapter: Place of previous birth, karma and remedial measures

- 14th chapter: Talisman, yantra and the type of chanted yantra to be worn

- 15th chapter: Remedies for incurable or hereditary diseases.

- 16th chapter: Planetary changes and the beneficial and malefic influences of planetary changes.

When I returned that afternoon, I was ushered into a bright, air-conditioned room by a small balding man wearing an ill-fitting navy-blue suit and fine, gold-rimmed spectacles, who was holding a plastic carrier bag in his hand. He motioned to me to sit on a large, mock-leather swivel chair on the far side of a large desk, on which stood an old Sony cassette recorder and a microphone. Staring down at me from the walls were more gaudy pictures of Ganesh, sitting fatly in various sylvan settings, surrounded by waterfalls and butterflies. There was also a large photograph of the Indian guru Sathya Sai Baba, draped with marigold garlands. The small man sat opposite, and informed me he was to be my interpreter and would translate the messages that would be read to me in Tamil by the ola reader. A few minutes later, a very large man of about thirty waddled into the room, wearing the white sarong and shirt uniform of the ola readers. He placed on the table a stack of narrow, rectangular pieces of what looked like yellowed parchment, bound between two pieces of wood and tied together with string. The reader began to undo the pieces of string and beamed at me through a thick moustache, as he began to separate the fine leaves. Scored very faintly into the leaves I could see a script of flourishes and dots, which looked like a cross between Arabic and Tamil.

'On these leaves,' began the interpreter, 'there are the informations regarding many people and, we hope, for you as well. But it may not be so. What he will do is read to you the informations about all the people on these leaves and if we think that one of them is you, he will go and fetch your specific chapter.'

The ola reader sat up straight, beamed again and started to read rapidly in a monotone in Tamil. After a few sentences he would stop, draw in his breath and, as he was doing so, the interpreter would translate what had been said into English.

'You are a spinster and this is not your home country.' I agreed, disliking the word 'spinster'.

'Your parents are both living, but not in this country.' I agreed again.

'You are in employment in Colombo.' I agreed a third time.

'You are not having any children.'

After I had agreed to these four, easily predictable facts, both the ola reader and the interpreter looked triumphant.

'You are holding a degree.'

'Yes.'

'In economics.'

'Um, no.'

'In languages.'

'No.'

'In sciences.'

'Yes.'

'Your name is Stella!'

'No.'

At this point the two men looked rather disheartened. The ola reader who had been reading rapidly in a monotone for several minutes, almost without breath, started breathing heavily and we all smiled at each other in silence for a few minutes, before continuing.

'Your mother's name begins with the letter K.'

'No.'

'S?'

'No.'

'P?'

'No.'

'D??'

'No.'

'J????'

'Yes!'

'Mother's name is Jasmine!'

'Er, no. Sorry.'

'Jerry.'

'No.'

'Julia.'

'No.'

'Gillian.'

'Almost... '

'Jill!'

'Yes!'

Well, they had got a few things right, but it seemed far more like educated guesswork and trial and error than the accurate statements that other people had reported. The ola reader seemed satisfied, however, that he had stumbled across evidence of my 'specific details' in the leaves and asked me which of the 'chapters' of my life I would like to be read to me. I retrieved from my bag the list of chapters I had been given that morning and tried to decide. As I had no brothers or sisters, no children, no pending lawsuits, no problems with my vision, was not planning to go on any pilgrimages, had no desire to know my lifespan or 'malefic' periods in my life, already had a profession and did not believe I had lived a previous life, I settled on the 7th chapter. 'Auspicious periods for marriage, causes of the delay of marriage, characteristics of prospective life partner'. The two men looked at each other and smirked.

'Very good, madam! Women are often wanting to know about what husbands they will be having. Also, it's good for you, because it is not a very expensive chapter.'

When the ola reader had waddled out of the room to go and find my set of leaves, the interpreter started fumbling in the plastic bag he had brought into the room with him and produced from it a small, paperback book, which he pushed across the table to me. The book was entitled *Ways of Knowing God* and had a picture of two palms, clasped in prayer on the front cover. The interpreter peered at me over his gold spectacle frames and whispered across the desk, 'Are you saved?' I was rather confused. Why was an evangelical Christian, who generally disapproves of the notion that anyone other than the Almighty has knowledge of the future, acting as an interpreter to a Hindu fortune teller?

'I am a preacher at a local Catholic church,' the interpreter whispered. 'Do you know God?' I had tried to explain the concept of agnosticism several times before in Sri Lanka and on each occasion it had just caused confusion. I decided to answer his question with one of my own instead.

'Do you believe that these people really know my future?' I asked him, as I pushed his book back across the table towards him. 'Surely you believe only God knows our future?' The interpreter started to look rather sheepish and hurriedly put the book back into his plastic bag. 'It is up to you, madam, whether you believe what these people say,' he said in a rather defensive tone. 'But when I was a young man they told me that I would not marry the lady I was engaged to and they were right. She was not a good lady and she married my friend instead.'

The reader shuffled back into the room with a new sheaf of wood-bound ola leaves. The interpreter started looking in a drawer under the desk, pulled out a blank TDK B60 cassette and started to undo its cellophane wrapping. When the cassette was unwrapped and ready in the Sony tape recorder, the ola reader took a deep breath and started reading in his rapid, monotonous Tamil, whilst the interpreter translated into the microphone.

'The subject hailed from a respectable family to good parents and was born in the year 1984, in the month of November, on the first day, which was a Thursday. On the day of her birth the planets were in the following positions: in the first place was Mars and the Moon and in the fifth place was Rahu. The Sun and Saturn were in the tenth position, in the eleventh was Mercury, Venus and Ketu, and Jupiter was in the twelfth place. These were the planetary positions at the time when the subject was born.'

Most of the names of the planets were familiar, but I had never heard of Rahu or Ketu. Whilst the ola reader stopped to draw breath, I asked the interpreter what they were. Rahu and Ketu, he explained, are the north and south lunar nodes, the two points of intersection of the sun and the moon as they move around the celestial sphere, which causes eclipses. According to Hindu mythology, the Hindu gods had an elixir which they drank to become immortal. One day, Rahu, a demon, disguised himself as a god and drank some of the sacred elixir. The Sun and Moon spotted Rahu in the act and passed on the information to the god Vishnu. Just as Rahu was swallowing the elixir, Vishnu arrived on the scene and cut off his head. Since the elixir had passed into the throat, the head of Rahu had already become immortal and remained alive. Rahu is now the immortal head and Ketu is the name given to his headless torso. Because the Sun and Moon were responsible for reporting Rahu's disguise, the immortal head of Rahu now chases the Sun and Moon across the sky for eternity. Occasionally he catches and swallows one of them, causing an eclipse.

The ola reader licked his fingers, cracked his knuckles, thumbed through the ola leaves and continued.

'On such formation of planetary positions, the subject was born overseas. She has much knowledgeable wisdom and her future life will be very prosperous. The subject is a follower of Christianity and, at the time of the reading of her first chapter, her parents are both living overseas. The father is serving as a research scientist, the mother is a teacher and the subject is not having any brothers or sisters. The subject is not married yet, but the parents are having grave concerns about her marriage prospects. The subject is holding degrees in connection with science. Presently she is employed as a teacher, in a country that is not her birth country and she is deriving a good sum as her remuneration. She will lead a good life during the ages of twenty-eight and twenty-nine and will live a very comfortable and contented life. Later in life she will visit so many countries around the globe and will be helped by her associates. She will be active and healthy and destined to live a very long life. The subject's name is Cherry, her father's name is David and her mother's name is Jill. After giving these details we will now close the first chapter.'

The ola reader took a swig of water from a small bottle on the table, gargled and cleared his throat, whilst the interpreter rewound the cassette and played back the last few lines to make sure it had been recording properly. The reader wiped his brow with a handkerchief and started to thumb his way through a second sheaf of ola leaves that were even more yellow and faded than the first. Clearing his throat, he started again.

'Here we will start the reading of the seventh chapter that contains information relating to the subject's marriage prospects. At the time of the reading of the seventh chapter Cherry is not yet married. Although we could say that Cherry will enter into wedlock, because of her pre-birth karma, many evil eyes are upon her by jealous people, due to which her married life will be delayed. She will have a marriage proposal, but it will come to a sudden end and she will not marry the person she expects. The subject may have an affair and this will also end with problems. To overcome all the badness indicated here, it is advisable for her to seek priestly advice and undertake the recommended religious performances accordingly. After the religious performances have taken place, all the badness will be overcome by her twenty-eighth year. From the ages of twenty-eight to thirty the subject will have a chance to marry.

'Now we will give a description of the person she will marry. The coming person is a handsome person, fair of complexion, active and healthy. He will be having the good attitudes and also the good morality. He will be a person who speaks very well, which will be appreciated and will attract people to him. His parents will be living and he will have two, or less than two, brothers or sisters. He is not the youngest, but will be the middle or the eldest in his family. He will be two or three years older than Cherry and he, too, will be holding a degree in connection with science. Possibly he will hold a PhD too. He will be a scientist and deriving a high sum as his remuneration. He will be of the same religion and culture as the subject and born in the same country. He will have visited many countries in the globe, and will have hailed from a very respectable and wealthy family. He will be living close to a city to the north or north-west of Cherry's house. From the subject's house to reach his house will take less than two hours. There will be a stream or a prominent religious place close to his house. His first name will contain three syllables or less than two. The first name begins with the letter P, S, N or D and the last letter will be N, M, T or Y. For example, his name may be Shehan, Naveen, Stugart or Stanley. With the parental blessing they will enter into wedlock. After the marriage Cherry will be blessed with children – both males and females. The subject and the husband will understand each other, which will mean that they lead a trouble-free family life. After giving these details we have now finished the seventh chapter.'

Here, the interpreter snapped down the 'stop' button on the tape recorder and they both flopped back in their chairs and looked at me expectantly. What did I think? Was I happy with what I had heard? Apart from the mysterious allusion to the 'evil eyes' that would be upon me and the affair that I hoped I would not have, none of it was particularly unnerving or even that unrealistic (although I wasn't sure how many people of my generation were named Stanley these days). Cynical as I had been about the ability of these men, or anyone for that matter, to predict my future, I had to admit that there had been a noticeable increase in my heart rate as I heard each prediction and a definite sense of relief when no imminent disasters had been forecast. I was now a little more sympathetic to the comfort and reassurance that many of my friends and colleagues derived from the various auguries Colombo had to offer. They rose, shook my hands enthusiastically, extracted 2,500 rupees (about £12) from me and cheerfully waved me off from the balcony of the apartment, as I cycled back home along the coastal road.

As I was turning the corner into the road on which my house stood, I heard the sound of a tuk-tuk pull up behind my bike and start to slow its engine. The men who drive tuk-tuks in Sri Lanka are regarded rather like the men who drive white vans in Britain: dodgy, sleazy, wise to regard with a certain amount of suspicion, yet unavoidably necessary in many situations. During my first meeting with my Sri Lankan landlord when I arrived in the country, he asked me whether I had found a trustworthy tuk-tuk driver that I could use on a regular basis. 'You must be very careful that you choose a good one,' he warned me. 'Some of these men can be most unscrupulous and also very unreliable.' I had even seen a Sri Lankan music video which centred around the story of a beautiful young woman who had been harassed by a mob of tuk-tuk drivers in a deserted field.

The man in the tuk-tuk behind me turned out to be Ajith, belonging to a crowd of particularly friendly and good-humoured drivers who occupied a stand under a large frangipani tree near my house. Ajith took me to school every morning and wherever I needed to go throughout the week. He was a mine of information about the city and I was completely dependent on him when I first arrived. He knew exactly where to take me to get passport photos, bicycle pumps, cheap flights, visas for India, cow hearts for school biology experiments and the cheapest place to get a washing machine fixed. He also kept a close eye on Sri Lankan politics, a subject on which he was very well informed, and would often keep me up to date on the island's current affairs on the way to school in the morning. Ajith was about the same height as me, 5 ft 2 inches and stockily built, and had a neatly trimmed moustache and thick black hair that was developing an increasing number of grey flecks. Unlike many of the tuk-tuk drivers, he refused to wear a sarong, and clinked about in fitted jeans and a pair of cowboy boots instead. Ajith came from a village in the Buddhist Sinhalese heartland, where he had a wife and two young sons. Every week he would leave his family, drive his tuk-tuk several hours north to the capital and stay in a dormitory throughout the week whilst he worked Colombo's roads. But Ajith had never planned to be a tuk-tuk driver. In 1989, as a young man, he had abandoned his education in his village school to follow his dream of becoming a singer and had spent a number of years singing in a band with a group of Sinhala musicians. He often used to sing when we were stuck in the interminable traffic jams and I could hear that he had a great voice. Unfortunately, after a few years of scraping by, he realised he could not make enough money to survive and bought himself a tuk-tuk instead.

Ajith pulled his tuk-tuk alongside me as we turned into my road and started waggling his arm to gesture that I should stop. 'Great news, Miss Cherry!' he called out of the side of the tuk-tuk. 'Next week I am recording an album in number-one recording studio with the best Sinhala lyric writer!'

'Ajith, that's amazing!' I said, getting off my bike and peering into the tuk-tuk. 'Where is it happening?'

'You don't know the place,' he said dismissively, knowing that if he had never taken me there I would not have a clue, 'but you can come and listen if you like. My friend Sarath knows the place and he can take you. Two o'clock on Monday is OK? This is very great day for me – I have been trying to break the Sinhala music industry since 1989!'

I met Ajith and his group of musicians on the top floor of a dingy house that smelled of burned coconut oil and damp carpet, in one of the particularly grey and depressing suburbs of Colombo. According to Ajith, this was the city's premier recording studio. It was not exactly Abbey Road and, on first impressions, it didn't seem very convincing. A large velvet wall hanging of the Hindu goddess Lakshmi sitting in a lotus flower, playing a large sitar, hung above a door off one of the landings, and I was ushered by a little man in a sarong into the recording booth. The recording was already in full swing and I didn't immediately recognise Ajith as he was dressed up in a long-sleeved cotton shirt and a pair of pressed suit trousers, wearing a pair of headphones and singing emotionally into a recording mic with his eyes closed. His backing band of session musicians were a group of ageing Sri Lankan rockers; all of them over forty and most of them with shoulder-length hair or thick, wavy mullets. One of the musicians was wearing a T-shirt that said, 'There are good girls in every corner of the earth, but unfortunately the earth is round.' Another had a

T-shirt with a picture of an elephant on the front – 'I support elephants at the Pinnawala Elephant Orphanage' was written underneath.

I sat myself in the recording booth, on the other side of a glass screen from the musicians, with the much younger sound technician, who was twiddling an enormous board of knobs and watching the oscillating sound waves on two large computer screens. He turned round and looked at me with confusion, evidently wondering who on earth this young European woman was and what she was doing at the studio. 'Are you here to sing too?' he asked with mild irritation. Ajith saw what was happening, and quickly came and explained that I was just a friend who was there to listen. The sound technician looked relieved and shook my hand. It had been a long session, he explained, and they were hoping to finish fairly soon. They were just going to run through the last track a few more times. Ajith disappeared back onto the other side of the glass and the music began again.

Like many Sinhalese songs, the track had a quick, lilting, plinky-plonky rhythm and a bouncy, synthetic melody that was mainly produced from the vibrato violin and trumpet settings of an electric Casio keyboard. Two men sat behind the keyboards, bobbing along with the melody and acting as conductors for Ajith, whilst three electric guitar players sat barefoot on the floor, strumming a repetitive series of chords and nodding their heads rhythmically. Over the top of this, Ajith was singing a vibrato melody, with his head cocked to one side and a pained, wincing expression on his face.

A small elderly man with greasy black hair, few teeth and a mouth full of blood-red paan had been shuffling around the studio ever since I had arrived. I had assumed from his stained shirt and sarong that he was some sort of water boy or cleaner, and wondered if I had seen him by the side of the road with a begging bowl; I would not have been that surprised. He shuffled into the recording booth whilst Ajith and the conductor were playing back the most recent take and Ajith introduced him to me. 'This is Shantha Deshanbadu – he wrote the lyrics for all my songs. He has written lyrics for many famous Sinhala artists and I hope his lyrics will make me very famous too!' Shantha beamed at me and produced a small black business card from a frayed wallet in the pocket of his shirt. The card had a flashy blue and orange logo that looked as if it should be hanging above the entrance of a cocktail bar. Underneath it read:

'Pearl in the World – Creative Creations

Shantha Deshanbandu

Lyrics writer, Scripts, TV commercials, Documentary, Event management'

I asked Shantha what the Sinhala lyrics of Ajith's song were about. 'They are about a young girl and a young boy,' he began, predictably. 'The girl was very clever and had always worked hard at school until one day she met a boy. The boy was a very bad influence and distracted her from her studies. She stopped reading books and would only read text messages. She started to fail and eventually threw her studies away altogether,' continued Shantha, looking at me solemnly. 'Love is like a spider's web,' he said as he shook his head sadly, 'those are the words of the chorus. Love is the spider's web and the girl is the insect trapped inside, unable to break free.'

Chapter Four

COLOMBO TO KANDY

Tennent only spent a few months in the capital, and in March of 1846 he and the rest of the colonial administration left Colombo to travel along the steep road cut into the hillside, to take up residence in Kandy. The hill town of Kandy, with its cooler, gentle climate, had been used by members of the colonial administration for many years as their second residence during the hot, wet season from March to July. During these months the lowland regions swelter in the high humidity and wearing sun until it is finally broken only by the cooling rains of the Yala monsoon. Even today, the wealthy families of Colombo retreat to their holiday homes in the hills at the weekend and those who are forced to remain in the capital lead an even slower pace of life than usual, their energy drained by the oppressive humidity and the inconveniences of rapidly rotting food, clothes that won't dry, and books and shoes sprouting furry, green mould spots overnight.

A few days before I headed out along the hill road to Kandy, I woke up to the depressing sight of a face full of small red pustules looking back at me from my bathroom mirror. Although I had been living in Sri Lanka for over a year, my skin had never really managed to adapt to Colombo's constant humidity and air pollution, which had sent it ricocheting back into an adolescence of oozing glands and blocked pores. When I miserably pointed out my condition to one of my colleagues, she suggested I try visiting one of the city's many ayurvedic doctors, who practise the traditional form of Hindu medicine developed in India thousands of years ago. 'I suffered from the most terrible phlegm for years and after I had used their treatments for a few weeks, it disappeared and has never returned,' she said. 'Ayurveda was much more effective than any of the western medicine I tried.'

Like many therapies that are considered 'alternative' in the West, ayurveda focuses on the balance of elemental energies, the removal of toxins using preparations containing plant extracts, animal products and minerals, sweating and massage, and takes a holistic approach to the body, mind and spirit. According to the ancient Sanskrit texts on the matter, the key to well-being is the doctrine of the tri-dosha, the fine balance of the body's three vital forces: wind, bile and phlegm. Although being a practitioner of western medicine is one of the most revered occupations in Sri Lanka, many Sri Lankans like to combine ayurveda with western medicine or simply put their faith in ayurveda alone when they are unwell. If someone breaks an ankle, it is not unusual for it to be X-rayed and cast in one of the western hospitals, and then smeared with a herbal preparation by one of the ayurvedic doctors. The government is also very keen to promote ayurveda and there is even a department of ayurveda and a minister for indigenous medicine.

I had walked past my local ayurveda hospital almost every day since moving to Colombo but, as open minded as I liked to think I was about the potential of traditional medicine, my suspicions had been aroused by the use of the word 'hospital' referring to a small colonial bungalow on a residential street. Nor was I entirely convinced by the huge, lime-green billboard outside which advertised Pranajeewa Miracle Oil, which it claimed 'cures all types of heart disease (for relief without bypass surgery), controls hypotension, flushes out cholesterol deposits from blood vessels, stops development and spread of all cancers, and controls side effects of all malignancies.' The list went on: 'controls diabetes and its side effects; proven to cure diseases and complications of the nerves, paralysis, asthma, catarrh, phlegmatic conditions, skin diseases, all kinds of pains in joints, rheumatoid and osteoarthritis, haemorrhoids, fistula, gastritis, kidney ailments, kidney stones, bladder stones, liver diseases; controls obesity; and improves general well-being and energy.'

But after another sighting of my face in the mirror that afternoon, I realised that things couldn't get much worse and decided to drop in to the 'hospital' on my way home from school.

It was empty when I arrived and I left my shoes with the small pile of sandals that had been discarded on a doormat outside. There was a line of wicker chairs and a statue of the Buddha, in front of which an incense stick was gently smouldering and a handful of star-shaped jasmine flowers floated in a jam jar.

I couldn't see anyone else in the building except for a bored-looking young woman behind the counter of the dispensary who waved me towards the doctor's room. The doctor was a woman of about thirty, who was sitting barefoot and cross-legged behind a large desk, absorbed in the local newspaper. She had waist-length frizzy black hair, pulled back in a child's hair clip, and was wearing a skin-tight purple T-shirt, studded with fake diamante. On the wall behind the desk were two large, laminated photographs. One showed a generic government minister dressed in a white shirt and sarong, beaming benignly, whilst the other was the intriguing choice of an action shot of eight armed soldiers riding motorbikes, shooting bullets into the foreground.

In the corner of the room was a bed, on which a few old cardboard boxes had been stacked, and, other than an old-fashioned, mercury sphygmomanometer and a tray of dessert spoons, there were no medical instruments in sight. The sparseness, the pale-blue, gloss-painted walls and the general lack of any convincing medical equipment reminded me of the sick bay inhabited by my placid secondary school nurse, who was not even allowed to dispense plasters or paracetamol due to some strange health and safety guidelines. The doctor motioned to me to sit down on a plastic chair by her desk and stared at me for a couple of moments in silence. Clearly I was supposed to start things off.

'I seem to be having a problem with my skin,' I began, pointing to the red spots on my face.

She peered at my face and frowned. 'You are having a rash,' she said decisively. 'You want to stop it from itching?'

'I don't think it's a rash, I think they're spots, aren't they?'

'Stop wearing sunscreen then. They will go away,' she ordered.

'But I haven't used any sunscreen for about two months,' I protested, wondering why we were suddenly talking about sunscreen.

'You are sure that your face is not itching?'

'Quite sure.'

She peered at my face again and pulled out a leaflet advertising the Pranajeewa Miracle Oil that could apparently cure everything.

'Have you been taking our herbal remedy?' she asked, pushing the leaflet towards me. 'It contains two-hundred herbs that are simmered for four and a half months. Maybe you could take it? Two tablespoons, once a day, at any time of day, with a glass of hot water.'

'Is it particularly good for the skin?' I asked.

'It can cure everything. If you are having any pains, they will go away too,' she said enthusiastically, opening up the leaflet and pointing to the list of ailments it was supposed to cure. 'Even our president and the American people are taking Pranajeewa,' she continued, pointing to a photograph of Mahinda Rajapaksa intently examining a bottle of the stuff.

The leaflet also showed a list of testimonials from various university professors and a Buddhist monk, who each claimed that their health had been immeasurably improved by taking a few spoons of the herbal oil every day.

I have been continuously using this oil – even when I was abroad on my sabbatical leave I took enough of this oil with me to last my two-year stint at Oxford University.

When I took to this oil it is not because I had any particular ailment to be cured but it was the faith in it that I developed as I experienced the beneficial effects of its use on my general health condition, my physical fitness and wellness. I found improvements in my heart condition which I would attribute to the protection against illness and diseases that was given to me by the use of this oil. To this day no major illness has been diagnosed in my body.

Buddhadasa Hewavitharana, emeritus professor of
economics, University of Peradeniya

'Do you wash your face?' she asked, closing the leaflet.

'Of course!'

'With chemicals?'

'Well, with face wash.'

'You must stop. All unnatural chemicals are very bad. You must find a natural face wash.'

'Ok, can you prescribe me one?'

'No. Maybe try a chemist.'

She pulled out a small prescription pad, typed in the coiling Sinhala characters and, after filling one of the sheets out, told me to go and pick up my prescription from the little dispensary outside.

The dispensary looked like an old-fashioned sweet shop that had been drained of its bright colours and was lined with shelves holding large glass bottles of little black pellets, unlabelled jam jars and smaller glass bottles of deep-brown goo. The young woman manning the dispensary took my prescription and began to select various treatments from the shelves behind the counter.

'Take two tablespoons of this every day, with hot water,' she instructed, handing me a bottle of Pranajeewa, 'and take two of these before food,' pointing to a small plastic bag of black pellets that looked like rabbit droppings. Then she climbed onto a chair and reached for one of the unlabelled bottles of black goo. 'Twice a day with meals,' she said, before finally passing me a small bottle of a thick brown paste, so thick it wouldn't travel out of the bottleneck, which I was somehow supposed to smear on my face for an hour before bed.

Unsure, but having paid 3,000 rupees, or £15, for my bag of herbal remedies, I decided to start my treatments that evening. With the aid of a narrow-handled marmalade spoon, I was able to extract enough paste from the little bottle to cover my face and downed a few tablespoons of Pranajeewa, which smelled like Bisto but tasted like the bitter, charcoal edges of burned toast. I spent the evening hidden in my house with a paste-covered face, packing my bags to leave for Kandy the next morning. When it was time to go to bed, however, the brown paste, which had the unhelpful property of being insoluble in water, refused to come off my face and I eventually gave up and climbed into bed, still coated in a gritty brown film.

A week later I threw away my pillowcases.

The next morning I caught one of the small, intercity buses to Kandy. Only one seat on the bus was unoccupied and most of the other passengers seemed to be on their way back to Kandy after having come down from the hills to stock up on goods in the capital. The two men sitting in front of me were battling with what looked like part of the disassembled frame of a bed and were trying unsuccessfully to cram the stainless steel legs and headboard in-between the luggage racks, so that it straddled the ceiling of the bus. A teenage boy across the aisle was trying to fit a whole cricket set consisting of a new bat, three stumps, shin pads, a helmet and a bag of cricket whites under his seat. Various cardboard boxes and plastic sacks filled the aisle, over which the bus conductor clambered and stumbled to collect the fares. It was approaching midday when the bus pulled out of the station, and most of the passengers looked tired and miserable in the mounting heat, as they slumped against the windows or propped their foreheads against the seat in front to try to sleep away the impending journey.

The road led out of the Pettah and through the dismal suburb of Kalaniya – a sprawl of billboards and commercial buildings that resembled giant, dirty Rubik's Cubes thanks to the architectural trend of covering the outer walls with large, colourful plastic tiles. The tiles had lost their lustre long ago and were now covered in a film of grey grime from the road. The beggars that had been cleared out of the city were sitting along the pavements on unfolded cardboard boxes with their arms stretched out limply in front of them, watching the sluggish traffic jam that led away from Colombo. When Tennent passed along the road through Kalaniya he was equally unimpressed by the place, but for a different reason; it used to be the site where animal products were unloaded before being distributed to the various bazaars of the capital.

It is chiefly from the country from the north of the Kalany that provisions are brought to the bazaars of

Colombo; and however scrupulously the disciples of Buddha may observe his injunction to abstain from taking life, a stranger in travelling this road is shocked at the callous indifference to the infliction of pain which characterises their treatment of animals intended for market. Pigs are suspended from a pole, passed between the fore and hind legs, and evince by incessant cries that torture which they endure from the cords; fowls are brought from long distances hanging from their feet; and ducks are carried by the head, their necks bent over the bearers' fingers to stifle their noise.

Nowadays, the only animals on the Kalaniya pavements are mottled, stray dogs, and it has become the site of one of Colombo's biggest slums, whose jumble of corrugated iron roofs straggle their way along the banks of the Kalaniya River and under its congested road bridge. As the suburbs of Colombo began to disappear, however, the roadside started to come back to life with the green palm trees and waxy banana leaves of the jungle. In places, the dark, dense curtain of jungle was broken to reveal wide, open spaces cleared for rice cultivation. Many of the square paddy fields were filled with rainwater and formed still, glassy mirrors reflecting the midday sun. Solitary figures were working in the middle, bent double over long-handled farm implements, whilst barefooted children skipped along the narrow ridges of earth that divided the land.

The road soon left the coastal plain and began to climb into the dense woods of hill country, which obliterated the horizon in every direction. Teetering on the edge of the road with their backs to the sharp descent to the jungle floor, women were tending small fires and crouching over steaming cauldrons, boiling corn on the cob to sell to the travellers plying the road. Every now and again a villager would emerge from the darkness of the forest and jump down onto the road below from the small settlements that clung to the hillside, hidden amongst the trees.

As the bus had been climbing up the steep mountain road, I had started to notice that much heavier and older-looking vehicles were starting to overtake us. As the road got steeper the bus seemed to be travelling more and more slowly, until suddenly, after a grinding gear-change and a spinning of the wheels, the bus stopped momentarily and slowly began to slide backwards. The other passengers, who had been fast asleep since we left Colombo, woke up at the sudden change in motion and looked out of the back windscreen in panic. The driver slammed on the brakes and brought the bus to a shuddering standstill, right in the middle of the road.

A couple of men got out of the bus and stood by the driver's window to give him words of advice and encouragement as he revved the accelerator unsuccessfully. Everyone else seemed pessimistic about the outcome and began to retrieve their luggage from the racks. Five minutes later, after the bus had slid several metres further back down the road, the passengers decided to give up and began to file off. I waited until everyone else had vacated the bus and then joined the small crowd on the roadside who had descended on the bus conductor, demanding their money back. The conductor seemed unfazed and pulled out the wad of notes he had collected in Colombo, which he started to hand back to the passengers. The whole process had the air of a standard procedure. 'This is my second trip to Kandy this month and this is the second time we have been failed by one of these buses,' grumbled an elderly gentleman.

The passengers, having now been reimbursed, stood by the roadside and started to wave their arms vigorously at any other passing buses heading for Kandy. 'These buses are all very full and we will all have to stand for several hours,' said one of the dejected owners of the disassembled bed frame, as he looked at the overcrowded vehicles, wandering how he could squeeze his bed on board. Eventually, an old, creaking government-run bus, which seemed to me to be already full to bursting, came to a stop. Somehow the twenty of us, and the bed frame, managed to squeeze in between the rows of people already crammed into the aisle. The driver's mate spotted me hovering uncertainly by the steps and pulled me onto the bus, pushed me into a space by the driver and, with my nose almost touching the windscreen, we set off again.

The road started to slalom around the curves of the hillside, through small villages that peeped through the trees. In the middle of the larger towns, tall, red-brick clock towers stood at the crossroads, showing the time on four digital clock faces that looked to the four points of the compass. I had seen similar clock towers in many other towns across the island and a Sri Lankan friend explained they were installed in the 1980s by President Ranasinghe Premadasa, who was reputed to be a great stickler for punctuality. During his presidency he was responsible for building garment factories in the rural areas, and when each village or town received a factory, a large clock tower was also erected in the town centre. For some, these were a symbol of the modernising changes that were taking place in the countryside, whilst others felt they were an attempt to improve the temporal discipline of the rural islanders who, the president hoped, would consult the clocks regularly, turn up to work on time and adopt the European habit of living a life that is constantly dictated by a timepiece. Unfortunately, over the years, many of the clocks began to break down and started to show erroneous times and, as with many broken things in developing countries, remained that way. One newspaper eventually conducted an outraged survey and found that in a number of the island's provinces, more clocks showed the wrong time than the correct time, and some towers showed four different times on their four different faces. More recently, most seem to have been fixed and the old analogue faces replaced with digital green numerals that glow through the night with the correct time.

As the bus neared Kandy the passengers began to get off and, eventually, I was able to get a seat next to a middle-aged gentleman with gold-rimmed glasses who, unlike most of the other passengers, was wearing trousers and a shirt rather than a sarong. He was engrossed in the matrimonial section of the Sri Lankan weekend newspaper, *The Sunday Times*, in which Sri Lankan parents advertise for suitable spouses for their unmarried children.

• Colombo, Buddhist, Govi caste parents seek a suitable, educated, handsome partner, non-malefic and devoid of all vices for their 5 ft 6 in, pretty daughter educated with

GCSEs and A-levels. Elder sister is to be married soon. Please apply with family details and horoscope. House will form part of dowry. Bankers especially considered.

• Galle, Buddhist, Karava caste parents seek for a Govi or Karava groom below thirty years for their eldest daughter – 5 ft 3 in, with two siblings, degree holder in social science (hons), expects a job and twenty-six years old. Only brother in medical college. Southern grooms especially considered. Write only if no malefic planets.

• Academically qualified Jaffna Tamil, Anglican Christian, Vellala caste, high net-worth parents seek a pretty educated bride below thirty-two years, with similar status for their son, non-smoker, teetotaller, graduated and well employed in Australia with sound financial background.

The gentleman saw me reading the newspaper over his shoulder and asked me where I was from.

'Ah, my son lives in England,' he said with a smile, when I told him I was British. 'He is completing a PhD at the London School of Economics.'

'Are you trying to find him a wife?' I asked, pointing to the matrimonial section in his hand. He shook his head and sighed.

'No, I have more or less given up on trying to sort out his marriage, but I still like to have a look and see if there is anyone that might be suitable for him. He has met a Sri Lankan girl in London and they have been together for six years, but unfortunately her parents won't accept him. They are strict Sinhalese Buddhists you see, and my wife and I are both half Tamil.'

'Have her parents found a Sinhalese boy for her to marry instead?' I asked.

He gave a laugh and folded up the paper.

'They have found several, but I think she must love my son because she has refused to marry any of them. We are not like the Pakistanis you know – we don't force our daughters to marry, it's more of a recommendation. I think that her parents may be giving up too. My wife and I can't understand it; after all we are a mixed Sinhalese-Tamil family. It is not even as if her parents are uneducated – her father is a university professor – but when it comes to marriage, some parents can be very funny.'

He looked me up and down and then glanced at the fingers of my left hand. 'You will choose your own husband of course and probably find our arrangements rather strange, but I think that you will find we have a much lower number of divorces than your country,' he said with satisfaction.

I agreed that given the sorry state of many marriages in Britain it was difficult to claim that our model was superior, and he nodded enthusiastically.

'For us, you see, the love affair begins after we are married. Our parents find us suitable partners, based on a deep understanding of who we are and where we want our lives to lead, and then they find us someone with the same background and aspirations so that things don't get difficult along the line. Choosing to spend your life with someone when you are in a haze of infatuation has always seemed much more risky to me.' It made a lot of sense.

I asked him how much of an issue caste still was in Sri Lanka. As a foreigner, it was something I had never encountered, but every one of the matrimonial adverts mentioned it in the first line. At the mention of the word caste, the gentleman began to look uncomfortable and glanced around to see if anyone else was listening.

'It's not something we really like to talk about anymore,' he said carefully, 'but it is still an issue. In the urban areas its influence is diminishing – it doesn't dictate which job you can do for instance – but when it comes to marriage, people rarely marry outside their caste.'

The caste system is usually associated with Hindu society in India, where it was introduced over 4,000 years ago by the Aryan conquerors. Given the proximity of Sri Lanka to India, and the frequent invasions and migration of Indians to Sri Lanka over the millennia, it was probably inevitable that a caste system came to evolve on the island too. A caste is essentially a group of people who claim descent from a common ancestor and only marry others within their caste. As your caste is the same as that of your parents and as it is impossible to become a member of a different caste, it can make social mobility difficult. In the past, people of the same caste usually performed the same role within their village – the people of the Govigama caste would generally be cultivators, members of the Salagama caste were cinnamon peelers and members of the Navandanna caste were artisans. The system also has an ingrained hierarchy with some castes being 'higher' or 'lower' than others. In the past not all castes had the same rights within society, even down to details such as the way they were allowed to dress, buildings they were allowed to enter and the nature of the houses they could build.

It is thought that the influence of Buddhism in Sri Lanka, which arose in India partly as a reaction against the caste system of Hinduism, prevented the Sinhalese system from being quite as rigid as in India; the Tamil Hindus in the north have their own caste system which is more restrictive and very different from that of their Sinhalese neighbours. Although the issue of caste is rarely mentioned openly in Sri Lanka and many Sri Lankans view its existence with a certain amount of shame, it has still proved almost impossible to remove from people's mindset.

The road to Kandy had been completed a few years before Tenennt's arrival and was part of over 1,200 km of roads that were built by the British in the first half of the nineteenth century. Tennent regarded these as one of the great achievements of the British Empire, and proudly claimed that the island's road network was adapted for carriages where it approaches the principal places, and nearly everywhere available for horsemen and wayfarers. The road to Kandy still passes through the same settlements as it did in Tennent's day and as it started to descend towards the Mahaweli Ganga, the wide brown river that cuts through the forest floor at the base of the hills, Tennent had his own encounter with the island's caste system. This section of the road to Kandy passed through a cluster of settlements that were home to the people of the Rodiya caste, who had the misfortune to be one of the lowest castes in the Sinhalese system, similar to the untouchables of India. Before the British arrived in Sri Lanka, the lot of the Rodiya was a particularly miserable one; they were not allowed to draw water from the village wells or enter the temples to pray, and neither the men nor women were allowed to wear clothing that covered their bodies above the waist or below the knee. The Rodiya were also not permitted to learn a trade and were forced to survive on the alms they could receive if they protected the villagers' fields from wild animals or if they buried the carcasses of dead cattle. Under the British, the Rodiyas were allowed to take up a trade, but according to Tennent's observations:

> After centuries of mendicancy and idleness they evince no inclination for work. Their pursuits and habits are still the same, but their bearing is a shade less servile, and they pay a profounder homage to a high than a low caste Kandyan, and manifest some desire to shake off the opprobrious epithet of Rodiyas. Their houses are better built, and contain a few articles of furniture, and in some places they have acquired patches of land and possess cattle. Even the cattle share the odium of their owners, and to distinguish them from the herds of Kandyans, their masters are obliged to suspend a coconut shell from their necks... Socially their hereditary stigma remains unaltered; their contact is shunned by Kandyans as pollution, and instinctively the Rodiyas crouch to their own degradation... They fall on their knees with uplifted hands to address a man of the lowest recognised caste; and they shout on the approach of a traveller, to warn him to stop till they can get off the road to allow him to pass without the risk of too close a proximity to their persons.
>
> Their habits are filthy, and their appetites omnivorous. Carrion is acceptable to them as is the flesh of monkeys, squirrels, civet-cat, mongoose and tortoises.

The members of the Rodiya caste were thought to be the descendants of an indigenous eastern Indian tribe and central to their folklore was a dancing, blue-haired deity named Ratnavali, who they worshipped in sacred, secluded tree groves. According to the legend told by the Rodiya, Ratnavali was the daughter of a king. The king was known for having fondness for venison and his meat was usually supplied by a Vedda – a member of the forest-dwelling, indigenous hunter tribe of the island. One day, when deer were scarce, Princess Ratnavali ordered a Vedda to go and find human flesh, as nothing else was available for her father's meals. The Vedda duly went away in search of human flesh and the unfortunate source he selected was the son of the royal barber. Later, when the royal barber requested an audience with the king to discuss the mysterious disappearance of his son, he was offered a meal of rice and 'venison' curry. When the barber discovered a human finger in his stew, showing the same knuckle deformity with which his son had been born, he feigned sickness and left the palace. When eventually the truth came to light, and princess Ratnavali's role was discovered, the king was furious. A Rodiya, or scavenger, from a neighbouring yard was called and the king banished the princess from the palace, ordering her to marry the Rodiya and spend the rest of her life as a scavenger.

Tennent commented that in spite of their low status, the Rodiya women were remarkably beautiful and he made a sketch of a group of the bare-chested, fine-featured females standing in a clearing of the palm trees. It was one of the many detailed and skilful drawings of people and landscapes that interspersed his written descriptions, and as I watched the undulating hillsides flying past the window, I could see both how accurate and detailed his sketches were and how little the landscape by the road had changed.

I got down from the bus in the centre of Kandy and walked through its network of narrow roads to find somewhere to stay. It was a Saturday evening, and most of the hotels were fully booked for the weekend as it was the season for most Sri Lankan families and foreign tourists to visit the hills. The town was a jumble of elegant colonial buildings that had escaped the anti-colonial demolition squads; wrought iron, Victorian lamp posts and ugly new, glass-fronted buildings that had been hastily thrown up and displayed synthetic clothes on headless, white mannequins. Foreign tourists usually rave about Kandy, mainly because the cooler air comes as a relief from the humidity of the coast, but most Sri Lankans take a much dimmer view of the city, complaining about the dreadful new 'architecture', the perpetual traffic jams and the cloud of pollution that hangs over the town.

The town is what remains of the once formidable Kandyan Kingdom, which ruled itself independently from the island's other fragmented kingdoms from the sixteenth century. The kingdom was unique in Sri Lankan history as the only region that successfully defeated the numerous invaders, and rejected the various treaties of both the Portuguese and the Dutch. Its success was largely down to its geographical position: the tough mountain terrain with its poor and often non-existent roads, mercurial weather and local diseases were all too much for the European armies to handle. Even during the brief periods when Kandy was temporarily captured, the Europeans struggled to maintain a steady supply of resources up to the hill country, allowing the Kandyans to quickly chase their armies back down to the lowlands.

The British, despite their access to more reliable sources of ammunition and superior weapons, launched a spectacularly unsuccessful invasion of the kingdom in 1803. Many of the British soldiers died from malaria, the monsoon rains cut off their supplies and a number of soldiers simply committed suicide when they realised that capture by the Kandyans was inevitable. Luckily for the British, however, the last king of Kandy, a paranoid alcoholic called Sri Vikrama Rajasinha, managed to make himself very unpopular with his bouts of erratic and violent behaviour. After he attempted to seduce, and then executed, the wife of one of his ministers, a devout Buddhist named Ehelepola, many of the Kandyans aligned themselves with the British. The king was eventually captured and lived out his days with his wife and children in a Sultan's palace in South India, whilst his kingdom was officially handed over to the British on 2 March 1815.

I eventually found a hotel with an empty room and was handed a key by two tearful receptionists. I had interrupted them watching a YouTube clip of Kate Winslet and Leonardo DiCaprio leaning over the deck of the Titanic to Celine Dion's 'My Heart Will Go On'. The corridors smelled of stale cigarette smoke, and I was shown to my room by a porter dressed in a grey jacket with brass buttons and a mandarin collar. He had recently returned to Sri Lanka after having spent five years working in Saudi Arabia. The heat and the sand had not been to his liking and he was glad to be back.

At the centre of Kandy was a large, artificial lake, built on a whim by the maniac Sri Vikrama Rajasinha on prime agricultural land against the recommendations of his advisors. Surrounding the lake were the white colonial buildings of the Victorian hotels and clubhouses built by the British, where they danced in the ballrooms and played croquet on the wide lawns. Now it was all faded grandeur with fraying carpets, foggy mirrors and cavernous reception rooms, filed through by coachloads of tourists in trainers and baseball caps, and the once elegant and refined town felt like the abandoned coastal resorts of England. The lakeside was still the most peaceful spot in the town, however, and I watched the evening sunlight skittering over its surface before it was extinguished by the growing shadows of the surrounding hills. A large white Buddha looked down from the light-studded hillside, watching the town as it disappeared into the darkness.

Back at the rooftop bar of the hotel, two men in their early twenties were sitting at a table in the corner of the room drinking bottles of Lion Lager. They waved over to me and asked how long I had been travelling in Sri Lanka. They had spent the past month surfing on one of the quieter stretches of beach on the west coast.

'The waves were great,' said one of the men, who had a scraggy mass of ginger hair and a nose that looked as if it had been broken in several places, 'but we stayed in this really racist place.'

'Racist towards who?' I asked.

'Racist towards Sri Lankans,' said his friend, who was wearing an England football shirt. 'We met up with a Sri Lankan mate that we used to go to school with and the manager of the hotel wouldn't let him share a room with us. Said the hotel had a foreigner-only policy.'

'Where was the manager from?'

'He was Sri Lankan too.'

'I don't think it had anything to do with our friend being Sri Lankan really,' his friend cut in with a smirk, 'he was just worried that he was a beach boy we'd picked up and didn't want us getting up to anything in one of his hotel rooms.'

I asked them what they were doing in Kandy and their faces became serious.

'Meditation.'

'Yeah, we're doing this really intense week-long course with the monks. We started at four this morning. I did one last year in India and it totally changed my life,' said the ginger-haired man.

'Really?' I asked. 'How?'

'Just totally changed everything, but in a really good way.'

'He's totally Zen, can't you see?' said his friend, looking closely at him. 'You're always chilled aren't you? All the time. It's kind of weird. Never gets stressed. Hoping it's going to do the same for me. I'm always stressed,' he explained, shaking his head, 'all the time.'

The man whose life had apparently been transformed in an Indian ashram started rummaging around in a rucksack and pulled out a print of an old sepia photograph of a Kandyan woman, thickly swaddled in a sari over a long-sleeved under-blouse with several long chains of beads hanging around her neck. 'I picked this up in one of the shops in the town,' he said pushing it towards me. 'Apparently they used to have loads of husbands.'

Many anthropologists had visited the region around Kandy to study the unusual local families in which the women had more than one husband, and Tennent, too, had witnessed, what he described as, the 'revolting practice of polyandry'. Although there are many cultures around the world where a man has several wives, the culture of polyandry, where a woman has several husbands, is relatively rare. The polyandry that existed in the Kandyan Kingdom was a topic of fascination for many who wrote about Sri Lanka, in particular the Englishman Robert Knox, who was imprisoned by the kings of Kandy for nineteen years during the seventeenth century. According to his records:

> ... in this country each man, even the greatest, hath but one wife; but a woman often has two husbands. For it is lawful and common with them for two brothers to keep house together with one wife, and the children do acknowledge and call both Father.

In most cases it was usually two brothers or two male cousins who would share the same wife, but some European visitors to Kandy claimed to have found women who had up to seven husbands. According to Tennent, polyandry had once been prevalent throughout the island but the Portuguese and the Dutch had largely stamped it out of the maritime provinces, confining the practice predominantly to the Kandyan Kingdom. Whilst polyandry initially sounds like a system devised by dominant, matriarchal women, Tennent suggested that its origins lay in the feudal structure of the Kandyan Kingdom and that in fact, the women probably didn't have a lot of choice in their growing number of husbands. When males from the villages had to leave their fields to work on those of the king or his lords, or when they were conscripted to fight in battle, their own fields would go uncultivated. If one of his brothers was invited to join the family, the new husband could cultivate the land and provide an income in his brother's absence. As a reward, he would also have access to his brother's wife. Other anthropologists also suggested that if several sons married the same woman it would prevent the division of the land that the sons inherited and if they cultivated the land together, it would be more productive.

Whichever was the case, the British took a very dim view of polyandry. Not only did it offend the sensibilities of the prudish Victorians, but as these marriages were not registered or formalised in any way, it was also an affront to the British love of order and systematic rule-following. Furthermore, the British often ended up with an administrative nightmare when they had to try to work out who was the legitimate father of the children in a household and, if one of the fathers in the house died, there were no rules to decide who should inherit what. In their wisdom, the British civil servants decreed that all polyandrous marriages were null and void. All marriages must be monogamous and officially registered if they were to be recognised. Unfortunately the new laws just made things worse. Most of the Kandyan women just ignored the new rules and carried on living with their multiple husbands, whilst the men, who were already unofficially married to one wife, essentially committed bigamy by deciding that they would register their marriage to a new wife and keep the old one too. In the end the British had to give up in exasperation and, although polyandry still remained illegal, marriage laws were eventually relaxed and the practice continued in some isolated rural communities well into the middle of the twentieth century. The Sinhalese television networks still like to use the stories of these Kandyan women in their costume dramas and many screenwriters have produced high-tension storylines about the complex relationships within these unusual families.

The next morning I paid a visit to Kandy's most famous building, the Temple of the Tooth, home to one of the island's most sacred treasures – a tooth that is said to have once furnished the gums of the Buddha. According to the legend, the tooth was rescued from the flames of the Buddha's funeral pyre in India in 543 BC and was smuggled into Sri Lanka almost nine hundred years later, in the hair of a princess. After being passed to and fro between India and Sri Lanka by various kings and invading forces, it was eventually captured in Sri Lanka by the Portuguese, who carried it back to their colony in Goa, where they claimed to have burnt it in a fit of Catholic zeal. The Sinhalese, on the other hand, claimed that the Portuguese had been fooled into stealing a replica tooth and the genuine tooth of the Buddha had remained on the island all along. Nowadays the tooth is very rarely shown to the public, but when Tennent visited Kandy in 1846, the tooth was unveiled and he was permitted to gaze upon it for long enough to produce a small sketch for his book. When he saw the tooth he was convinced that there was no way it could possibly have belonged to the Buddha, or any human for that matter, as he estimated it to be two inches long and almost an inch in diameter; he concluded that it was either a piece of carved ivory or the tooth of a crocodile. Either way, the Temple of the Tooth is still one of the most sacred Buddhist monuments on the island and pilgrims flock to worship the tooth every day and to see its annual procession through the town on the back of an elephant, under the light of the full moon.

I walked to the temple through narrow backstreets that were already clogged with the quotidian traffic. Men were pulling small wagons, from which they sold small plastic bags filled with chopped mango or pineapple, seasoned with red chilli powder and salt. The road that led towards the temple was lined with open doorways, above which 'Attorney of Law' was written in hand-painted white letters on little blackboards. Small, elderly gentlemen were leaning against most of the doorframes wearing white floor-length sarongs and white shirts. Each dark, Dickensian office was lined with shelves holding stacks of dusty ledgers and piles of yellowing papers, and contained an old, wooden desk on which a large book was open and a fountain pen waited in a pot. Nobody seemed to be requiring their services and most of them were staring blankly at the streets outside, occasionally stroking their beards or leaning across their doorway to chat to one of their neighbouring, septuagenarian attorneys.

I walked past the stalls selling buckets of purple lotus flowers to offer to the tooth, towards a large octagonal building with a ribbed white wall and a red roof supported by pillars. The temple was surrounded by lawns, and local families were sitting in the shade of blossoming trees whilst their children played on the grass. As I was about to enter the temple through a large white archway, a voice from behind me asked, 'You are needing a guide, madam?'

I turned round to see an elderly Sri Lankan gentleman grinning enthusiastically at me, exhibiting the only two yellow teeth that were left in his gums. He waved a small laminated identity card in my face. 'I am being very good, cheap guide, madam. I am working in Kandy temple for thirty years. I am knowing all histories and special areas. Very small price. Come!' All around me Sri Lankan men and women were streaming through the gate of the temple clutching offerings of lotus flowers, bags of white jasmine flowers, bottles of coconut oil and baskets of fruit. With the exception of a couple of tourists who were looking in bewilderment at the pages of their guidebook, trying to work out how to get into the temple, I was the only person without an offering. I decided that I might as well behave like the tourist I was and accept the offer of this guide. If I didn't, several others were waiting to pounce anyway.

My newly hired guide, who told me that his name was Bertram, seemed in a hurry to get round the temple, and had very little time for the Sri Lankan devotees who were making their way slowly through the crowded gates and up the congested stairways into its halls. He thrust his way through the crowds, pushing the devotees aside, and grabbed my wrist to pull me along with him. We came out of the crowds and into a courtyard where men in Kandyan costume were performing the morning puja. Wearing baggy white trousers gathered at the ankle and red bands of cloth wrapped round their torsos, they were beating large barrel drums that hung round their necks and rested on their bellies. Others were playing staccato melodies on small shrill flutes. The courtyard surrounded the temple's main shrine, hidden behind a pair of ornate, gold doors. The roof of the courtyard was supported by stone pillars decorated with intricate carvings of arabesques and flowers, while brightly painted wooden beams showed illustrations of mystical creatures and dwarves. Bertram pushed me through the people reverently watching the puja towards the drummers and shouted, 'Take photo, madam! Good photos, this place!' Within a few minutes my wrist was grabbed again and I was pulled up a flight of stairs at the back of the courtyard and into a large, dark room.

The room was hot and stuffy, and was filled with devotees standing shoulder to shoulder, with their palms placed together in front of their heads in prayer. At the back of the room, groups of elderly ladies and younger women holding children were sitting on the floor with their eyes closed, quietly murmuring. Winding its way round the edges of the room and down the stairs, a long queue of men and women were waiting to be ushered into a small enclosure in the centre, in which twenty or so worshippers were allowed to stand for a few minutes to meditate on a large, gold casket, the shape of an upturned hand bell. After a few minutes that group would be ushered out of the other side and a new group entered.

Bertram shoved me into the enclosure from the exiting side, much to the irritation of the people queuing to enter from the correct side, and shouted loudly as he pointed at the casket, 'There is tooth!' When I looked confused, he shouted even more loudly, 'Inside, madam. Tooth is inside! Lord Buddha's tooth!' I had brought Tennent's sketch of the enormous tooth, which looked more like a rhino's horn, to see whether he had exaggerated its size, but this was clearly not one of the few days on which it was to be unveiled. The Buddhist pilgrims who had travelled for miles to cherish a few moments in front of the concealed tooth began to glare at Bertram and at me. I was so embarrassed by the disturbance that it was now my turn to drag Bertram out of the muggy, claustrophobic room and into the sunshine of the temple grounds.

As we strolled through the neatly tended grounds, Bertram, bored with his factual repertoire of the temple, turned to me and asked, 'Madam, what is the only city in the world that people are not living in?' Mistaking this for a question, I pondered it for a moment and asked him what he meant. 'It is electricity madam!' he explained with glee. 'Now give me sentence having all letters of the alphabet.'

'The quick brown fox jumped over the lazy old dog.' I tried, vaguely remembering a school handwriting test.

'Slow dog madam. Not old dog. Old dog is not having any letter S.'

Bertram continued to amuse himself by asking me a series of other riddles that he had presumably picked up during his many years as a guide, as he led me out into a large courtyard by the side of the road where we said goodbye. In the centre of the courtyard stood a large, old bodhi tree, its wide branches laden with delicate, heart-shaped leaves fluttering in the wind. The Buddha is said to have reached enlightenment under a bodhi tree in Bodh Gaya in India 2,600 years ago and a bodhi tree sits in the courtyard of every temple on the island. The trunk of this bodhi tree was surrounded by a wide wooden platform reached by a narrow set of steps, and men and women were climbing up with offerings of fruit, coconut oil and banana leaves full of jasmine flowers, which they placed under the branches. I climbed up to the platform and sat amongst the families who were looking up through the branches of the bodhi tree as they sang prayers in unison from small printed pamphlets. Some were not singing but simply gazing at the leaves in meditation, their hands clasped in front of their heads. On the ground, devotees were lighting small terracotta oil lamps, which glowed with hundreds of tiny flames and filled the air with the smell of burning coconut oil. The slow singing was soporific and I spent twenty minutes sitting with them, staring up the through the fluttering bodhi-leaves and watching the clouds drifting across the sky.

Before Tennent left Kandy he made a visit to the Royal Botanical Gardens in the small town of Peradeniya, a few kilometres away. Many of the buses that enter and leave Kandy pass through Peradeniya so early the next morning I made my way to the central bus station. Dark clouds had been gathering and by the time I arrived a dank English drizzle had begun. Kandy has a reputation for being the most polluted town on the island and, after spending a few minutes in the bus station, it is easy to see why. The road by the entrance was four lanes thick with tuk-tuks, buses and trucks, causing gridlock. Each vehicle was emitting blue clouds of noxious fumes so pungent that the passengers and tuk-tuk drivers were pulling their scarves and handkerchiefs over their faces. I was not sorry to be leaving Kandy; its mighty and unique past had made the humdrum, polluted tedium of the modern town all the more disappointing. I found a bus that was heading in the right direction and slumped in a seat in the corner, watching the swarms of passengers, many of them barefooted, dodging in and out of the puddles, as the sky darkened and the rain became heavier. I bought a handful of lentil patties from one of the hawkers, who handed them to me in a small paper bag pasted together from the pages of a schoolchild's exercise book. An old man started to hobble down the aisle, shaking a begging bowl at the passengers who were already seated. Many of them were shrinking away from him in disgust and as he walked past me I saw his thin hands were bent into contortions and deformed with the clawed fingers of leprosy.

The Royal Botanical Gardens were planted by the British in the nineteenth century and, under the chilly grey sky, the order and symmetry of the gardens had something akin to a disappointing visit to an English country house on a dank autumn day. The pathways led through avenues of regimented palm trees, perpendicular and equidistant, as they had been planted by the Victorian horticulturalists. The wide-open lawns were closely cropped and the geometric flower beds carefully tessellated – it felt very un-Sri Lankan. Later, when the sun came out, young female students from the local university came into the garden to sit cross-legged, studying from textbooks rested on the sprawling roots of ancient trees. In amongst the canes of the giant yellow bamboo that lined the wide lawns, teenage couples were hiding, passionately groping each other, whilst out on the stone benches around the edges of the lawns, the more timid couples were holding hands and looking shyly into each other's eyes. I walked through the damp gardens, watching the park attendants chasing the courting couples out of the undergrowth, and sat on a bench under an avenue of trees. The trees seemed to be screaming. As I looked up through the branches I saw large, furry creatures hanging upside down and staring at me, as they shrieked to each other through the damp leaves.

Chapter Five

PUSSELLAWA TO NUWARA ELIYA

Soon after Tennent had settled himself in his new residence in Kandy, he travelled by horse and carriage along a newly built mountain road, further into the hill country, to explore the new British coffee plantations. Although Sri Lanka has long been famed for the tea estates that have exported tea leaves throughout the world for almost 150 years, for a short period of time in the middle of the nineteenth century Sri Lanka was the world's premier supplier of coffee beans. Nowadays very little coffee is grown on the island and it is one of the more expensive imported items in the supermarkets. Sri Lanka is also one of the few countries in Asia where Starbucks is yet to make its mark and, with the exception of a few trendy cafes in the capital, it's not that easy to find a place that serves a decent cup of coffee.

Tennent reports that coffee was brought to Sri Lanka by the Arabs long before any Europeans set foot on the island, and although the Sinhalese never brewed the seeds as a drink, they used the young coffee leaves to flavour their curries and gave the delicate, jasmine-like flowers as offerings in the Buddhist temples. When the Dutch arrived on the island they made a brief attempt to cultivate coffee along the humid, lowland coast, where the climate was unsuitable and the natives uncooperative. As coffee was being grown much more successfully in their other colonies, the Dutch soon gave up on their small plantations in Sri Lanka and turned their attention to their coffee empire in Indonesia.

When the British arrived on the island many years later, they discovered that the Sinhalese were still growing coffee plants in the temples and gardens of the hill country. The British had made unsuccessful attempts to cultivate both indigo and sugar on the island, and with mounting pressure to keep up with the booming colonial industries in India they decided to give coffee a try. Luckily for the British, almost as soon as the first coffee was harvested in Ceylon, the slaves who worked on the plantations in Jamaica, Dominica and Guiana paralysed the Caribbean coffee industry in their struggle for emancipation, leaving a serendipitous gap in the coffee market for Ceylonese coffee to fill.

When Tennent arrived, the Ceylonese coffee boom was at its peak and half of the British civil servants, the military and even a few Anglican clergymen had rushed to invest their savings in prospective coffee land on the hillsides. News of this great investment scheme spread back to Britain, and soon many Englishmen and Scotsmen were rushing to board steamships, lured by the promise of wealth and a new, exotic way of life. Some of these were lone adventurers with money to spare, thrilled by the journey into the unknown; some were military men who had spent years of service in Ceylon; but many were bands of brothers from the area around Aberdeen, who came out to Ceylon to risk the lives and finances of their families in the desperate hope of a better future. Whilst these early coffee pioneers were an odd assortment of men who initially had very little in common, they had one similarity that came to bind them together: they all knew absolutely nothing about the cultivation of coffee.

When they finally arrived after spending three months at sea, they trekked into the hill country by foot or bumped along rough roads in bullock carts, to find that the 'coffee estates' they had purchased in Britain were in fact acres of virgin jungle that had been stolen from the Kandyan peasants. There was nowhere to live and no coffee plants to cultivate. Most of the pioneers spent the first year on their 'plantation' living in the palm-frond huts they had built with their own hands, nervously clutching a musket to protect themselves from the local leopards and hoping that their hut would not be trampled by elephants. In the years that it took to fell the trees, burn the vegetation and plant the first bushes, many died from disease, snake bites or simply from loneliness on the isolated hillside.

Only a few decades after Tennent's arrival, *Hemileia vastatrix*, or 'coffee rust', a fungus of the coffee leaf which had already devastated the coffee plantations of Java, East Africa and South India, began to appear on Ceylonese coffee estates. By the 1880s it had laid waste to the majority of the island's plantations and many of the pioneers watched the coffee bushes to which they had devoted years of their lives wither and die on the hillside.

I was on my way to visit a plantation in Pussellawa that had once been owned by two brothers, Maurice and Gabriel Worms, a pair of Victorian yuppies from the London Stock Exchange, who left Europe to invest in a large coffee plantation in the hill country. When Tennent was touring the plantations, the Worms brothers gave him a bed for the night in the bungalow at the top of their estate. They had also had the foresight to collect some tea seedlings a few years earlier during a trip to China, which they cultivated in a small nursery on their estate.

> On this fine estate an attempt has been made to grow tea: the plants thrive surprisingly, and when I saw them they were covered with bloom. But the experiment was defeated by the impossibility of finding skilled labour to dry and manipulate the leaves. Should it ever be thought expedient to cultivate tea in addition to coffee in Ceylon, the adaptation of the soil and climate has thus been established, and it only remains to introduce artisans from China to conduct the subsequent processes.

It was probably the descendants of these tea seedlings that eventually came to save the island's economy. By the end of the nineteenth century, when the coffee rust had swept through the hillsides, many of the planters had uprooted their dead coffee plants and begun to replace them with tea bushes. As someone who drinks a minimum of eight cups of tea per day, the prospect of spending a few days amongst the bushes of these tea estates was an appealing one.

Most of the buses that head out of Kandy further into the hills follow the same road that Tennent took in 1846, a great feat of structural engineering in its day, which has not significantly altered course in the intervening 160 years. I boarded a bus early the next morning that was heading in the direction of Pussellawa along the hill road, one of the quietest on the island. As the old bus crawled up the increasingly steep road, very few vehicles passed in either direction. This was just as well; on one side was the rock face of the hillside, on the other side a steep drop down to the valley below. As the driver did not seem able to steer his bus sharply enough to stay on his side of the road, any other vehicles would have been in trouble. Away from Kandy and its haze of pollution, the air smelled healthy and clean. The dark, waxy foliage of the wetlands had disappeared and willowy trees with pale, delicate leaves covered the hillside.

Earlier that morning, I had walked into one of the branches of the Vijitha Yapa bookshop opposite my hotel. I had managed to leave the novel I was reading in Colombo and I wanted to find something for the journey. Vijitha Yapa is the Sri Lankan equivalent of Waterstone's, with small branches in most towns on the island, but, unlike Waterstone's, it stocks very few novels that were written after 1900. All the branches of Vijitha Yapa stock the same variety of cheap Asian editions of particularly dry English classics and translations of obscure Greek and Latin works that I couldn't imagine many people who lived in the smaller Sri Lankan towns having much interest in. I flicked through a couple of Dickens novels and had decided I couldn't face either of them when I spotted one of the most modern novels on the shelf, *A Portrait of the Artist as a Young Man* by James Joyce. I had read it when I was sixteen, but as I scanned through the first few pages I realised I had forgotten almost everything and decided to reread it.

I had been reading for about half an hour when I was tapped on the shoulder by the man sitting behind me. He smiled and handed me a torn bus ticket. I turned the ticket over and found that '*Ulysses!*' had been written on the reverse in a spidery, cursive hand. I looked up at the man and he hastily pointed to an elderly Sri Lankan gentleman who was sitting diagonally behind me, wearing a threadbare tweed jacket with leather elbow patches and an Englishman's flat cap. The old gentleman beamed at me from under a whiskery, grey moustache and began scribbling something on another scrap of paper. This was then passed along the rows of people sitting in between us and on the reverse he had scrawled '*Dubliners!*'

When the bus stopped at Pussellawa's collection of fruit and vegetable stalls, both the James Joyce enthusiast and I got off the bus. 'I am so happy to meet someone who is a fellow lover of James Joyce!' he said, as he shook my hand violently. 'I have never seen anyone in this country reading such a high calibre of literature on one of our buses.' He told me that he had once lived on a tea estate at the eastern end of the hill country, but when his wife died he couldn't bear to live in their bungalow of memories and had retired to the capital.

'But I had such an extensive library in my bungalow,' he said nostalgically, 'probably one of the best on the island. I imported books from all over the world, I even had first editions of Henry Miller sent out from America. But when you are the only person who has read these books you don't have anyone to share the stories with,' he explained dolefully. 'That's why I was so excited when I saw you reading on the bus – I always wanted someone to share James Joyce with, but nobody else was interested.'

I stood with him by the side of the road, whilst he talked about Molly Bloom and his favourite works of European and American literature. He talked about his cramped house in Colombo, his hatred of the constant humidity and the noise of traffic, and how he missed the space and isolation of his tea plantation. He insisted on finding a tuk-tuk to take me to the tea estate and I felt a twinge of regret to leave the lonely intellectual standing in the road, as he watched us drive off through the hills.

The forests that once covered the slopes around Pussellawa had been cleared by the pioneer planters almost two centuries earlier and now rows of squat, deep-green tea bushes formed a ribbed, leafy carpet over the hillsides. They sprawled as far as the eye could see and each estate looked identical to the next, except for the little hand-painted signposts that stood in the middle of the bushes, displaying the un-Sri Lankan names of the Rothschild and the Delta estates. Tea pluckers were standing amongst the bushes with woven baskets full of leaves strapped across their foreheads, and scarves draped over their heads and shoulders to shield themselves from the afternoon sun. Those who had already filled their baskets were carrying them on their heads along the narrow, red earth paths between the bushes.

The tuk-tuk turned off the road and bumped up a narrow track to the top of the Hellboda estate, and I was dropped outside a low wooden gate which was opened by a security guard. I walked down a path shaded by a narrow avenue of eucalyptus trees and came to a large bungalow, which would not have looked out of place in a leafy village in the Home Counties. The bungalows were built by the pioneer planters at the top of their plantation, where they lived with their families, overlooking the estate below. Standing in his back garden, the planter could see the sweeping views of his whole plantation, set against the hazy backdrop of the soaring hills, and surrounded by the undulations of his neighbours' estates. This bungalow now belonged to Osanka, a wealthy Sri Lankan from Galle, who had restored it to its colonial splendour of Persian rugs and porcelain bathtubs, turning it into a luxury boutique hotel and one of the most expensive places to stay on the island.

I left my bags on the polished wooden floor of the hall with one of the house servants and was led through an airy conservatory, past a baby grand piano and out onto a wide lawn. I sat on one of the rush-bottomed seats on the veranda and looked down at the lines of emerald tea bushes.

I was joined by a grey-haired, soft-eyed lady called Rose and her pink-cheeked husband, John. My fellow guests sank down onto the chairs next to me, streaming with perspiration and began to fan themselves with straw hats. They had just finished a game of tennis on the old, clay court that belonged to the estate. A young boy cautiously carried out a tea set of heavy china and a large teapot, which he began to lay out on the table, as if he were following some kind of non-intuitive, mental list about where everything should be placed. Given that he had probably only been hired from the village a few weeks ago, it was not surprising that he seemed baffled by the alien etiquette. As soon as he had poured the tea, he smiled nervously around the table and dashed back into the house. The three of us drank the delicate golden tea that had been brewed with leaves from the estate, enthused about the view and shared our feelings of middle-class guilt about the price we were paying for just one night in such a luxurious hotel.

John had grown up on a nearby tea estate that had been in his family for generations, where his father had been the superintendent. His family came to the island from Scotland and his ancestors had been among the pioneers who had cleared the land and planted the first, fated coffee bushes. I asked John about his childhood, but he seemed reluctant to talk and preferred to sit alone, lost in thought as he gazed out over the tea bushes.

His wife left a book for me on my chair that afternoon, which had the initially misleading title, *The Suicide Club*. It was the memoirs of a Sri Lankan planter, Herman Gunaratne, who had made his way up through the ranks to run one of the biggest plantations on the island. His grandfather had been a member of the Suicide Club, an elite group of gamblers who would stake the entirety of their family's money and possessions on a single game, and he was the source of inspiration that drove Gunaratne to take the risks that pushed him through the plantation hierarchy. He described the superintendents, who were initially all British men and oversaw the running of the estates with a gin and tonic in the morning, whiskey with lunch and claret in the evening. They fed their staff on roast beef and Yorkshire puddings, and taught their aspiring Ceylonese assistants how to waltz to Strauss and sing the words to 'Jingle Bells'. Later, some of the estates were managed by high-caste Sri Lankan superintendents, who had worked their way through the plantation hierarchy under British men, and had adopted their habits and tastes. They swapped their sarongs for lounge suits, mastered the confusing array of dining room cutlery, hoped that their wives could produce a decent bread-and-butter pudding, and developed an enthusiasm for European wine and Highland whiskies.

As the sun started to fall behind the hills and the tea bushes disappeared into the shadows, groups of pluckers who had finished for the day were trooping down the hillside together towards the small Hindu temple on the road below for the evening puja. Many tea pluckers were Hindu Tamils of Indian origin and although the surrounding area was a Buddhist region, the plantation Tamils built small temples or *kovil*, with red-and-white striped walls and pyramidal towers covered with their multi-limbed Hindu gods climbing into the sky.

John's parents had left the plantation and emigrated to Australia when he was eleven; I asked him why.

'Well, after Sri Lanka became independent there was a wave of socialism in the country's politics and my father could tell that one day they would nationalise the plantations. He knew that if this happened our lives could become very difficult so he decided it would be best to start a new life elsewhere.' His father was correct – a few years later the government had taken control of the island's prospering estates in a move which many people felt was one of the most disastrous decisions a Sri Lankan government has ever taken. But more about that later.

Early that evening, after spending an hour soaking in my deep, porcelain bathtub, I joined the other guests outside on the dimly lit lawn for a drink before dinner. Subtle jazz was drifting through the open French windows from the conservatory and the house servants were hovering in the background ready to drop more ice cubes into guests' glasses of gin and tonic. Everyone in Colombo seemed to think that I was writing a gritty narrative about a country reeling from civil war but this was far more enjoyable. A Canadian couple, Marius and Hannah, both slender, both attractive, both on their second marriages, were recovering from a trip to Orissa in East India, which Marius had persuaded Hannah was the best place to purchase interior decor for the house they lived in on their cool-climate vineyard.

'Hannah had her divorce lawyer on speed dial,' joked Marius, as Hannah described, still shuddering at the memory, the budget hovels in which she had been forced to stay in India.

'Yeah, Sri Lanka is cleaner, quieter and you can't get places like this in India,' Marius continued, waving his hand across the lawn, 'but there's not much to buy here, is there? I go on holiday to buy stuff to put on my walls and over my sofas, but I haven't found anything here that I actually want to own.'

John and Rose were standing with a couple of friends they were travelling with, who were members of their book group in Australia. Liz and Ruth were tall, confidently spoken Australian women in their late forties, who wore the linen tunics and ethnic-print shawls of the kind of well-educated, broad-minded women who have spent recent holidays in Tehran and Karachi. They were listening carefully to Marius, adjusting their shawls and looking slightly uncomfortable about his blatant consumerism.

Liz and Ruth both worked for the immigration authorities in Australia and had come to Sri Lanka with their Kindles, to spend time at a literary festival and to try to find out more about the country. Every year hundreds of Sri Lankans without visas climb onto unregistered boats and make the long voyage to Australia in search of what they believe to be a brighter future, only to be placed in detention centres to await a decision as to whether they will be granted refugee status. Liz is one of the people who makes that decision and she had come to Sri Lanka to try to form a more accurate picture of the terror from which the asylum seekers claim the need to escape.

'Since the end of the civil war the number of people arriving on the boats has dropped,' Liz explained to the small audience that gathered around her on the lawn, 'but we still have large numbers of Tamils from the north who claim that their position is still not safe in their home towns. Have you spent much time in the north?' she asked me.

I told her I had travelled to the former warzone on a couple of occasions and that the situation still seemed fairly grim for many people.

'Grim in what way?' she pressed.

I explained that some of the people who had been driven from their houses during the war were still living in refugee camps, waiting to be rehoused, and that the Sinhalese army were still watching over many of the Tamil towns.

Liz pondered this for a moment. 'But whilst you were up there, did you ever see anyone being physically beaten by the army or abused in any way?' she asked. I said that whilst I had heard of isolated incidents from other people, I hadn't ever witnessed it myself.

Liz sighed. 'But the problem is, that unless they can prove that their lives are in immediate danger, we can't let them into Australia,' she said despondently.

One of the house servants came out onto the lawn and struck a large brass gong telling us it was time to eat. We were ushered into a deep-red dining room and seated around a large mahogany table laid with heavy silver cutlery. As we ate, the conversation turned back to immigration. Although Marius and Hannah were technically Canadian, neither of them had been born in Canada, and both had entered as illegal immigrants and spent years dodging the immigration authorities before they were finally granted citizenship. Marius proudly launched into the tale of his own attempts to obstruct the immigration process, whilst Liz and Ruth continued to rearrange their shawls, stopped looking uncomfortable and began to look annoyed.

'I had been living with a woman and working for two years before they found me,' said formerly half-German, half-US citizen Marius. 'We even managed to have a kid before they got hold of me! I was just lucky that the person judging my case took a liking to me,' he said, winking at Liz. 'He said to me, "Marius, you've fucked up here, really fucked up my friend, but I can see that you're a good guy. Leave the country for a month, we'll wipe your slate clean and then when you make a legit application, I'll pull a few strings to make sure you get in." And I did!' he finished triumphantly, giving Liz a supercilious smile.

His current wife, Hannah, was a British-passport-holding Zimbabwean, who had also spent a number of years making trips in and out of Canada, via the visa offices of England, Zimbabwe and Canada, before she was finally allowed to settle there. Listening to the stories of the people around the table, it all seemed absurd: Hannah, the grandchild of the white colonisers of Africa, pleading for citizenship in a country made up almost entirely of immigrants, and John, the grandchild of a British planter in Sri Lanka, moving to a land that would not grant citizenship to the Sri Lankans that many of their ancestors had been instrumental in dividing and ruling many years before.

The grass was covered in dew the next morning and the servants were padding around the wet lawn in their bare feet, picking flowers for the house and raking up the leaves that had fallen from the trees during the night. The air, too, was heavy with moisture and clouds of mist were tumbling through the valley, as the weak morning sunrays shone through the haze, bathing the lower tea terraces in the pale morning light. The female tea pluckers were standing amongst the tea bushes chattering to each other and nipping at the leaves, which they flicked over their shoulders into sacks that hung on their backs from a single strap over their foreheads. Some were in saris but most had abandoned them in favour of more practical loose cotton skirts, with a long-sleeved T-shirt to protect their skin from the sun's rays. Pickers who had already collected a sackful of leaves were tramping in wellington boots to the plantation office where the leaves would be weighed. When they had offloaded their sacks, the women slumped down together in the shade of the bushes and passed a large water canister around, which they held above their thrown-back heads, and poured into their mouths and over their faces.

Many of the pluckers on the tea estates are the descendants of the 'coolies' from India, who filled the labour shortage on the estates in the nineteenth century. In the 1830s, the economic situation in the Tamil-speaking regions of South India was so bad that many boarded the ships of the British India Steam Navigation Company and travelled to Ceylon as deck passengers. Many died on the voyage and, for those who didn't, the grim crossing was followed by a several-hundred-mile trek uphill from the coast to the tea estates. This journey into the hills by foot could take up to six weeks and many more died from disease, lack of sustenance or exhaustion along the way. When the coolies eventually reached the end of their gruelling journey, the pay on the estates was a pittance and they had to live on top of each other in small hovels.

The Sinhalese who lived in the hill country worked alongside the Tamils on the estates, but the relationship was not always a happy one. According to the British, the Sinhalese were lazy and unreliable, often not appearing for work, especially in the rain. The Tamils, on the other hand, were good grafters, keen to get ahead and happy to work in any conditions. Sinhalese historians protested that the Sinhalese also had their own land to cultivate and often chose to leave the plantations rather than put up with the dreadful conditions. And why should they exert themselves for the British, on land that was rightfully theirs and had been stolen from their ancestors? The Tamils, the Sinhalese argued, had no land of their own to deal with and nowhere else to go, and simply worked hard because they were bound to the estate by a contract and had nothing better to do.

The quiet outside in the garden was suddenly broken by a stream of expletives in a Canadian accent, which sent the house staff running into the bungalow, dropping their rakes on the lawn. Ten minutes later, Marius hobbled out onto the lawn with bandages wrapped around the fingers of his hand that he had somehow managed to catch in the spinning metal blades of an electric fan. He and Hannah had intended to leave early to try to find some antiques in Colombo, but Hannah was now lying in the porcelain bath tub in their room, fully clothed, having fainted at the sight of his blood.

I left the tea estate after breakfast and flagged down a tuk-tuk on the road that was heading in the direction of Nuwara Eliya, the highest and coldest town on the island in the heart of the tea district. As the road wound steeply up the hillside, the solid concrete buildings began to disappear and were replaced by flimsy wooden shacks with corrugated-iron roofs. Many of these little lodgings were surrounded by neatly planted vegetable plots, which formed a patchwork in shades of green. As we climbed higher, the air began to cool, and the men and women who were trudging up and down the road, carrying bundles of firewood and sacks of vegetables on their backs, were wrapped up in woollen hats and scarves. Tennent recorded that the British found it almost impossible to persuade the lowland Sinhalese, who had a horror of the cold in these elevated situations, and still more of the rain, to move up to the hills to provide labour on the mountain roads. As a result, the government had to employ a body of men they referred to as Caffres, the remaining descendants of the Africans brought by the Portuguese from their colony of Mozambique.

Although Tennent's name may have disappeared into obscurity over the years, his record of an incident that took place on the road to Nuwara Eliya did earn him a place in the *Oxford English Dictionary*. The incident occurred at the Ramboda Pass, a sharp ascent along the hill road, which was the home of a violent elephant that had become separated from its herd. Tennent referred to the creature as a 'rogue elephant', a translation of the Sinhalese phrase used by the locals for such an animal, and was credited by the *Oxford English Dictionary* as being the first person to use the term in printed English.

On the occasion of my first ascent, the Rangbodde [Ramboda] pass was rendered dangerous by the presence of a 'rogue' elephant which infested it. He concealed himself by day in the dense forest on either side of the road, making his way during the darkness to the river below; and we saw, as we passed, marks on the trunks of the trees where he had rubbed off the mud, returning from his midnight bath. On the morning when I crossed the mountain, a poor Caffre, one of the pioneer corps, proceeding to his labour, came suddenly upon this savage at a turning in the road, when the elephant, alarmed by the intrusion, lifted him with its trunk and beat out his brains against the bank.

The high plain on which Nuwara Eliya now stands was discovered about thirty years before Tennent arrived in Ceylon by a party of English officers, whilst they were out in the hills on an elephant-hunting expedition. When they reported this to the governor of the island, Sir Edward Barnes, and he saw the cool, breezy landscape with a bleakness reminiscent of home, he decided to transform it into a sanitary retreat, where his British troops could recover from the disease and exhaustion of the tropical lowlands in newly built whitewashed cottages surrounded by rose gardens. I was dropped in the centre of the town and, as I looked around, I was disconcerted by just how English the place still felt. Travellers are always on the lookout for anything that is different from their own country and, standing in the middle of a place that felt so similar to home, the absence of difference was unnerving. But although Nuwara Eliya felt incredibly English, I couldn't immediately work out why; in many ways it was typical of every other Sri Lankan town I had visited, with its large dusty bus station, market stalls selling bananas and coconuts, and the moustachioed men smoking in the back of their tuk-tuks; and yet I kept thinking of holidays I had spent in the Lake District. Maybe it was the roundabout that was covered with geraniums or the leaded windowpanes and chimneys of the semi-detached houses. Maybe it was the large plastic conservatories and neatly mown front lawns surrounded by low, conifer hedges and flower beds; or the cardigans over the saris, the anoraks over the sarongs and the hunched shoulders, tensed against the cold.

I had intended to spend that night in Nuwara Eliya, but after walking through the streets for an hour I began to find its dilapidated Englishness depressing and decided to move on, as soon as I had made a brief visit to the town's famous Hill Club.

The Nuwara Eliya Hill Club's half-timbered, grey stone building looked as if it had been dragged off a golf course in Scotland and I was escorted into the leather-upholstered library by a porter wearing pressed trousers and a button-down tunic. Every town in the tea district had a club where the estate managers and the more senior assistants on the plantations could socialise together, away from their tea bushes. During the evenings the managers and their wives drank in the club bars with the couples from the neighbouring estates, and at the weekends village fetes were organised, prizes were awarded for the best roses, and fishing outings and sports matches took place in the hills. Many of the tea estates selected their aspiring Ceylonese workers not just on the basis of their qualifications but also on their skills on the pitch, and the young men recruited from the most prestigious schools in Colombo soon found themselves rugby tackling and drinking whisky with their British managers, who slowly moulded them into English gentlemen. The Hill Club in Nuwara Eliya was regarded as the most prestigious and for many years membership was only given to British families. Nowadays it is a private club for wealthy Sri Lankan bankers and estate managers. The porter led me through the dark corridors of the club where photographs of prize-winning trout and the heads of various stuffed mammals still hung on the walls. I asked if it would be possible for me to have lunch in the club bar but was told apologetically that it was still members only and it would be best if I ate elsewhere.

As I was being ushered out past the receptionist I overheard a fair-skinned lady with wild, black hair and a mouth painted in deep-red lipstick also being politely refused lunch in the club. As we walked out of the gloomy clubhouse into the sunshine of the garden together, she glared back at the receptionist, muttering expletives under her breath.

'They wouldn't let me eat lunch either,' I sympathised.

'It's just one thing after another with this place,' she muttered, scowling, 'I really wish I hadn't bothered coming.'

'To the Hill Club?'

'No, to Uva,' she said, using the name of the easternmost province of the hill country.

I asked her why she was visiting the area and she said she had come to see the tea estate and the rubber plantation that her family had once owned.

'How long ago did you sell it?' I asked.

'Sell it!?' she exploded, glaring at me. 'We didn't sell it. It was stolen from us nearly forty years ago.'

'Who stole it?' I asked, wondering how anyone could steal a tea plantation.

'The government stole it, that's who,' she continued angrily, shaking her head.

Her name was Julia and, although she spoke with a clipped, Oxford English accent, she had lived in Sri Lanka her whole life. Her German father and Sri Lankan mother had owned many acres of tea and rubber estate in the hill country, but when the government had nationalised the plantations in the 1970s, her parents were left without an income.

We walked out of the grounds of the Hill Club into the town together and I asked Julia if she knew anywhere we could find something to eat.

'Let's go in here,' she said decisively, nudging me into a small hotel in the middle of the town. 'There will be cake. Cake calms me down.'

We sat in the hotel's restaurant, which was a few tables and chairs in a conservatory looking towards Nuwara Eliya's little play park, hidden behind rows of Scots pines. When our tea and a fluorescent green, cream-filled cake arrived, Julia continued angrily with her story.

It had all started in 1970 when Sirimavo Bandaranaike, the world's first female prime minister – 'Mrs B', as she was referred to – was voted into power in a coalition with the Communist Party, promising the islanders radical, socialist reforms. Her supporters were young, Sinhalese, rural and poor. Many were from the lowest castes and were the ancestors of the Kandyans who had been turfed off their land by the white pioneers in the nineteenth century. Their idol was Che Guevara, and they called for the redistribution of wealth and land. When Mrs Bandaranaike's reforms didn't go far enough, they rose up against the government with weapons they had paid for by cultivating cannabis and mining gemstones.

Waiting in the wings was the minister of agriculture, a proud Kandyan named Hector Kobbekaduwa, who had an axe to grind. As Herman Gunaratne, the Sri Lankan tea-industry guru, wrote in *The Plantation Raj*, Kobbekaduwa's targets were the two groups of people he believed had shafted the Kandyans: firstly the British, who stole their land to build their coffee empire, and secondly the low-country Sinhalese, who migrated to the hill country and took control of many of the estates. He called these men the Brown Sahibs and hated them for the British habits they adopted and their decadent, non-Buddhist way of life. He openly mocked them in a famous speech in parliament for decorating their houses at Christmas, eating sardines on toast and for serving large quantities of liquor 'to the strains of "The Blue Danube" and the "Moonlight Sonata", deep into the "Silent Night"'. He persuaded Mrs Bandaranaike that the only way to prevent further insurrections from the unemployed youth was to allow the government to repossess the estates and redistribute the land. When the Land Reform Act was passed, the masses in the hill country celebrated throughout the night, whilst the estate owners buried their heads in their hands. Soon the estates were handed over to new Sinhalese managers, favourites of the government, many of whom not only had no experience of managing a tea estate, but no management experience at all.

Many of the former estate owners watched in despair as the new managers let the neat tea bushes and tea factories fall into decline. A number also embezzled money from the plantations and almost bankrupted their new businesses in the process.

John, who I had met in Pussellawa, had also alluded to the problems that had followed land reform. When he had visited his family's old estate and spoken to some of the staff, they told him that after the plantation was taken over by the government, the new Sinhalese manager was not only incompetent but treated the pluckers very badly. He was so unpopular that one night the pluckers set fire to the bungalow whilst he was asleep and he only just escaped from the flames by scrambling up the hillside.

'There were no legal proceedings and I could even show you my father's deeds to the land,' Julia grumbled, as she stabbed another piece of cake with her fork. 'The problem was that we were living in Colombo and couldn't put up a fight. We were just told that we were forbidden any access to the land and given a pitiful sum as compensation. Not that there was anything for us to buy even if we had any money.'

'There were shortages too?' I asked, envisaging Soviet-era queues.

'Yes. We probably lived on one of the most fertile islands in the world and we couldn't even produce enough food to feed ourselves. Everyone had to have ration cards and it was very difficult to get hold of sugar, butter or clothes. I think that's why I have this unhealthy love of cake,' she said, as she helped herself to another lurid confection. 'Because of the communists, I never had a birthday cake.'

As Julia ate her cake she lowered her voice and outlined her own theory that Sri Lankan government had never really bought into the Marxist world view, and had just used it as a way to nationalise the industries and siphon money off for themselves. She talked of her father's battles with the government, their life in their cramped house in Colombo and the food rations they had to share with their stateless Tamil servants. She cursed the communists, ridiculing their world view and citing historical failures of their systems. Her tales and conspiracies were Soviet ones, but less well known and set under bluer skies.

Chapter Six

INTO THE
FORMER WARZONE

In the spring of 1848, Tennent embarked on one of the longest trips he took during his stay in Ceylon. The route took him from the cool, arboreous slopes of the hill country, due east through the forested peaks, down to the arid coastal plain and finally north, along the east coast to the Jaffna Peninsula, where the land disintegrates into small islets that float out into the Palk Strait towards India. On modern maps of Sri Lanka the route begins in a jumble of contour lines, surrounded by the polysyllabic names of overlapping settlements, which diffuse into the uncontoured expanse of the sparsely inhabited east. The people, too, change with the topography. The north and east of Sri Lanka is home to the majority of the island's Tamil population, described by early anthropologists as a taller, darker people, who trace their ancestors to the Dravidian Tamils of South India. Their language and culture is distinct from that of the fairer Sinhalese who populate the south and west of the island, and are the descendants of Aryan invaders from northern India. When Tennent embarked on this trip the majority of the area had been ignored by previous European travellers – deterred by the dense forests and indigenous tribes – and was simply shown on maps as an 'unexplored district'. Nowadays, the north and east of the island are still relatively unknown to European travellers – and a whole generation of Sri Lankans – as much of the twenty-six-year civil war was waged on its barren, thirsty land.

Like many separatist movements, the desire of the Tamil Tigers for an independent north-eastern state can be traced back to ancient events. For centuries, waves of South Indian Tamil kings led armies over to the island, and wars raged between the Tamils and the Sinhalese, the Hindus and the Buddhists. Other Sinhalese kings married Tamil princesses from India and built their wives Hindu shrines in their Buddhist temples so they could worship together. Later, when the island became a fragmented hotchpotch of kingdoms, the statues of Shiva and the Buddha crumbled side by side in the ground. By the thirteenth century the north existed as the Tamil kingdom of Jaffna and was separated from the kingdoms of the south by a wide belt of impenetrable forest known as the Vanni. As a result, the two populations gradually evolved completely separate cultures and never learnt to speak each other's language.

The differences between the two communities deepened during the nineteenth century, when a group of American missionaries turned up in Jaffna and began preaching the gospel and educating the locals in English. The Tamils were keen to learn. When the British arrived on the scene and made

English the island's national language, the Tamils, with their linguistic advantage, quickly became the backbone of the civil service and the majority of the local doctors, lawyers and engineers. When the British departed from Sri Lanka in 1948, the descendants of the old, fractured kingdoms were left to try to get along together as a unified country. Meanwhile, the Sinhalese had been growing jealous of the Tamils' dominance under the British and, as independence progressed, various Sinhalese presidents took it upon themselves to redress the balance. Under a series of parliamentary acts, Sinhala, a foreign tongue to most Tamils, became the national language, Tamil students were told they had to achieve higher marks than Sinhalese students to get into university and Buddhism became the official state religion.

As Tamils all over the island began to feel threatened, many decided that the formation of a separate state was the only way they could protect themselves from an openly racist government. Under their violent and bloodthirsty leader Velupillai Prabhakaran, angry and disillusioned Tamil youths grouped together to form the LTTE – the Liberation Tigers of Tamil Eelam, or the Tamil Tigers. They were disciplined and determined, renouncing alcohol, drugs, cigarettes and sex. They were casteless, genderless and ageless; untouchables, Brahmins, mothers and children. For their identity they looked to their ancestry and adopted the emblem of the ancient Tamil Chola invaders, a tiger on a red background; for their methods they looked to the Palestinians. The 'Black Tigers', a group of elite LTTE suicide bombers, attacked aircraft, naval vessels and oil-storage tankers. They blew up temples, schools and buses, using arms that were funded by an international network of wealthy diaspora that stretched from Paris to Yangon. For twenty-six years they fought against the Sinhalese and the soldiers of the Sri Lankan army, until the war officially ended with the death of their leader on the banks of a lagoon in May 2009.

When I came to Sri Lanka in 2010 the war had ended just over a year earlier. Although it was celebrated as a great victory in the Sinhalese regions of the island and Mahinda Rajapaksa's government was triumphantly re-elected, questions were being raised in the international community about the final stages of the war – a bloody showdown that killed an unknown number of civilians in the north-east corner of the island. There were murmurs of war crimes and ethnic cleansing. Channel 4 produced a documentary, narrated by a grim-faced Jon Snow, which interviewed survivors of the war's final phase and showed video clips of the shelling of civilian targets, including in no-fire zones, taken on the mobile phones of the victims. The video went global and caused uproar in Sri Lankan communities around the world. The Sri Lankan government responded with indignation and claimed the evidence was fabricated. The human rights wing of the UN began poking around and issued a report stating there were credible allegations that the Sri Lankan army shelled no-fire zones, denied humanitarian assistance to the area, and violated the human rights of journalists and critics of the government. It also found evidence that the LTTE had committed human rights violations, including the forced recruitment of children. The UN panel suggested that the government should get a move on and organise an internationally credible investigation. Not surprisingly, the government was not keen to let many more foreigners into the region.

Getting military clearance to travel through the north and the east was going to be my first challenge.

Whilst Sri Lankans were now able to move freely throughout the island, foreign passport holders had to obtain military clearance to travel to any areas north of a small town called Omanthai, or along the roads of the east coast. There was also no guarantee that if you requested permission to travel to the restricted area it would be granted. I only knew one European in Sri Lanka who had successfully travelled to the north, a British journalist who had made the journey to write a newspaper article. I met her for lunch one day in Colombo and asked for some advice about the application I had to make to the Ministry of Defence. 'Whatever you do, don't say you are going there to write about what you see,' she advised me. 'The government is still very sensitive about what happened in the area and they are worried about what foreigners might report. The government is making a lot of noise about rehabilitating the warzone, but there is still a long way to go. When I went there I just said I was going to visit Jaffna as a tourist, to make life easier. I knew my bags might be searched at the checkpoint in Omanthai so I didn't risk taking my camera and I tried to disguise my notebooks.'

As I showed her Tennent's route on the map and ran my finger along the narrow east-coast road that would take me north, she began to shake her head. 'Although they are letting people up to the north now, I have no idea whether you will be able to travel there via that coastal road. The big checkpoint where you present your military clearance is on the central A9 road that runs through the middle of the Northern Province,' she said, pointing to the thick red line of the main artery, miles inland. 'You will just have to apply for the general military clearance to go to the north and hope they recognise it in the east when you get there. Be careful though,' she said, putting her hand lightly on my arm. 'Nobody really seems to know what is going on in the east and there will be a large military presence. Even if they don't give you any trouble, you will still need to be careful about the landmines. Make sure you travel with someone who knows the area well and, whatever you do, don't leave the main roads.'

So the next day, I filled in the 'Clearance Application to Travel North – Form A', stating that I wanted to visit Jaffna by an unspecified route as a tourist. I then called Ajith, who was not in the recording studio that day, and asked him to drive me to the office of the Ministry of Defence in his tuk-tuk.

I was expecting a high-security compound behind tall granite walls – like most of the other government buildings in the city – with iron gates flanked by rigid uniformed guards. Instead, Ajith drove me to Galle Face Green, a desolate strip of windswept land by the sea, and pulled up in front of a little single-storey building, not much larger than a garage.

'This can't be the Ministry of Defence, Ajith,' I said.

'Yes, this is it. You call when you're finished,' said Ajith hastily, looking uncomfortably at a couple of moody adolescent soldiers leaning against the wall in camouflage uniforms and green berets. I stepped out of the tuk-tuk to ask the soldiers for directions to the correct building, but before I could say anything, Ajith had turned the tuk-tuk around as fast as he could and was speeding back to the road.

'Yes, madam,' said one of the soldiers as he walked over the tarmac towards me. 'What are you wanting?'

'I want to travel to Jaffna,' I replied uncertainly.

'In there, madam. You wait here,' said the soldier, pointing to the doorway of the small building.

Inside, it did not look like the headquarters of an army that had managed to wipe out one of the most violent and well-funded terrorist groups of the twentieth century. A few mismatching, battered desks sat in the middle of the room and loose wires hung through holes in the ceiling, where the square ceiling panels had either rotted away or fallen out. There was not a computer or piece of electronic equipment in sight and, instead, large cardboard folders of paper were being passed between more acne-ridden members of the military, who clomped around the office in ill-fitting boots and baggy camouflage uniforms. A couple of girls stood behind a table by the door 'checking' the bags of everyone who entered and left the room, by quickly opening and closing them, whilst they continued their conversation without glancing at what was inside. A couple of young men in uniform sitting on the desk nearest to me were absorbed by the challenge of trying to peel an unripe mango without a knife, by smashing it repeatedly on the edge of the desk.

Meanwhile, a large group of weary looking people had gathered around me, many of them old men in sarongs, holding Indian passports and handwritten letters on thin, lined paper, pleading for access to the north. We sat together in silence on a line of plastic chairs, in a salty gale that blew through the open windows from the ocean. An hour later, another uniformed man, who looked no different from the rest, walked into the room. Immediately he was clearly identified by everyone else but me as the person to give your paperwork to. As he sat down at a desk in the corner of the room, the twenty people around me made a stampede for the table and surrounded it, standing over him, as they shouted and thrust their passports in his face. As I had been the first person in the office that morning by a margin of about twenty minutes, I was enraged by this affront to my British sense of fair queuing etiquette. Fuming, I hovered around the edge of the jabbing elbows and kicking legs until, realising that this could be a very long process, I elbowed my way to the front and threw my passport and application form under the nose of the beleaguered man.

Several days later I received a fax from the Ministry of Defence granting me permission to travel to Jaffna. Whilst this was a relief, the document specified that the route must be along the A9 road that was miles away from the east-coast road I wanted to take. It also stated that some of the districts that lay along Tennent's eastern route were strictly out of bounds as they were still being de-mined. I decided it would be wise to delay my trip for a few months.

In the meantime, the government announced it was relaxing travel restrictions to the north, having cleared up most of the war evidence that lay along the A9 road, but restrictions to the east still applied. I spent the next few months asking people in Colombo who worked at the various embassies whether they had any idea about the level of security in the region and the probability that I would be stopped en route. The answers were all the same: security was still high, there were military checkpoints on all roads, vehicles were still being searched, some areas were still landmined and there were still refugee camps outside some of the towns. But as to whether foreigners were allowed through, nobody knew. After a few months, I decided I couldn't wait any longer. If the government was relaxing restrictions in some areas it was a promising sign, so I decided to try my luck, to head out for the east coast and hope for the best.

Whilst Tennent did not need any official permission to travel to this 'unexplored district', he spent many weeks preparing for the trip before he was able to leave his residence in Kandy. He had to find elephants and coolies to carry the tents, beds, food and water that his party would need for their month-long expedition. They needed cooks and servants who would run ahead to set up camp and provide the explorers with their meals. Horse keepers had to be found to care for the animals they rode, and grass cutters were employed to slash through the undergrowth and forge the paths ahead. The whole party came to 150 men and, as they set out from Kandy, they had very little idea of what they would find or how easy it would be to get hold of provisions along the way. The Kandyans were very reluctant to sell Tennent's party any of the produce from their land, so the band of explorers had to rely on the small villages along the route. Finding enough food to feed a party of 150 men in the little jungle settlements proved very difficult and in the end the party had to resort to shooting any unfortunate wildlife for food – including flamingos and parrots, which, Tennent reported in his account of the trip, made particularly excellent pies.

A few days before I set off for the east, I bumped into Mr Sinniah, the diminutive, impeccably presented gentleman who lived on my lane in Colombo, as he was supervising the gardener attacking the large hedge outside his house. He had read James Emerson Tennent's *Ceylon* as a teenager and asked me how I was getting on tracing his footsteps. I told him I was planning to head to the east later that week and asked if he had ever visited the region himself.

'I did go to the beach at Trincomalee as a child many years before the war,' he replied, as he looked with concern at the large chunks of vegetation the gardener seemed to be removing from the hedge at random. 'I don't remember much about it, except for the spotted deer that I saw paddling in the water of China Bay early one morning. But since the war, and everything that happened to us in Black July of 1983, I have no real desire to go back.'

Although tensions and skirmishes between the Sinhalese and the Tamils had been taking place on the island since soon after independence, many people regard the summer of 1983 as the official start of the civil war. After a handful of Sinhalese soldiers were killed in an ambush by Tamil rebels in the north of the island, Sinhalese mobs took to the streets all over the island and turned on their Tamil neighbours, murdering, looting, and burning their houses and businesses to the ground.

Mr Sinniah and his wife were Tamil, although they spoke both Sinhalese and English fluently, and their families had lived in the south of the island for generations. They had moved to the capital soon after they were married and had never really regarded themselves as 'Tamil' or shared an identity with the Tamils in the north. I asked Mr Sinniah if he would mind telling me the story of what happened to his family in Black July and he invited me to listen to his tale over a cup of tea with his wife that afternoon.

I sat with the Sinniahs later that day on their wide, shady veranda that looked over a receding lawn. We were all sitting on old wicker rocking chairs that had been coated in white gloss many years earlier and were now dropping stiff flakes of dry paint onto the red tiled floor. The Sinniahs, like many other families in Colombo, were helped in the house by a 'boy', who was not a boy at all, but a spindly, thirty-year-old man who wore thick, milk-bottle glasses that distorted his eyes. He lived in a single room in the Sinniahs' house, which overlooked the front gate. He had been with the family since he was a boy, and spent his days opening and closing the gate to visitors and running occasional household errands. The window of his room looked out over the lane and if I ever had friends visiting the house, I would often see his curtains twitch as he peeped out to watch what was going on. Whenever I passed him in the lane I always said hello, but he usually avoided eye contact and shuffled past shyly, focusing steadily on the ground through his thick lenses. The Sinniahs also had an elderly maid, a rotund, round-shouldered lady, with a grey straggly ponytail and a large number of absent teeth, who always wore a loose, white cotton dress that looked like a Victorian nightgown. After the maid had brought a tray of full teacups to the table and waddled back into the house with her white shroud billowing in the breeze, Mr Sinniah began to recount their story.

'We had decided to go on holiday to Europe during that summer of 1983. It was the first time we had ever been to

Europe and we did a grand tour, travelling through England and France, and eventually we caught a train to Rome, from where we were going to fly back to Sri Lanka. Whilst we were on the train, an Italian gentleman came up to us with a copy of the local newspaper and asked if we were Sri Lankan. On the front page there was a photograph of some of the buildings in Colombo on fire and people fighting hand-to-hand in the street.'

'But we weren't worried, were we?' said his wife.

'Oh no, not to begin with,' Mr Sinniah agreed. 'There had been small riots between the Sinhalese and the Tamils every few years for as long as we could remember, and we thought it was just another period of unrest that would have blown over by the time we got home. She was six months pregnant with our daughter,' he said, smiling at his wife, 'and we had been travelling for weeks. Our suitcases were full of dirty clothes and we were exhausted.'

'I said that I would sleep for a week when we got back to Colombo, do you remember?' said his wife with a wry laugh.

'When we landed in the airport,' continued Mr Sinniah, 'we could tell that something was wrong. There were crowds of people sheltering in the terminal, camping on the floor, and you could feel a tension in the atmosphere. Whilst I was trying to find us a taxi I overheard a group of Sinhalese men behind me saying, "We really gave them the works this time. Fort is going to burn to the ground." I can still remember those exact words,' he said, shaking his head, 'even thirty years later. It was at that point that we started to become scared. I told my wife that we must only speak English to each other, not Tamil or Sinhala. We began pulling the luggage labels off our bags and

I buried our passports in the suitcases so that people wouldn't see our Tamil names.'

'I was so worried about our little boy who was also with us,' said Mrs Sinniah, 'he was only two and he used to call us mother and father in Tamil.'

'When we took a taxi back through the suburbs to Colombo, the air over the city was thick with smoke and through the smog you could see the flames of buildings that had been set alight. As we drove through the city, past the shells of looted buildings that were still smouldering, I could see Sinhalese men, standing in a daze, staring at the destruction around them. It was almost as if they could not believe what they had done. There were rumours that some were rural villagers from the area around Galle and they had actually been hired by the government. They were apparently loaded onto a train, given copies of the electoral registers so that they knew which buildings belonged to Tamils and unleashed on the city. They set occupied cars alight, bludgeoned people in the street, and burned and looted the city whilst the police stood by and watched. The same thing happened in towns all over the country, not just in Colombo.'

'All I wanted to do was to go back to our house,' said Mrs Sinniah, looking at her husband. 'My ankles were so swollen and I was so tired, but you wouldn't let us, would you?'

'I just had a feeling that something terrible had happened,' he said, quietly, looking into the distance across the lawn. 'I don't know why, but I just had this strange premonition that our house wasn't there anymore. I was so worried that the sight of it would cause her to have a miscarriage that we went straight to some of our relatives instead. When we got there they confirmed that our house had been burnt down and said that we could stay with them.'

'It was kind of them, but their neighbours, however, did not want to have us there. They were worried that the village would be accused of harbouring Tamils and their houses would be attacked too,' explained Mrs Sinniah. 'We went instead to a refugee camp that had been set up in a convent near the railway line. It was July and it was baking hot – we were all packed together, sleeping on the floor and there were not enough toilets.'

'After a few days, I felt that it was time for us to face up to what had happened to our house,' said Mr Sinniah, 'so I walked through the ashes and ruins of the city, along the coastline to our road. As I turned the corner, our dog, who had somehow survived, ran out to meet me. He led me up the road to the house and as I walked through the gates, I was almost knocked down by a few men running out of the shell of our house, carrying the grills that they had pulled out of the windows and a set of taps that they had smashed out of the bathtub. The roof of the house had caved in and all of our belongings had been stolen. The first wave of looters stole our jewellery, the second wave took the furniture and the final wave ripped out whatever was left. I still remember the wineglasses that we had left on the table had warped and melted in the heat of the fire, and were welded to the ground. They were practically all that was left.'

As Mr Sinniah had been describing the ruins of their house, his wife's face had started to harden. 'It was on that day, for the first time in my life, that I really felt like a Tamil,' she said quietly. 'Before that summer, I had never really felt any different from my Sinhalese neighbours, but suddenly I began to feel different. I couldn't look my Sinhalese friends in the eye any more, people I had known for years, and they were too embarrassed and ashamed to speak to me.'

'But we went back, didn't we?' said Mr Sinniah. 'Even though we had lost everything, she was pregnant and exhausted and just wanted to go back to our house. We stayed in the house for weeks, with no windows and no doors – we didn't need them after all as there was nothing left for anyone to steal. Little by little we rebuilt the place, first with the roof, then the doors and finally we started to replace our possessions.'

'What happened to the people who didn't have the money to rebuild their houses?' I asked.

'Well, a lot of those people are the Tamils who live in your country,' replied Mr Sinniah with a laugh. 'That's the irony. The government thought that they would make the Tamils weak by driving them out of the country, but instead they went abroad and many became wealthy doctors, lawyers and businessmen. They were the diaspora, some of whom sponsored the LTTE. And those who could not leave the island were driven into the north, arrived with nothing and went straight to the LTTE camps, where their anger and frustration turned into violent desires for revenge.'

'You must be careful on your trip to the north-east,' warned Mrs Sinniah, furrowing her brow, 'the war may be over, but so much has happened in that region that it will not be peaceful for a long time.'

The first leg of Tennent's journey was due east of Kandy, through the dense forests of the central highland mountain range and down to the town of Mahiyangana on the eastern plain. The bus to Mahiyangana from Kandy trundled slowly along the sharp hairpin bends of the narrow mountain road and climbed steeply through the trees. The road looked out over the deep green undulations of the hills and valleys below, and down to the sluggish brown river that cut its way along the base of the wooded peaks. Travelling by road in Sri Lanka can often be a claustrophobic experience; most of the roads run through dense jungle where the trees meet overhead, obscuring the sky, and it feels as if you are travelling through a dark, herbaceous tunnel. But as the road broke through the treeline and looked down towards the eastern plain rolling out to the horizon, I felt a sense of uninhibited space for the first time since I had begun the journey.

The bus paused briefly at a small muddy settlement at the highest point of the road, which consisted of a few concrete houses with corrugated-iron roofs, surrounded by tall spindly fir trees. Two teenage boys jumped onto the half-empty bus carrying woven baskets filled with small green citrus fruits. As the passengers started to roll the little green balls between their hands and pulled away their tough skin, the bus was filled with the sharp smell of unripe oranges. Up so high, the wind moving through the alpine trees had a sharp chill, and the villagers were traipsing through the mud in woolly hats and garish polyester cardigans. A group of teenage boys, who had climbed down from the bus to share a single cigarette, leant against a wall, watching me through the bus window, and started to smirk and make obscene gestures. I couldn't imagine that many tourists would come along this road and the presence of a single white female must have been something of a novelty. I thought about getting out of the bus and sticking up for myself, but I had a feeling my anger would just amuse them further. 'It's not just because you're foreign,' a female Sri Lankan friend told me later, 'it's the same for us too. I've been groped and leered at on so many buses in Colombo that I don't take them anymore and spend lots of money taking taxis instead. Many Sri Lankan men just have very little respect for women.'

As the bus descended to the flat plain, the gentle, muted green of the scrawny alpine trees was replaced by the waxy leaves of the banana plants and furry emerald paddy fields, bathed in late-afternoon sunshine. By the time we arrived in Mahiyangana, the sun had almost disappeared from the sky and the town had an air of desertion. All the buildings seemed to be either disintegrating and decrepit or so new they were not yet fully built. A tall, half-constructed statue of the Buddha stood in the middle of the town, surrounded by scaffolding, in front of a crumbling, red-brick, colonial clock tower. Many of the narrow concrete shops had metal girders sticking out of their roofs, ready to support higher storeys that were waiting to be added, whilst the ground floors were already patched with peeling posters and looked tired enough to be demolished. A couple of tuk-tuk drivers were asleep in the back of their vehicles by the roadside, sprawled across the back seat with their feet pressing on the windscreen. I tapped on a windscreen to wake one of the drivers, who drove me along a grassy track that led out of the town, to a small hotel surrounded by dusky paddy fields, humming with cicadas.

As I sat in the small reception area, waiting for someone to find me a room key, I noticed a large portrait hanging on the wall. The background was a bluish watercolour of a sylvan landscape, and pasted into the foreground was a cut-out photograph of a sinewy old man with shoulder-length hair, wearing a green loincloth and carrying a small axe over his shoulder. When the manager returned with a key I asked him about the photograph and he confirmed what I had suspected, that it was a portrait of one of the headmen of a local tribe of Veddas.

The Veddas are the island's indigenous people and are thought to be the descendants of an early people who walked into Sri Lanka several millennia ago from India, at a time when the two countries were still connected by a narrow strip of land. These aboriginal people were the first humans to inhabit the island and lived in tribes as hunter-gatherers. Thousands of years later, according to the ancient Sri Lankan chronicle 'The Mahavamsa', the ancient Lala kingdom in north-west India was ruled by the son of a legendary union between a young princess and a lion. His unfortunate wife gave birth to thirty-two sons, the eldest of which was a wild and unruly boy named Vijaya. Vijaya and his band of 700 followers wreaked such violent havoc in the kingdom that the king was forced to banish his son and shaved the heads of his followers as a mark of shame. The disowned Vijaya and his bald disciples set sail from West Bengal and eventually washed up on the shores of north-west Sri Lanka, on the same day that the Buddha reached enlightenment under his bodhi tree at Bodh Gaya. After defeating Kuveni, the demon queen who ruled the island, Vijaya – who is now regarded as the first king of Sri Lanka

– and his followers went on to colonise the island and are regarded as the founders of the Sinhalese race. Although the legend is not, of course, entirely true, there is evidence of the arrival of a wave of Aryan-speaking immigrants in Sri Lanka at a similar time, from whom the Sinhalese are descended. As they colonised the island, they drove the indigenous Veddas deep into the forests. Over the centuries that followed, the two communities began to mix and many of the Veddas abandoned their tribal lifestyle, started to live in villages and intermarried with the Sinhalese. There were, however, always a number of 'pure' Veddas who continued to live their hunter-gatherer existence, resisting contact with the outside community, and a number still survive to this day. Most live in a small region of the island that stretches from the eastern slopes of the hill country to the shores of the east coast, in the area around Mahiyangana.

It was Tennent's desire to observe this 'harmless and uncivilised tribe, who live in caves or inhabit rude dwellings constructed of bark and grass', that drove him to lead his party of 150 men on such a difficult trek through the forests of the island's interior. The Veddas have held a fascination with travellers, both before and since Tennent, and over the years members of the Vedda settlements have been paraded in front of the curious eyes of foreign visitors, to be observed, questioned, drawn, recorded and used in anthropological experiments. The British explorer Robert Knox produced a sketch of *A Vaddah or Wild Man* in the seventeenth century, showing a muscular man with long hair tied in a knot on the top of his head, wearing a wide loincloth, and holding a bow and arrow. Tucked into the loincloth was a small axe and he held in his mouth a long, elegant pipe, from which clouds of smoke billowed. In *An Historical Relation of the Island of Ceylon in the East Indies*, the volume he produced when he finally returned to London, he wrote about this area.

> In this Land are many of these wild men: they call them Vaddahs, dwelling near no other Inhabitants... They kill Deer and dry the flesh over the fire, and the people of the countrey come and buy it of them. They never till the ground for corn, their food being only flesh. They are very expert with their bows. They have a little ax, which they stick by their sides to cut honey out of hollow trees. Some few, which are near inhabitants have commerce with other people. They have no towns nor houses, only live by the waters under a tree, with some boughs cut and laid round about them, to give notice when any wild beasts come near, which they may hear by their rustling and trampling upon them.

When Tennent arrived in the region, the colonial government and a group of Wesleyan Methodist missionaries were experimenting with an early kind of development work, to try to introduce 'civilisation' amongst the Veddas. Cottages were built on their old hunting ground, and they were shown how to cultivate rice, dig wells and plant coconut trees. A small school was also built to teach the Veddas how to speak the Sinhalese language and the Wesleyan missionaries made various attempts to convert the tribesmen to Christianity. Whether the Veddas had expressed any interest in adopting the more developed, Sinhalese way of life was not mentioned and, unsurprisingly, a number refused to move into their new cottages and continued their wandering, hunter-gatherer way of life. Tennent did record with pride, however, that the missionaries had been surprisingly successful when it came to religious conversion, and in one of the new settlements the whole community had professed themselves Christians and abandoned their addiction to devil dances.

The morning after Tennent arrived in Mahiyangana, a group of sixty Veddas were rounded up for his inspection. In his record of the episode he made little attempt to hide the disgust with which he regarded the poor tribesmen, who had been dragged out of the forest to be paraded in front of him.

> … they were miserable objects, active but timid, and athletic though deformed, with large heads and misshapen limbs. Their long black hair and beards fell down to their middle in uncombed lumps, they stood with their faces towards the ground and their restless eyes twinkled upwards with an expression of uneasiness and apprehension… They danced for us, after the exhibition of their archery, shuffling with their feet to a low and plaintive chaunt, shaking their long hair, till it concealed the upper part of their body; and as they excited themselves with their exercise they uttered shrill cries, jumping in the air and clung round each other's necks. We were told that the dance generally ended in a kind of frenzy, after which they sunk exhausted to the ground; but the whole scene was repulsive and humiliating that we could not permit the arrival of this denouement; and dispersed the party with a present of some silver.

As I stood looking at the photograph of the Vedda in the reception area, the manager asked me if I would like to visit a Vedda settlement in the nearby village of Dambana. For $40 I could join a group of 'ethno-tourists' to gawp at some of the last remaining Veddas in their 'natural environment', as they danced and spoke in their native tongue. There would also apparently be the opportunity to buy 'genuine' Vedda handicrafts. I had misguidedly done something similar several years earlier in Tanzania, when I took a group of white middle-class teenagers from the boys' boarding school in which I taught in England to see a Maasai village in the Serengeti, supposedly to broaden their horizons. The terrified students were immediately surrounded by a group of spear-toting Maasai men, who danced, leapt in the air and then, in the darkness of their huts, rinsed the boys of their pocket money in return for flimsy spears and beaded necklaces. The whole experience was somewhat humiliating for both parties and particularly disappointing for the boys when, as we drove away, the Maasai retrieved their hidden mobile phones from under their red robes and started to check their text messages.

One hundred years earlier, in 1911, two anthropologists named Charles and Brenda Seligmann spent many months with the Veddas of Ceylon and produced a lengthy account of their social organisation, religion, language and music. The couple recorded with great frustration their difficulty in finding 'genuine Veddas' and claimed that the tribes had been regarded as a curiosity by Europeans for so long that, even then, many of the Veddas exhibited to travellers returned to their villages to speak Sinhala and wear conventional clothes as soon as the white men had departed. It seemed unlikely that a century later the $40 Veddas of Dambana would be any more genuine and, if they were, it was probably best to leave them to it.

My hotel room was sparse and dark, and reeked of disinfectant, ineffectively masked by a synthetic, rose-scented air freshener. Yellow water dripped through a rusted-up shower head, whilst fat black mosquitoes droned around the bathroom. I was too tired to eat after the long journey from Kandy and, after trying to kill the swarm of mosquitoes around the bed, I crawled under the mosquito net and fell straight to sleep.

I woke up early the next morning feeling painfully hungry and ordered a Sri Lankan breakfast in the open-fronted dining room of the hotel, which looked out onto a leafy garden. The waiter brought me a large plate of string hoppers – flat, circular knots of thin white noodles, which are eaten for breakfast with fish and lentil curry. He set down the plate in front of me and asked again if I was going to visit the Veddas. Whilst I was eating my hoppers and curry, I heard strange, shuffling footsteps on the tiled floor behind me and turned round to see a large, spotted deer strolling through the dining room. I wondered if I was hallucinating. The animal moved between the tables, sniffing the chairs and the crockery, stopped at the table next to mine and stared at me. There was no one else in the dining room to confirm that the deer was not some strange figment of my imagination, so we just looked at each other in silence for several minutes. When the deer had tired of the dining room, it turned round and sauntered into the garden, making its way over to the small swimming pool, from which it began to drink. 'His name is Kiri,' said the waiter who had just emerged from the kitchen and was eyeing the deer fondly. 'He is boy deer; pet of the manager.'

I spent the afternoon walking along the banks of the Sorabora tank, an enormous reservoir that was built over a millennium ago by the island's ancient engineers to irrigate the fields of the lowlands. Like the mystery that surrounds the construction of the Egyptian pyramids, nobody knows how the islanders were able to dam the river that flowed between two mountains to the north to form the large body of water they called 'Sea of Bintenna', or how they were able to cut the sluices and channels out of the rock that directed the water to the fields below. It was a Saturday afternoon and the local families had come to have picnics on the banks of the tank, looking out over its still, grey surface surrounded by golden trees. Young couples walked along the grassy banks arm in arm. Old men in sarongs sold ice-cream from cool boxes strapped to the back of their bicycles and beeped old, rubber bicycle horns to remind the picnicking families that they were there.

Complex irrigation systems like the Sorabora tank were built all over the dry zone of the island and are regarded by many historians as some of the most impressive engineering feats of the world's ancient civilisations. But as invaders came and went, the organisation of their upkeep was neglected by each generation and they slowly fell into ruin. When Tennent visited the tank, the retaining walls had worn away, the basin had been taken over by crocodiles and the embankments subsumed by the jungle. He was, however, so moved by the beauty of the ruined tank and the idea of its former grandeur, that as soon as he returned to Colombo he recommended that the British government restore it, to give the provinces a way of improving their agriculture. The island, he said, had been exploited by colonisers for their own gains for long enough and it was time someone did something to help the Ceylonese people. In fact, it was Britain's moral obligation. Although Tennent's suggestion was adopted, rebellions broke out in the region soon after, causing the restoration plans to be shelved, and Tennent left the island before they were resumed. A paper published in the scientific journal *Nature* in 1877, however, stated that a work apparently pregnant with the largest and most beneficent results to the native population of Ceylon had been launched by the colonial government to restore the ancient irrigation systems, and quoted a passage from Tennent's book as the source of the project's inspiration.

The next morning, I continued my journey towards the town of Batticaloa on the island's eastern coast. I had not slept well and had woken up tangled in the mosquito net and covered with the puffy, red blotches of mosquito bites. It was mid morning by the time I arrived at the bus station and in my sleep-deprived, itchy state I was not looking forward to the bus journey. On my map, Mahiyangana and Batticaloa were connected by a thick red line which indicated a major road, yet I was repeatedly told by the bus drivers hanging around outside their battered vehicles that there was no direct bus. Instead, I would have to take a detour south, to a large town called Ampara, where I could then catch another bus that was heading up the coast to Batticaloa.

The Ampara bus was only half full, but already all of the window seats, which would provide the breeze needed to make the journey bearable, had been taken. I sat at the back near the open door and hoped that the hot, stale air would cool when the bus started to move. Most of the people around looked hungry and slightly malnourished. Their limbs were spindly, their skin was spattered with pockmarks, and the feet in their rubber sandals were splay-toed and cracked. The bus was showing no sign of filling up and I couldn't see anyone who looked like the driver or his mate. A group of teenage boys climbed onto the bus, traipsed down the aisle and left again. Four teenage girls sat down, whispered conspiratorially for several minutes and disappeared. After I had been sitting on the bus for an hour, sliding around in a pool of perspiration, the driver finally jumped on and began to rev the engine. As he slowly started to edge out from under the corrugated-iron awning of the bus shelter, the roof of the bus somehow managed to collide with an overhanging metal sign. The driver and his mate jumped off the bus in a panic and stared gesturing wildly at the dented sign, whilst they tried to decide what to do. Several of the male passengers on the bus also got off to give their thoughts on the matter. After ten minutes of inching the bus backwards and forwards, whilst people shouted conflicting instructions and banged on the front and back windscreens, the bus finally left the station and headed out of the town.

As the road ran east towards the coast, the last traces of the wet-zone jungle disappeared. Under their splayed, brittle branches, desiccated thorn bushes crawled over the ground. The road crossed great expanses of open plain, dotted with cattle, beneath miles of cloudless sky. The settlements were few and sparse, formed by lines of lonely, concrete boxes that had a single dark hole for a door and palm-thatched roofs. There was no running water in these remote villages and groups of women stood by the roadside, bending over the walls of the wells to draw buckets of water. Elderly men with sinewy backs burnt black by the sun herded long-eared goats down the middle of the road, whilst their grandchildren scampered alongside the herd, hurrying the goats along with wooden sticks. As we passed through the small town of Maha Oya, it was clear that we had crossed over into the land of the Tamils. The curvaceous Sinhala characters had disappeared and the signs that hung above the shops were written in the sharper, more angular Tamil script. The serene white figure of the Buddha had also disappeared from the landscape and small, black statues of Ganesh sat by the side of the road, swaddled in knotted lengths of red and gold silk.

The bus had only been travelling for an hour when it pulled over and the driver disappeared into a gloomy tea shack. The other passengers took this as a cue to start pulling their bags from the overhead racks and climbing down onto the road. I had estimated from my map that the journey to Ampara would take at least four hours and after the hour of hanging around at the bus station my irritation was starting to grow. A short gentleman, with very long thumbnails that curved inward towards the palm of his hand, explained that the driver needed a teabreak and suggested I get off the bus and have one too. 'But we have only been going for an hour!' I wanted to scream, 'how can he need a break already?' As I stood by the bus and watched the passengers diffuse into the roadside food stalls and dig into plates of rice and curry, I could see that we were not going to be leaving any time soon. Anyone who has lived in a developing country knows that to remain sane, you need to abandon your western susceptibility to the pressure of time and on most days you manage to do it. But there are some days when, in spite of your best efforts, you find yourself overwhelmed by the feelings of frustration you have been repressing for months – and today was turning into one of those days. The bus journey was clearly going to take forever and I didn't even want to go to Ampara. So, to the confusion of the watching passengers, I retrieved my bag from the bus and agreed to pay one of the town's tuk-tuk drivers as much as it would cost for him to take me directly along the road to Batticaloa.

Batticaloa is a floating town, surrounded by glassy lagoons and flat sandy plains. It is arid and exposed, bleached by the sun and blown by the Eurus that sweeps inland from the Bay of Bengal. My guesthouse was a few simple rooms hidden in the palm trees on the sandy banks of a large lagoon. Although it hadn't seen tourists for many years, the rooms were permanently occupied by groups of NGO workers involved in the rehabilitation of the east after the war. Four gleaming four-wheel drives displaying the logos of US Aid, CARE, Save the Children and GTZ stood outside in the sunlight, whilst groups of European and American aid workers tapped on laptops in the shade of the dark cafe. The Sri Lankan owner of the guesthouse was sitting at a small table at the back, showing a menu to a pale American woman with frizzy, ginger hair.

'Sorry, madam, we are not cooking the green leaf curry today. Only vegetable curry,' he was saying apologetically.

'But the menu says you have green leaf curry and that's what I ordered this morning.'

'Yes, madam, but the cook didn't come to work today, so nobody has had time to go to the market to buy the green leaves. We are sorry, madam.'

The woman gave a short grunt of irritation and walked back to her laptop, cursing under her breath. I ordered a lime juice with soda water and sat down on the table next to hers. The groups of NGO workers all looked to be in their thirties and each group seemed determined to work alone and ignore the members of the other NGOs. Some were frowning into the screens of their MacBooks, whilst others were talking earnestly or annotating sheaves of paper with red pens. When the ginger-haired woman gave a yawn and snapped down the screen of her laptop, I asked her what she was doing in Batticaloa. She had spent the day with some nearby villagers who were having trouble with the local elephants, which were trampling their farmland during the night. She had been teaching the villagers how to write letters to the local government representatives to request motion-sensitive lights to frighten the elephants away.

There were lots of NGO workers in the area, she said, focusing on different projects, including some who were working with the young women who had been forcibly recruited into the Tamil Tigers as children. The Tigers had recruited anybody and everybody from the Tamil areas they controlled, irrespective of gender, caste or age. Some had joined voluntarily but many were forced. Tamil women made up almost a third of the fighters, cutting their hair short, and wearing vials of cyanide around their necks. Whilst many people associate child soldiers with the guerrillas of Central Africa, thousands of children were also absorbed into the ranks of the Tigers during the twenty-six years of war. Some were the orphans of martyred parents who had been raised and indoctrinated in orphanages run by the Tigers, some were teenagers lured by the glamour of war and the promise of a better future, but many were simply abducted on the way to school or dragged from their parents' arms.

When there was a leadership conflict towards the end of the war between the northern and eastern LTTE commanders, the eastern Tamil Tigers commander disbanded his forces and went into hiding. Many of the young girls from the east who had been separated from their families simply drifted into the war-torn towns on the coast where they had to somehow try to survive. Now that the war has ended, many of those children are psychologically scarred young women. They were robbed of their childhood, forced into conflict and have no sense of identity in the absence of the war. Various charities are now working with these women, trying to get them back into education so they can gain some skills and try to forge a new identity.

I knew a lot of NGO workers in Colombo, many of whom had worked in the country for several years. Whenever I talked to them about how their projects were going, many, though not all, had admitted to a certain amount of disillusion with development work. I asked her how she felt about things.

'I've been working in the east for a while now,' she replied, 'and there is still so much resentment of the Sinhalese in some communities that I wouldn't be surprised if the area descends back into conflict in the future. Some days I work with the local people and I'm hopeful, other days I overhear the things the Tamils say about the Sinhalese and I'm not. I don't really know if my work will make any difference, but at least I feel like I'm trying.'

As she was talking, a tall, good-looking man who sounded as if he might be Dutch had walked over to the hotel manager to query something on his bill. 'The bill's fine,' he was saying to the manager with embarrassment, 'but could you give us a separate one without any of the alcohol on it?'

'Ah, of course, sir,' said the manager with a knowing smile, 'NGO people often want us to do this. We know your charities are not happy about paying for all the bottles of Lion Lager.'

When the sun had gone down I sat by the edge of the lagoon in the warm, muggy darkness. The NGO workers had packed away their laptops and were lying in hammocks by the water's edge, drinking and talking together softly. A fisherman had moored his narrow canoe to a small, wooden raft that floated a few metres from the bank and was sifting through his fishing nets by the flame of a candle-lit lantern. Tennent had paid a fisherman to row him into the middle of the lagoon when he visited Batticaloa in 1848, so that he could investigate a strange phenomenon in the town known as the 'singing fish'. According to the local fishermen there was a species of fish living in the lagoon which, at certain times of the year, on nights when the moon was full, would emit a sweet singing sound that resembled the notes of an Aeolian harp. When Tennent crossed the lagoon in the moonlight, he claimed he distinctly heard sounds that came up from the water like the gentle thrill of a musical chord, or the faint vibrations of a wine glass when its rim is rubbed with a wet finger. I walked away from the voices of the NGO workers, through the palm trees that fringed the lagoon, and listened. I could hear the gentle sploshing of a few fishermen paddling their canoes through the dark waters, but other than that and the sound of the traffic crossing the new bridge I could hear nothing else. I asked the owner of the hotel about it the next morning as I was leaving but he laughed and shook his head; the fish that had sung a century ago were now long gone. When Tennent returned from Batticaloa, he wrote to Dr Robert E. Grant, a member of the Wernerian Natural History Society of Edinburgh, to see if he might have any idea about the source of the music attributed by the people of Batticaloa to the singing fish. His only suggestion was that it was caused by *Tritonia arborescens*, a small marine creature he and his colleagues were studying.

> My two living trintonia, contained in a large clear colourless glass cylinder, filled with pure sea water, and placed on the central table of the Wernerian Natural History Society in Edinburgh, around which many members were sitting, continued to clink audibly within the distance of twelve feet during the whole meeting. These small creatures were individually not half the size of the last joint of my little finger. What effect the mellow sounds of millions of these, covering the shallow bottom of a tranquil estuary, in the silence of the night, might produce, I can scarcely conjecture.

Although news of the supposedly musical creatures caused excitement back in Britain, the source of the music remained a mystery.

I went to Batticaloa's bus stand early the next morning to try to find a bus that was heading directly north, up the coastal road to the largest town on the east coast, Trincomalee. As Batticaloa and Trincomalee were the two major towns in the east and were connected by a single road, I had assumed that there would be frequent buses running between them. The station was almost empty when I arrived at 7.30 a.m. and other than a couple of tall, dark-skinned women wearing gold nose studs, there was nobody around. Several concrete benches looked out over the waters of the lagoon. A couple of men carrying canvas bags of wood-working tools sat down on the twisted roots of a tree in the shade of its leaves, and asked me where I wanted to go. The next bus to Trincomalee would not be leaving for two hours, they said, as they closed their eyes and slumped against the tree trunk. I had not eaten much for breakfast and the journey up the coast would probably take several hours, so I walked into the town in search of food.

The main street of Batticaloa was sleepy and sand-strewn. The saris of the Tamil women were made of richly coloured, gold-embroidered silk and were the only spots of colour on the otherwise pale, sun-bleached streets. They were darker and more statuesque than the Sinhalese women in the south, and wore pieces of thread tied tightly around the flesh of their upper arms and gold jewellery studded with coloured stones.

The shops and stalls by the side of the road were opening for the day and many of the women were already sweeping the pavement in their never-ending battle against the dust. I walked past the pyramidal kovil of the Hindu temple as the men and women of the town were leaving the morning puja with ceremonial ash smeared across their foreheads.

As I was walking back along the road to the bus station I heard a series of loud bangs behind me and turned around to see the road filled with clouds of smoke. The smoke was coming from small firecrackers, which were being thrown into the road by a group of men, who emerged from the smoke, throwing more down road the ahead of them. As it began to clear, a pair of men walked out of the haze towards me, rolling a large length of sari material along the tarmac to form a sort of carpet. Behind them was a group of pall-bearers carrying a coffin on their shoulders, staggering from side to side to make sure their feet followed the silk and didn't touch the bare tarmac. A huge procession followed, filling the road. Crowds of schoolchildren were wheeling their bicycles behind tuk-tuks that played loud music from speakers strapped to their roofs. Farther behind, families held hands together and walked along in silence. I didn't follow for long, but as the bus headed up the coastal road towards Trincomalee we passed the coffin where it had come to rest, shrouded in silk and enveloped by flames, blazing on the sand by the sea.

Chapter Seven

TRINCOMALEE TO MANKULAM

The road to Trincomalee ran along the coastline, across a dry shadeless plain that stretched towards the horizon under the hard blue sky. For miles there were no other vehicles except for the occasional pick-up truck crammed with slender Tamils, who were holding umbrellas and scarves over their faces to protect themselves from the sun. A few villagers huddled by the roadside in the precious shade of the scattered palmyra palms, clutching faded plastic carrier bags and waiting for a bus or truck to carry them to the next town. As the road drifted inland, wide paddy fields began to appear, worked by men ankle-deep in the water, who were turning over the dripping, muddy land with heavy shovels. Young children swam in a narrow canal that ran along the edge of the road, thrashing and ducking each other under its surface whilst their mothers swirled frothing clothes in the murky brown water.

As we neared Trincomalee, evidence of the war littered the roadside. The roofs of the simple concrete houses were patched up with sheets of white plastic bearing the blue olive branches and cupped hands of the logo of the UN's refugee agency. A pair of wrought-iron gates embellished with crosses that had once opened onto a churchyard hung loosely from their hinges, in front of a bare patch of land scattered with rubble. Weary cattle with dark silky hides tugged at the few sprigs of vegetation around the abandoned shell of a village library, whose pink walls had been worn smooth by the dry, dusty wind. Many of the Tamils who lived in this section of the east coast had been forced to leave their land during the fighting and some families were still living in the corrugated-iron shacks of an internally displaced persons (IDP) camp by the side of the road. Groups of women and children were slumped in the doorways of the shacks, looking out through tired, empty eyes, as packs of stray dogs ran between the huts, sniffing at the piles of rubbish.

The road ran along the sweeping coastline of China Bay, a flawless blue pocket of the Indian Ocean surrounded by rolling green hills. Tennent saw it and thought it looked like Lake Windermere. Lines of fishermen were standing on the beach, pulling on long ropes attached to heavy nets submerged beneath the surface of the water. With their heels dug into the sand and their bodies flung backward as they hung off the ropes, it looked as if they were engaged in a tug of war with the sea. The slippery, silvery bodies of the fish that had already been emptied from the nets were drying in the sun on large mats by the side of the road, and men with large knives were hacking the fish into fleshy pink steaks.

Trincomalee is now trying to re-establish itself as a tourist destination and investors are rushing to buy up land by the sea to build boutique hotels for Europeans. As the bus drove across a brand-new bridge, the passengers craned their necks out of the windows at the sound of the little seaplane chugging overhead that was carrying the first trickle of tourists back to Colombo. It was almost as if the war hadn't happened here and the famished coastal plain felt a long way away.

When the British had captured Trincomalee in 1795 they had great plans to turn its capacious port, the only harbour of refuge to the east of Cape Comorin, into a grand emporium of oriental trade and the arsenal of the East. The night before Tennent reached Trincomalee, his party had set up camp under the tamarind trees that lined the Topoor tank and gazed at the Southern Cross constellation hanging above them in the dark, cloudless sky. When he reached the town the next day it was something of a let down. With the attention of successive governors being occupied by the colony's precious cinnamon plantations on the other side of the island, the town had fallen into neglect.

> ... an extreme feeling of disappointment is excited now by looking upon its incomplete fortifications, its neglected works, and its reduced military establishment – utterly unequal to any emergency... With the exception of the official buildings, the town is poorly constructed and the bazaars the least inviting in Ceylon. There are a couple of Hindu temples, with the usual paraphernalia of idols and cars, for religious festivals and processions; but these are in such barbarous taste as to stifle and repel curiosity.

I liked Trincomalee, however. The streets were a narrow, labyrinthine bazaar of sequined fabrics and gold jewellery, and I lost my bearings almost immediately. The town was surrounded by deep-green, wooded hills that rose above the narrow streets lined with one-storey, higgledy-piggledy houses, each of a unique design, painted in different bright shades. It was one of the few towns on the island where nobody stared at my fair hair and pale skin, and I got the impression it was not out of any particular politeness, but because most of the inhabitants had something better to do. There were a large number of slender police women strolling in unmenacing groups, dressed in khaki-coloured skirts and shirts, but very few police men. A man who had wrapped his naked body in polythene bags stood mumbling to himself by a post box, before he disappeared behind an ox-drawn cart piled with boxes of vegetables.

By far the strangest thing about Trincomalee, however, was the spotted deer with long antlers, teetering along the pavements on their dainty hooves, with the precarious motion of a woman balancing on stiletto heels. Like the stray dogs on the rest of the island, they appeared everywhere, gently nuzzling the tarmac or sitting tidily in the doorways of the shops with their legs folded up under their bodies. Unlike their canine counterparts, they were not regarded as pests and the Department of Wildlife Conservation had erected signs around the town encouraging the residents to take care of their elegant, hoofed pets by resisting the temptation to feed them polythene.

Getting lost in a maze of streets was evidently a problem for everyone, and it seemed that a number of lives had been lost during the tsunami because some disoriented inhabitants of the town had made the catastrophic mistake of running frantically towards the beach and the advancing wave, instead of away from it. To try to avoid this problem in any future tsunamis, small blue signs have been nailed to the walls of the buildings that show the 'Tsunami Evacuation Route' in big white letters, with a picture of a wave and arrows pointing in the direction that leads away from the sea. As I wanted to get out of the bazaars and down to the seafront, I decided to walk in the 'wrong' direction every time I saw one of the signs and eventually ended up at a small beach where local families were enjoying the late-afternoon breeze. I sat down on the sand and watched the mothers and young women standing waist-deep in the sea in their sequined saris and *salwar kameez*. I bought a 'cream soda' in a heavy glass bottle – which looked like washing up liquid and tasted like vanilla essence – from an elderly gentleman who was pushing a refrigerated wheelbarrow along the sand.

I had intended to head straight to a small guesthouse on the beach that had been recommended to me by an NGO worker in Colombo, but the driver of the tuk-tuk I hailed from the sand had his own ideas. How exactly the miscommunication arose, or whether it was a wilful misunderstanding, I was not sure, but the little three-wheeler drove me instead along the seafront road to the outskirts of the town and up the hillside to Trincomalee's only tourist attraction, Swami Rock. The rock, which towers 130 m above the Bay of Bengal, was once home to the Koneswaram Temple, a prominent Hindu shrine that attracted pilgrims from all over the Tamil regions of the island and across the sea from India. It was briefly known to the Portuguese as the 'Temple of a Thousand Columns' before they demolished it in 1622 and used the debris to build a set of fortifications around the base of the hill, which became known as Fort Frederick. The fortifications were captured a few years later by the Dutch, who added their usual long barn-like buildings with small shuttered windows and wooden verandas. The fort is now used as a military base by the Sri Lankan army and groups of soldiers in tracksuits were jogging between the buildings whilst officers in uniform sat on the verandas making calls on their mobile phones.

The temple that now stands on the spot where the original Koneswaram temple was destroyed had been renovated again recently and gaudy, carbon-fibre statues of the Hindu gods, painted with lurid gold gloss paint, lurked in the crevices of the Swami Rock that plunged down into the sea. A few Hindu women in saris and men in sarongs were wandering in-between the statues in bare feet, whilst groups of irreverent teenage boys posed in front of some murals of phallic images and took photographs of each other. A few of the resident swamis were strolling in and out of the temple, their fat, bare bellies wobbling over the edges of their sarongs and their foreheads smeared with streaks of ceremonial grey ash. A couple of the teenage boys spied me standing at one of the rock's vantage points, as I was looking over the edge at the white tips of the waves that were swirling below, and came over to recite to me a garbled version of the sad legend that gives the rock its other name of 'Lover's Leap'.

The story goes that the daughter of a Dutch general was engaged to a young officer who was spending his period of foreign service on the island. The engagement did not last and, after the officer had broken it off, he left the island to return home. As the ship that was carrying him back to Europe sailed under the precipice, his abandoned fiancée threw herself from the sacred rock into the sea below.

The tuk-tuk driver who had taken it upon himself to bring me up to the Swami Rock was beginning to look restless so, after I had paid him a few hundred rupees and assured him I could find my own way back to the town, I sat on the sprawling roots of one of the trees in the temple courtyards and started to read through Tennent's description of the rock. The evening puja was beginning and a wailing, reedy melody played over rhythmical drumming came from a group of fat musicians sitting on cushions on the floor of the temple, slumped heavily over their instruments. A couple of Australian tourists, on hearing the music, dashed into the temple and began to distract the musicians by sticking large SLR lenses several inches from their faces, and taking rapid shots with a blinding flash in quick succession.

When Tennent visited the rock he recorded that 'a procession, attended by crowds of devotees, who bring offerings of fruit and flowers, repairs, at sunset, to the spot where the rock projects more than 100 m above the ocean; a series of ceremonies is performed, including the mysterious breaking of a coconut against the cliff; and the officiating Brahman concludes his invocation by elevating a brazen censer above his head, filled with inflammable materials, the light of which, as they burn, is reflected far over the sea.'

When I arrived at the guesthouse later that afternoon, I was greeted at the gates by Sebastian, a middle-aged Swiss man, with dark rings under his eyes and a cigarette dangling carelessly from his fingers. He showed me to a simple, tiled room, full of large, lethargic mosquitoes, and suggested that I join him and his deeply tanned wife Maria for 'the only cappuccino you'll find outside Colombo' in his cafe under the palm trees. Whilst Sebastian and Maria chain-smoked over their cappuccinos and gave friendly orders to a band of local women who were sweeping the fallen leaves in the garden, I asked them how they had come to live in the middle of Sri Lanka's warzone. Sebastian raised his eyebrows and gave a mirthless laugh. He glanced up at me over his coffee cup, through the dark circles around his eyes, and looked as if he was still suffering from exhaustion from his past.

'We didn't really have a lot of choice,' Sebastian explained as he ground a cigarette into the bottom of an ashtray. 'We used to own a hotel on the beach over on the west coast, but we lost all of the front rooms of the building during the tsunami. We stayed around for a while and thought about trying to rebuild the hotel but we were so sickened by what was happening with foreign aid in the area that we just wanted to get as far away as possible.'

Sebastian put another cigarette between his lips and crouched under the table to try to light it out of the breeze. 'We just drifted across the island and spent two months living on the beach to begin with. When we found this place we thought we had really landed on our feet and decided that it would be a great place to start again.'

Only two weeks later, however, a bomb exploded in the market in Trincomalee and the whole area descended into war. He flicked ash onto the ground and gave a short, irritable sigh.

'It wasn't safe to leave the hotel for months, as the Tamil Tigers began to encroach on the region. This area was shelled, too, and on some nights we had to use the rooms to shelter people from the shells that were falling from the sky.'

Had I been in Sebastian's situation, my inclination would have been to jump onto the next plane out of the country. I asked Sebastian whether he had been tempted to leave, but he shook his head.

'We had lost all our money in the tsunami and it just wasn't an option. You need a lot of money to move back to Europe and we had practically none.' He gave a short laugh. 'But, at the same time, business here was actually the best it had ever been. OK, there were obviously no tourists, but the area was full of NGO workers who needed somewhere to let their hair down.' He pointed to the hotel's small bar that was being tickled with a feather duster by one of the women who worked in the kitchen. 'Every single night, for the last three years of the war, we were full of young Europeans and Americans who came here to dance and drink late into the night to try to forget the stuff they had seen during the day. Even now, as much of our business is from aid workers as it is from tourists.'

Sebastian looked over at Maria who had wrapped herself in a towel and announced she was heading down to the beach for a late-afternoon swim. 'I know this country has got some real problems – we've lived here for long enough to see them all. But I don't think we'll ever go back to Europe, it's just not where we belong anymore.'

I decided to take a break from travelling and spent a few days lying on the village's empty beach. I chatted to a couple of local men who had a little hut on the sand that sold small bottles of Coca-Cola, and they told me they were expecting the eastern beaches to be inundated with tourists in the next couple of years. Wealthy Europeans and men from Colombo had bought strips of the coastline, and would build luxury hotels to draw the tourists away from the crowded resorts on the west coast. A group of sunburnt Russians were the only other people on the sand, but they gave the sea a wide berth and spent most of their time sprawled under the palm-frond umbrellas trying to shield the screens of their iPads from the sun. I ate every evening in Sebastian's little cafe. Like me, many of the NGO workers ate alone at their tables, reading through reports and staring at their laptops. Sebastian served up three-course meals whilst Maria tried to ease the loneliness she seemed to sense in the NGO workers by talking and flirting with them. She was warm and friendly with the local workers from the village who helped to run the cafe and the hotel, joking with them in Tamil and embracing their children.

Tennent also paused from his journey for several days in Trincomalee, recruiting new 'foot runners' and 'coolies' from the town to continue with his expedition party. The next leg of the journey followed the coastline directly north to Mullaitivu, the last large town on the east coast that sits on the banks of the Nanthi Kadal Lagoon. This region more recently lay deep in the land of the Tamil Tigers and was the site of the final showdown between the Tigers and the Sri Lankan army in the spring of 2009. This north-eastern corner of the island had been worrying me; the region was still rumoured to be a no-go area, littered with landmines and under heavy military surveillance. Back in Colombo nobody had known if the road to Mullaitivu still existed, let alone whether foreigners were being allowed into the area.

Whilst I was having my breakfast the next morning, I asked Sebastian whether he had any idea what was going on 100 km up the coast from his guesthouse. He gave a shrug and called over to Aravindan, his young and adoring assistant, who lived in the bungalow next to Sebastian's with his wife and family.

'I think the road is open,' said Aravindan, with a frown, 'but I don't think it would be safe for you to go there.'

'Why not?' I asked, 'has the area not been cleared of landmines yet?'

He shook his head slowly and rubbed his fingers across his brow. 'They say they have cleared the landmines now, but that is not what I am worried about. I don't think you would be safe alone. Mullaitivu is being run by the Sri Lankan army now – they have complete control and seem to be able to do whatever they like.' He began to look embarrassed and turned to Sebastian, speaking rapidly in Tamil and gesturing over to me.

Sebastian kept nodding his head in agreement as Aravindan spoke and when he had finished he turned to me. 'The bottom line is, you're a female, you're alone and you're very small. There have been some pretty nasty stories about what bored young soldiers have done to women up there. If you ask me, you would just be looking for trouble.'

When Sebastian and Aravindan had gone, I unfolded my map of the island and looked at the pale pink 'minor road' that connected Trincomalee with Mullaitivu. The north-east stretch of coast looked bare and empty; a large expanse of flat plain flooded with lagoons and dotted sparsely with settlements. There were no major roads anywhere near the coastline and if there was any trouble along the way there was no escape route inland. I had heard rumours in Colombo about the ongoing abuse of Tamils by the Sri Lankan army in the area and I had seen the mutilated stumps of people in the town who had come into contact with landmines. Aside from my personal safety, I was also beginning to wonder whether it was just insensitive and naive to go snooping around in a warzone, which had been a living hell – that I was incapable of grasping – for many people. I went to bed that night, still unsure of what to do and hoped that some sleep might make the matter clearer.

The next morning I had managed to reach a compromise with myself. I had come so far that I was not prepared to turn back, but I would not risk the journey north to Mullaitivu alone. Instead I asked Sebastian if he could find me a driver that he trusted.

Early the next morning Sebastian knocked on my door and introduced me to Balasankar, a good-looking man in his early twenties with a square, stubble-dusted jawline and a shy smile that was directed towards my feet rather than my face. He spoke very little English and I spoke virtually no Tamil, so it was going to be a quiet journey. As I put my rucksack into the back of Balasankar's small van, Sebastian watched us from the shade of the veranda, chewing the inside of his cheeks.

'What are you going to say if you are questioned by the army?' he asked as he came over. 'You may need to have some kind of story ready.' He looked at the notebook and pen I was holding so that I could make notes on the journey. 'And I would hide those too. Whatever you say, make sure they don't think you are a journalist,' he said with a wry smile. 'We all know what happens to them.'

The freedom of the journalists of the Sri Lankan media had been compromised for so many years that it was common knowledge, and almost accepted, that anyone who attempted to publish anything that criticised the government was taking a grave risk. It had all started several decades earlier when the then president, Sirimavo Bandaranaike, had used the government's emergency powers following an insurgency to control one of the country's largest newspaper groups, and forced several others to stop publishing. Since Mahinda Rajapaksa had come to power, however, things had become far worse. Any journalists who attempted to criticise either the Rajapaksa regime or the war against the LTTE now knew that they were risking their lives. Death threats would be issued by groups of masked men who appeared at the doors of their family homes. Some journalists were bundled into white vans in broad daylight on suburban streets and taken away to be tortured or killed, whilst a number were simply shot dead or assaulted on the streets. The publishing houses themselves were also targeted: printing presses were smashed up and paper supplies were cut off. Even international publications were not spared and crate-loads of publications like *The Economist*, containing anti-government articles, were withheld from circulation at customs. The government named and shamed dissenting journalists on various websites, labelling them as LTTE sympathisers, and government hitlists began to circulate in the capital. As journalists became increasingly nervous, those who wanted to continue to work on the island toned their articles down and self-censored, whilst the rest fled abroad. It was easy to see why the British journalist I had spoken to in Colombo had chosen to hide her camera and notebooks.

The coastal road was a deserted strip of smooth tarmac that cut across the sparse grassland and wound around the mirror-like lagoons of the coastal plain. Whereas the coconut palm trees in the land of the Sinhalese have slender trunks that bend gracefully towards the land and tapering, feathery leaves, the palmyra palms that are scattered across the arid land of the north and the east have thick vertical trunks, black fruit and rigid, serrated, angry-looking fanned leaves. The small, concrete houses and thatched shacks by the side of the road were surrounded by fences made from the desiccated fans of palmyra leaves, tessellated together and stitched with wire thread. Women walked barefoot along the road carrying bulbous water pots under their arms towards the village well, where groups of women crouched on their haunches, with their cotton saris pulled low over their faces against the sunlight and dust. A crowd of young Muslim boys played football together on a bald field, kicking the ball through mounds of litter and rubble. As the road skirted the sea, children peered out from the ruins of a house that had fallen to the tsunami, whilst their mother swept the bare, sandy earth with a palmyra broom.

When Tennent travelled through the region, his party encountered groups of nomadic tree-fellers, who made their living moving along the coast, harvesting the valuable wood from the ebony and satinwood trees, which was then floated down the rivers and round to the sea in Trincomalee, where the logs were collected. These wanderers travelled in bullock carts, carrying their axes, cooking utensils and sacks of rice, and slept under the stars, with only the light of their fires as protection from the wild elephants and leopards. The heat of the coastal plain was so intense that Tennent's party were forced to do most of their travelling before sunrise. In the tropics, these cooler, muted hours are the time when the wildlife is at its most active and Tennent recorded many encounters with the local fauna during his early rides on the eastern plain.

Sometimes our horses were frightened by the sudden plunge of a crocodile, as we disturbed him on the sands; but, more frequently we ourselves were startled in the morning twilight by a deer bounding across our path into cover, or an elephant shuffling out of our way, and trampling down the jungle as he leisurely retired. On one occasion, an hour before sunrise, we rode suddenly into the centre of a herd of wild hogs, at least a hundred in number, that were feeding amongst some clumps of acacias, and gave battle immediately in defence of their young, which the coolies laid hold of without hesitation or pity. Our guns brought down two or three full-grown ones, that provided an acceptable feast for our people.

Although we had only been travelling for half an hour, I was already beginning to feel calmer about the journey ahead and Sebastian's concerns were starting to seem melodramatic. The road was the best I had encountered on my whole trip and the van was eating up the tarmac at twice the speed of the buses I had taken over the past few days. Balasankar rarely spoke, and was an attentive and careful driver, constantly scanning the roadside and horizon for any moving figures that might wander out into his path. Pairs of wild peacocks, with sapphire breasts and long trains of feathers, strutted out into the road from the undergrowth and the villagers padded barefoot down the white lines in the middle of the road. As we passed through the small town of Nilaveli there were signs that life might be looking up in the area; we had crossed several newly built bridges that spanned the lagoons, and large areas of the roadside displayed signs showing that they had been earmarked for development. There were clusters of newly built houses with the conspicuous uniformity of foreign aid creations and cultivated fields sprouting rows of adolescent mango trees. It all seemed a bit too good to be true; then, a few kilometres later, the even tarmac disappeared and the road disintegrated into a rutted track of wet, orange earth. As the van flew off the end of the road and ground its wheels into the mud, Balasankar jammed on the breaks and tried to steer between the potholes. The van slowed to a crawl of 5 km per hour as Balasankar laboriously wound the steering wheel from one extreme to the other, trying to keep to the even sections of track.

Although my map showed the road from Trincomalee to Mullaitivu as a single, straight line, we came to an unsigned T-junction in the middle of a small town a few miles later. When Balasankar stopped the van and jumped out to ask for directions, I realised he had never travelled along this road before either. Sebastian had led me to believe that Balasankar was familiar with this area of the coast and as I realised he knew as little about it as I did, the optimism and relief I had felt a few miles before started to fade.

As we continued along the rough road, we passed several army barracks and groups of soldiers peering out at the road from corrugated-iron watchtowers. The van was stopped several times by military officials at small checkpoints by the side of the road. As they saw us approaching, one of the officials would rise to his feet and saunter into the road, languidly waving his arm up and down to indicate to Balasankar that we should pull up in front of the barrier. When we came to the first checkpoint my heart rate rose, as I searched in my bag for my passport and mentally began to rehearse the set of reasons I was going to give for being in the area. Each time, however, only Balasankar was made to leave the van and, whilst he walked over to the roadside hut to have his papers checked, I was given a polite nod by the officers who glanced briefly over the van.

At the centre of a small town a few kilometres further north, a large Buddha looked out from under the arches of the town's clock tower. This was an unexpected sight, as the Tamils of the east are not Buddhists, and worship in Hindu temples or Catholic churches. Although there had always been a small number of Sinhalese settlements in the predominantly Tamil regions of the country, since independence an increasing number of Sinhalese families had been encouraged to move to the north and east of the island. This was initially as part of a government scheme to resettle Sinhalese peasants, who had lost their land under the British, on new swathes of land that were emerging as forests in the north were cleared. In addition, it was hoped that the peasants would cultivate the area and improve the island's productivity. This is still happening today and Tamil newspapers mutter bitterly that the Sinhalese government is colonising the region and complain that new waves of immigrant Sinhalese fishermen are ruining the trade of the Tamils. There were rumours that the new Sinhalese inhabitants had dubious, criminal backgrounds and that their Buddhist monks were stealing land from the Tamils on which to erect new Buddhist temples. Like the Buddha under the clock tower, brand new dazzling white Buddhist shrines had gradually begun to appear in the northern and eastern towns and added to the Tamils' convictions that their culture was under threat.

The road had been getting narrower and more uneven and, by the time we were 50 km away from Trincomalee, it had disappeared altogether. We were now driving through overgrown fields and Balasankar was finding his way by trying to follow wheel ruts in the grass. We had also taken several unexpected turnings on the advice of the soldiers in huts by the side of the road – and the route we had taken bore no resemblance to the straight pink line on the map in my lap. When we had not seen any other vehicles for several kilometres I started to get worried: I was pretty certain that Balasankar had no idea where we were and I was haunted by the warning I had been given by the journalist in Colombo, never to leave the main road in areas that had been landmined. Just as I insisted we go back to the last turning so I could speak to the soldiers myself, several motorbikes overtook us and, in the rear-view mirror, I could see a large bus on our tail. Even if we were no longer heading for Mullaitivu, at least we were not driving through a minefield, so I asked Balasankar to carry on and hoped that we would reach a town soon.

We continued to follow the track through the fields until a few miles later, when the road ended at a small military base. A middle-aged soldier with a friendly, pock-marked face asked us both to get out of the van and led us over to a small wooden building with a sloping veranda. Several young men, who looked little older than teenagers and were wearing the dark blue and white uniforms of the Sri Lankan navy, lounged on plastic chairs in the shade. There had been no other signs of habitation for miles and it felt like a distant, solitary outpost, known only to the jungle birds, who occasionally dipped down to the veranda from the trees.

'Madam, this is a highly sensitive military area ahead of you,' said the middle-aged soldier, as he flicked distractedly through the pages in my passport. 'I'm afraid it is not within my power to allow you access. Are you a tourist?'

I told him I was teaching in Colombo and handed him my school ID card to prove it.

'Ah, you are working in Colombo. I know this school, it is next door to the cemetery?' he asked, as he peered at my identity card. Slowly he turned it over and read out the printed address of the school. 'And what about this man,' he asked, pointing to Balasankar, 'he is your driver?'

After he had spoken to Balasankar for a few minutes and checked his identity card and bundle of papers, he pulled out a mobile phone and spoke rapidly in Sinhala, reading out my personal details from my passport and identity card.

'Madam, I have spoken with the general at my headquarters,' he said, when he had finished the phone call. 'He will ring me when he has made a decision. It may take some time. Please sit with us,' he offered, motioning to some empty chairs on the veranda.

According to everyone in Colombo and Trincomalee, the soldiers roaming around the north-east are bigoted, violent animals who rape young women and make the lives of the Tamils a daily misery. As Balasankar and I sat on the veranda, the soldiers were friendly and respectful to both of us, and didn't seem to show any outward hostility towards Balasankar for being Tamil. The young men in naval uniforms had been manning the checkpoint for several months and admitted that it was a very boring existence. As we were sitting, waiting for the phone call from the headquarters, a quiet chirruping sound came from a cardboard shoebox that had been tied to one of the wooden columns supporting the veranda. One of the young soldiers jumped up from his chair and gently began to untie the box. Carefully, he carried it over to the other officers who had also risen expectantly. They placed the box on a wooden desk and crowded around it, as one of the soldiers snipped away at the string and slowly opened the lid. Inside, a clutch of fluffy baby birds were hopping around on a nest made from straw, as they screwed up their eyes at the harsh mid-morning light and opened their raw, pink throats to the sky. The young soldiers smiled at each other and cooed over the birds, gently tickling their feathers as they fed their pets crumbs of wafer biscuit.

After we had waited for half an hour, a phone call came through from the headquarters to tell us that we had been granted permission to continue. I was relieved. I was also surprised. Given that this was supposedly such a high-security area, why had nobody thought to questions my motives for wanting to pass through? Maybe the fact that I was an innocuous teacher was simply enough to reassure the army that it didn't matter what I saw. The middle-aged soldier shook our hands warmly as he said goodbye and opened the barrier across the road, waving our van towards a narrow track that disappeared into the forest.

I had been so preoccupied by the possibility that I would not be allowed to travel all the way to Mullaitivu that I hadn't really tried to imagine what the road ahead would be like. A wide, earth road – so smooth and even that it looked as if it had recently been steamrolled through the forest floor – opened up ahead of us. On either side of the road was the Vanni, the impenetrable tract of forest that had divided the north and south of the island for centuries. Its trees have dry, gnarled trunks and fine, sprawling branches, bound together by a dense meshwork of thorny shrubs that grow up and around the trees in a prickly haze. People talk of dense jungles in the south of the island but, as vast and deep as they are, there is always a way through the waxy leaves and hanging vines. As I looked at the Vanni, I could see how it had divided the island for so long. There was no way through the solid tangle of branches and thorns that would easily lacerate the skin of anyone who tried to forge a path.

This was a ghost land that people had been driven from long ago. Its only inhabitants now were the army and the only buildings were their barracks. There were tall watchtowers every kilometre, each manned by a solitary soldier whose head and rifle butt peered at the road from under the high, corrugated-iron roof. More camouflage-clad men paced silently up and down the roadside, whilst heavy military trucks filled with soldiers or towing construction machinery rumbled past. The road continued through the Vanni for kilometre after kilometre, passing the high walls of large military bases, and patches of blackened land that had been recently cleared by slash and burn. It had been the start of the Sinhalese New Year celebrations a few days earlier and, as we passed one of the army bases, I could see crowds of soldiers and a few dignitaries outside in the grounds. A speech was echoing through a tinny PA system and the soldiers were playing the traditional games of the New Year celebrations. A group of blindfolded officers were trying to pin a fabric tail onto a large picture of an elephant that was hanging on an easel, whilst adolescent soldiers were cheering on a pillow fight. A couple of young men were trying to climb their way up a fireman's pole, which had been lubricated with some kind of oil, and kept sliding their way back to the ground.

As the road neared Mullaitivu, remnants of the villages that must have existed before the war began to reappear and there were the first signs of civilian life. A few houses stood in the middle of bare patches of land, surrounded by the crumbling walls of buildings that had been taken over by the encroaching forest, with branches growing through the roofs and leafy tendrils pouring out of the windows. A lone building stood in a field, set far back from the road, and inside a young boy was sitting on a barber's chair, with a sheet tucked into the neck of his T-shirt, whilst an elderly man shaved away the hair on the back of his head. A few cows grazed by the roadside and a barefooted lady was crouching by a small, dark, Hindu god that was wrapped in red silk at the base of a tree.

We arrived at the devastated centre of Mullaitivu, which had been heavily shelled during the final stages of the war, and quickly decided there was no reason to stay. Clouds of cement dust were rising from the miles of roadworks that were reconstructing the damaged route that led back to the main A9 artery. Vegetable stalls stood amidst the dust and toppled buildings by the roadside, and a few dusty locals were tramping through the rubble carrying woven rubber shopping bags of withered vegetables. It was hard to tell what was being demolished, what had been damaged by shells and what was being rebuilt. As a police officer, who had been interrogating a man about his motorbike, began to walk over to our van, Balasankar glanced quickly at me and cocked his head towards the road, knowing that it was time to leave. We drove for several more hours along the partially constructed road, inland from the coast towards Mankulam, a small town on the A9. There I had arranged to meet Sarah, a friend and NGO worker from Colombo, who had invited me to visit.

Balasankar dropped me in Mankulam and, although he had barely said a word all day, I was grateful to him for the security his presence had provided on the strange journey we had taken together. When I had waved him goodbye and watched him drive off back towards Trincomalee, I wandered through Mankulam to try to find Sarah. She was waiting for me in a minibus with a group of Sri Lankan women who worked with her at the NGO in Colombo and they were on their way to deliver some donations to a village further north towards the Jaffna Peninsula. 'It will probably take us a while to get there as some of the roads are being rebuilt, but you are welcome to join us,' Sarah said. 'It will give you an idea of what life is like in the north.'

The minibus bumped along for a couple of hours, over a series of roads that became progressively narrower and more potholed, until it pulled up outside a small village school. Most of the government schools in the rural areas consist of a few long, barn-like buildings, with grilled, unglazed windows and plastered facades painted in various shades of peach or pink, usually displaying a large mural of the island, divided into its nine provinces. We were greeted at the gates by an army general dressed in full uniform and beret, and a few of his juvenile-looking subordinates who didn't seem to have quite grown into their uniforms.

'It's impossible to do anything in the north without Sri Lankan army supervision,' whispered Sarah. 'It adds tension to everything we do with the people up here, but without the army's blessing, we wouldn't be allowed through.'

The general led us towards one of the school buildings, outside which three middle-aged men were waiting for us. Although they were Sri Lankan, the Ralph Lauren polo shirts, chinos, deck shoes and expensive aftershave they were wearing suggested that they probably spent most of their time abroad. The eldest of the three men was introduced as George; he had thinning grey hair, trembling wattles of skin under his chin and a distinguished air. He shook my hand warmly and asked if I was an NGO worker. I explained that I was a friend of Sarah's and asked him why he was here at the school.

'I was born in the Jaffna area and so were these men,' he said, with a faint US drawl, gesturing to the two younger men who were leaning against the angular black four-wheel drive Porsche that they had driven ahead of the minibus. 'We all moved to the USA in the 1980s, when the war started, but we still have family in the north. We heard about this charity through our Tamil network in the States and we have donated large sums of money to try to help this region since the end of the war. I'm a neurosurgeon and I have a very successful practice in Washington state, and I have not been back to this region for fifteen years, but I have been told that the house that I grew up in as a child has now been consumed by the jungle.' He looked around him with a look of lost distraction. 'Since the war ended, my friends and I have often talked about visiting Sri Lanka to try to find out what happened to our ancestral villages, but it is only recently that we thought it would be possible. We are going to try to travel to them tomorrow, but we thought we would come and see what all the money we have donated is being used for today.'

I had not heard any sound from the building so I had assumed that it was empty. When we walked inside however, rows of local villagers were sitting in the darkness, completely still, in mute silence. There were over a hundred of them, sitting on plastic chairs and staring directly ahead at a small PA system that had been rigged up at the front of the room, under garlands of lurid plastic flowers suspended from the ceiling. The NGO workers and their three donors were led by the general to some seats at the front of the room, whilst one of the young army boys fiddled with the microphone and tapped it worriedly with his fingers. As the general approached the mic, the young boy stood to attention with such vertical enthusiasm that his knees were in danger of dislocating his jaw, before he span on his heel and marched stiffly out of the room. The general proceeded to address the Tamils sitting in the audience in English and gave a rambling speech about peace, reconciliation and his great faith in the principles of Buddhism, to his Hindu audience, some of whom had probably lost family to his army's shells. The villagers stared back at him in motionless silence. One by one, the villagers were called up to the front of the room to be 'presented' with a mosquito net, a bottle of insect repellent, and a pack of books and stationery for the children. As each donation was presented, the nervous villager was asked to pose for a photograph as they shook hands with one of the donors. Some of the children seemed happy to prance out to the front and accept the gifts, but several just gazed at the NGO workers through dark, empty eyes, before returning mutely to their seats.

We stood outside afterwards, drinking tea that had been provided by the army, and the villagers seemed to suddenly come to life as they returned to their houses with the smirking, boisterous energy of teenagers who had been released from a long and boring school assembly. As I watched them almost running out of the school grounds, mosquito nets tucked under their arms, I saw a boy of about ten loitering quietly in a corner waiting for his mother. The other children had shoved off together, but this one, who had large staring eyes and an expressionless face, had not joined them. George, the neurosurgeon, saw me looking at him and said into my ear, 'Look at his neck and he'll make sense.' There was a large scar on the boy's neck, just above his collar bone, that ran down his chest and below the neck of his T-shirt. 'I spoke to his father earlier,' said George. 'It's a bullet wound and he was lucky not to die. It just missed an artery by a few millimetres. His dad kept telling him to smile and lighten up, and be happy about the books and pens he'd just been given, but you can see that the kid's got issues. There's a whole generation of children up here who have witnessed things from which they will struggle to recover.'

Chapter Eight

ONTO THE JAFFNA PENINSULA

Whereas the roadsides around so much of Sri Lanka are lined with brightly painted bungalows and huts selling coconuts, soft drinks and vegetables, the land that bordered the road from Kilinochchi to Jaffna was deserted, covered with the tangled, brittle, torn bushes of the Vanni. The only sign of habitation was the occasional corrugated-iron shack thatched with desiccated palm fronds; apart from this, there were merely the scattered shells of abandoned buildings. Every few kilometres, more army watchtowers appeared, out of which a couple of young soldiers with rifles strapped across their chests stared in soporific boredom at the empty road. Clusters of identical breeze-block bungalows were being constructed on the empty land by various aid organisations, to resettle families who had been forced to leave during the war. The only large, well-maintained buildings were the huge bases belonging to the Sri Lankan army, set far back from the road inside gated compounds surrounded by high, granite walls topped with coils of razor wire. The soldiers trooping up and down outnumbered any civilians and it was easy to see why many people felt the persistent army presence was oppressive to the Tamil civilians of the north.

The government had also erected a number of roadside memorials to commemorate their victory over the Tamils. Just outside Kilinochchi, a large statue of a cracked wall with a bullet passing through it, topped with a lotus flower, sat on a conspicuously manicured green lawn, the only piece of lush vegetation in the province. Further along the road, a 20-m water tank that had been toppled during the war by the LTTE now had a stone tablet standing by its side, declaring it a 'public attraction' in three languages. Whether the insensitivity of these monuments was deliberate, it was hard to tell. Were they genuinely intended to be the tourist attractions of the future, or a simply a constant warning to any potential Tamil Tigers of the might of the Sri Lankan army?

As the bus headed north, the filmy clouds that had been moving slowly across the sky began to gather and darken, and the heat of the afternoon was soon dissipated in a heavy downpour. The people hanging out of the doors of the bus tried to squeeze themselves further into the jammed aisles and twisted their heads towards the interior to shield their faces from the gritty spray coming off the road. As the rain grew heavier, long, creaking thunderclaps boomed and the children that had been sleeping in their mothers' laps began to whimper. The soldiers who were still trudging up and down the road had donned long, dark, rubber sou'westers with pointed hoods that covered their heads, and as they clutched their rifles to their chests under the inky sky, they looked like an army of Grim Reapers patrolling the land. Then, as we neared the Jaffna Peninsula, the sky brightened again and the passengers began to tug open the windows to let in the clean, organic-smelling air that had been cooled by the rain. The dusty soil was soon replaced by powdery white sand and the land began to dissolve into still, shallow lagoons that merged with the wide expanse of the Indian Ocean.

It was late afternoon by the time we arrived at the central bus station in Jaffna. I sat down on one of the stone benches and looked at my map, in an attempt to work out how to get to the only large hotel in town that had reopened after the war. None of the bus stations I had passed through on my trip had been anything short of grim, but this one was the most godforsaken of the lot. Groups of men sat on the stone benches dribbling and spitting vermillion paan from their stained mouths onto the filthy tarmac. Many of the people drifting through seemed to be physically deformed in some way. A slow-moving lady, whose baby-pink sari was trailing along in the dust, carried a melon-sized goitre on the front of her throat; a man with no hair dragged behind him a withered leg without a foot; and many of the older generation had large patches of albino skin on their arms and faces from vitilligo, a skin condition in which the brown pigmentation disappears. A young boy sat down on the bench opposite me, slowly bent his torso over his knees and spewed a large puddle of vomit onto the ground. His mother appeared and dragged him off to the reeking toilet. A few minutes later, a barefoot, blind beggar shuffled through the lumpy puddle that was beginning to steam in the sun. The buses, too, were as decrepit as their passengers. They had cracked windshields and flimsy, cardboard signs, handwritten in felt-tip pen, showing their destinations. Most of them looked unlikely to make it to the exit of the station. It had been a long, tiring day and, sitting lost in the middle of Jaffna, I felt depressed.

Luckily, as usual, the town improved beyond the dirty walls of the bus station and I began to walk through the bazaar towards the hotel. Small Hindu gods, carved from black stone, were tucked into crevices in the bazaar walls. The stall owners were burning incense on the pavement in front of sacks of small red onions and dried chillies, and men with small barrows were kindling charcoal braziers to barbeque skewers of meat and the local prawns. The landscape and the people had been gradually changing since I had left the hill country days earlier and here on the peninsula it was as if the subtle differences had suddenly crystallised; it felt like I had arrived in a different country. Jaffna is known for bearing more similarity to the neighbouring subcontinent than it does to the Sinhalese regions of the south of the island and the jewelled saris, the cows in the road, the Tamil film posters, even the more obvious poverty, were undeniably reminiscent of towns I had visited in the south of India.

I dropped my bags at the hotel and went for a walk along the main street that ran along the coast and past the walls of the old Dutch fort. During the civil war, the control of Jaffna passed through the hands of the LTTE, the Indian Peace Keeping Force and the Sinhalese Sri Lankan military, each battle for power killing civilians and destroying buildings and infrastructure. Before the war, Jaffna was the most prosperous city on the island after the capital, but the years of conflict slowly wrecked Jaffna's economy and forced thousands of residents to leave.

When I had spoken to people who had visited Jaffna in the previous year, they had reported an oppressive military presence, with soldiers standing on almost every street corner monitoring activity. A year on, there were still a few armed soldiers hanging around on the pavements, but the vast majority seemed to have disappeared and the town felt much more relaxed. A few streets still had ruined, bullet-riddled buildings and rusty coils of razor wire as persistent reminders of the conflict, but most of the civic buildings that had been destroyed had now been rebuilt. One of the most famous buildings to be destroyed in the war was the public library, reputed to have been one of largest and most important in South Asia – containing 97,000 books and valuable historical documents, many of which were destroyed in the fire. The restored white Mughal-Gothic building is now one of the most beautiful in the city and groups of students were being shooed out of the grounds before it closed for the night.

Historically, the position of the Jaffna Tamils, stuck out in the Palk Strait close to India, meant that they were particularly exposed to bands of Christian missionaries looking for converts. They were also very receptive and there is still a somewhat bizarre collection of religious establishments interspersed with the dark terracotta-tiled bungalows that line the quiet lanes off the main street. There were Catholic convents next door to Hindu ashrams; Methodist, Jesuit and Seventh-day Adventist churches and a Church of the Diocese of South India had all established places of worship within a few streets of each other. As missionaries had been at work on the peninsula for a number of years before Tennent arrived, he was surprised to learn that the Tamils of Jaffna were still particularly keen to use the services of the local witch doctors and, 'in spite of the labours and achievements of so many Christian teachers and ministers', the belief in sorcery was as strong as ever. One particularly gruesome case was brought officially to Tennent's notice and concerned the goings-on in the house of a witchdoctor in one of the villages.

In December 1848, the police vidahn of Vannarpannai in the suburbs of Jaffna came to the magistrate in much mental agitation and distress, to complain that the remains of his son, a boy of about eight years of age, which had been buried the day before, had been disinterred during the night, and that the head had been severed from the body to be used for the purposes of witchcraft. Suspicion fell on a native doctor of the village, who was extensively consulted as an adept in the occult sciences; but no evidence could be produced sufficient to connect him with the transaction.

The vidahn went on to explain to the magistrate that the witch doctor could be paid to perform a ceremony, involving the skull of a child, which was believed to induce the death of whoever you wished.

The skull of a male child, and particularly a first born, is preferred, and the effects are regarded as more certain if it be killed expressly for the occasion; but for ordinary purposes, the head of one who has died a natural death is presumed to be sufficient. The form of the ceremony is to draw certain figures and cabalistic signs upon the skull, after it has been scraped and denuded of the flesh; adding the name of the individual upon whom the charm is to take effect. A paste is then prepared, composed of sand from the footprints of the intended victim, and a portion of their hair moistened with their saliva, and this, being spread upon a leaden plate, is taken, together with the skull, to the graveyard of the village, where for forty nights the evil spirits are invoked to destroy the person so denounced.

A month later, a second complaint was brought before the magistrate of Jaffna, concerning the same witch doctor. That morning, discovering he was short of skulls, he had apparently resorted to murdering a child in order to harvest its skull. A second child was reported to be hidden in his house, awaiting the same fate. When his house was searched and a headless corpse was discovered, the evidence was conclusive (although a female assistant, who apparently aided the doctor in his sideline of abortions, suggested that the head may have been removed by a dog). Unfortunately, the doctor somehow managed to escape, but the papers that were seized from his house made interesting reading.

His papers were seized by the magistrate, among which was a volume of receipts for compounding nefarious preparations and poisons; and along with these a manuscript book containing the necessary diagrams and forms of invocation to 'Siva the Destroyer' for every imaginable purpose, 'to seduce the affections of a female – to effect a separation between a husband and wife – to procure abortion – to possess with a devil – to afflict with sickness' – and innumerable directions 'for procuring the death of an enemy'. In this remarkable treatise on domestic medicine, there was not a single receipt for the cure of disease amongst the numerous formulas for its infliction; nor one instruction for effecting a harmless or benevolent purpose amidst the diagrams and directions for gratifying the depraved passions, and encouraging the fiendish designs of the author's dupes.

It was Friday evening and as the sun was beginning its descent to the horizon, the teenage boys of the town were playing a football match in a stadium by the ocean. There are very few cars on the peninsula and the groups of men who were cycling home on old, steel bicycles stopped and piled up their steeds on the grass by the stadium, and sucked on ice lollies as they watched the match in the dimming light.

I walked back to the hotel in the dwindling twilight and went straight to the restaurant in search of food. It was still quite early and there was only one other person in the restaurant. The waiter led me to the table next to the other diner, a heavy-set Sri Lankan man with a fine gold chain around his neck, who was engrossed in a bowl of seafood soup.

'It's a Jaffna speciality, madam,' said the waiter, as he saw me looking at the soup. 'Would you like us to prepare some for you?'

'It's really very good,' said the man, looking up from his bowl, 'I haven't tasted it since I left Jaffna, but it is even better than I remember.'

Not feeling that I had much choice in the matter, I ordered a bowl from the waiter and asked the soup-eating gentleman where he lived now.

'I have lived in Melbourne since 2001,' he said, as he drained the last of his soup from the bowl, 'as do most of my family.'

'You left because of the war?' I asked.

'Yes,' he replied, wiping his mouth on a serviette, 'we stuck it out in Jaffna for the first part of the war, but after a while we just couldn't go on any longer. Our house had already been damaged in one bomb blast, which cost us several thousand dollars to repair, and we knew that the situation in Jaffna was going to get worse before it got any better. We were living round the corner from one of the city's LTTE camps and, like many families who lived near us, we had a large bunker dug into the floor of our living room. We lived in fear like that for several years – but a life like that is not worth living, so we started making applications to leave.'

'Did you ever consider moving to the south of the island, out of the warzone instead?' I asked. I knew a few Tamils in Colombo who had moved there from Jaffna during the same period, but they were quite unusual and most of their families had opted to move to a different continent instead.

'We did think about it,' said the gentleman, nodding his head slowly, 'but I had a rather strange experience when I was at university, which made me reluctant to go south. When I was at university in Jaffna I played badminton for the university team. Every year all the universities on the island join together for the Sri Lankan University Games, or "SLUG" as we used to call it, and a different university would host the event every year. One year it was held at Rohana University, down in the south near Galle; a very Sinhalese area where the majority are Buddhist. We had to fly to Colombo to get there I remember, because the roads from the north were all impassable because of the LTTE. There were about sixty of us from Jaffna who travelled there that year and on the evening that we arrived we were all sitting together in one of the university dorms, speaking in Tamil. Slowly, we became aware that a crowd of Sinhalese students from Galle were gathering outside the building and staring in at us through the windows.'

'Did you feel threatened?' I asked.

'Yes we did, in fact we were very scared,' he continued. 'We sat in silence and looked out at them, until we realised they were not doing anything, they just wanted to have a look at us. Many of them had never even seen a Tamil before and they thought all Tamils were members of the LTTE – they were expecting some kind of violent warriors.' He began to laugh. 'They just stood there watching us in silence, it was very strange. Although none of them spoke Tamil, a few of us spoke Sinhala, so we invited them in and shared some of our food with them. In the end, we spoke all evening and they were very kind to us whilst we stayed there, but it made me realise just how many suspicions my family could face in other parts of the island. It was especially my children that I was worried about. Even if they were born in Colombo they would still have been issued with identity cards that stated they were Tamil. I was worried that they would be at a disadvantage, even before they were born.'

The next morning I was up early to meet Taarun, a tuk-tuk driver who had agreed to drive me around the peninsula to visit some of the smaller towns Tennent had passed through on his journey. When Tennent arrived he discovered an extensive network of roads, a well-organised market system and a constant hive of activity that reminded him of the market towns in England.

Jaffna is almost on the only place in Ceylon of which it might be said that no one is idle or unprofitably employed. The Bazaars are full of activity and stocked with a greater variety of fruits and vegetables than is to be seen in any other town on the island. Every one appears to be more or less busy; and at the season of the year when labour is not in demand at home, numbers of the natives go off to trade in the interior... Large bodies of them also resort annually to the south were they find lucrative employment in repairing the village tanks – a species of labour in which they are peculiarly expert, and which the Sinhalese are too indolent or too litigious to perform for themselves. If the deserted fields and solitudes of the Wanny are ever again to be re-peopled and re-tilled, I am inclined to believe that the movement for that purpose will come from the Tamils of Jaffna, for, looking to their increasing intelligence and wealth, their habits of industry and adaptation to agricultural life, I can have little doubt that, as population increases, and the arable lands of the peninsula become occupied, emigration will gradually be directed towards the south, where, with the natural capabilities of the soil and the facilities for irrigation, one half of the exertion and toil bestowed on the reluctant sands of Jaffna would speedily convert the wilderness to a garden.

Like many other British men who lived and worked on the island during the colonial era, Tennent seemed to have more respect for the Tamils in Jaffna, and more faith in their ability to play a part in the running and development of the colony, than he did for the Sinhalese in the south. The notion amongst the colonial government that the Tamils were harder working, easier to communicate with and generally more capable, led to the dominance of the Tamils in positions of responsibility and the beginnings of the tensions with the Sinhalese that would culminate in the civil war over a century later. Tennent's conviction that the Jaffna Tamils would eventually come to expand their sphere of influence and develop the region to the south seemed a sad irony in light of their suppression by the government in later years, and the actions of the LTTE which drove so many Tamils away from their country and led to the decline of their prosperous homeland.

Although it was 7 a.m. and the sun had only risen an hour earlier, the air was already so humid that I was feeling stifled and my thin clothes were starting to cling to me as I walked over to the beige tuk-tuk. Taarun, my driver, had a mop of oiled, corkscrew curls that hung over his eyes, and effeminate hands with slender fingers and long, curving nails that dangled languidly over the controls as he drove. We were heading for Point Pedro, the small town that teeters on the tip of the Jaffna Peninsula at the northernmost point of the island. As we drove along, groups of women glided past on bicycles, sitting bolt upright and holding open umbrellas over their heads to protect their faces from the ageing glare of the morning sun. Everyone seemed to be wearing spectacles, which gave the people an erudite and refined appearance. Elderly tuk-tuk drivers peered intently at their newspapers through fine, gold-rimmed frames and teenage girls gossiped in the streets from behind angular, plastic-framed lenses. I wasn't sure whether the reputation of the Jaffna Tamils as hard workers had just given me a heightened awareness, but wherever I looked, people we passed seemed to be engaged in something productive and it was hard to find many simply lounging in the shade watching the world go by.

After we had been driving for twenty minutes, Taarun turned to me and asked if I was a Catholic. He clearly was, from the pale-blue rosary hanging from the tuk-tuk's rear-view mirror, and the stickers of the Virgin Mary and St Francis on the dashboard and windscreen. Before I had a chance to answer, he slowed the tuk-tuk and pulled up outside the red-and-white striped walls of a small Hindu temple. 'One minute,' he whispered to me as he walked over to a large tree a few yards in front of the temple. Inside a hollow halfway up its trunk someone had wedged a gold-framed picture of the Virgin Mary and a small terracotta pot, holding a deep-yellow paste, which Taarun carefully spooned into his cupped palm with a tiny earthenware spoon. A half-naked holy man with matted, waist-length hair mumbled up at him from his slumped position by the base of the tree. Taarun came back to the tuk-tuk and, using his index finger, began to work his way round the vehicle, smearing spots of the yellow paste on the number plate, the hubcap of each wheel, the front and back windscreens, and finishing with a dot in the middle of the dashboard. 'Later, when I come home, I will go to church and pray, but for now, this will give us a safe journey,' he explained.

Point Pedro was hot, dusty, corrugated and ramshackle. We drove through narrow alleys full of cross-legged women with gold nose studs, sitting amidst piles of vegetables, brandishing pairs of weighing scales. Behind the town, the white sand beach was littered with razor wire, tsunami rubble and upright wooden crosses, driven into the sand to commemorate the dead. The fishermen sat under palm-frond shelters, whilst their children played on the sand, watching the turquoise tongues of the ocean licking the shore.

We followed the coastline east, through a series of small villages dwarfed by symmetrical Catholic churches the colour of fairy-cake icing, to Valvedditturai, the birthplace of Velupillai Prabhakaran, the supreme leader of the Tamil Tigers, known as the Sun God. The shadow of the enigmatic leader had hung over Sri Lanka for three decades, until his death on the marshy banks of the Nanthi Kadal Lagoon in 2009. He was born in Valvedditturai in 1954 to a lower-caste family and, although his parents were followers of Mahatma Gandhi, he was rumoured to be a sadistic child who played alone with homemade weapons as he looked over the waters of the Palk Strait towards India. Photographs of the adult Prabhakaran show a plump, moustachioed man dressed in a tiger-striped military uniform, staring at the camera with distant, thoughtful eyes that belie his doctrine of cold, single-minded brutality. As a young Tamil man he had witnessed the continued oppression of Tamils on the Jaffna peninsula and developed a deep mistrust of the Sinhalese people and the government. His life's mission became the formation of a separate Tamil state of Eelam, a dream for which he was prepared to take as many lives as was necessary. Those who met him described a shy, softly spoken man whose rigid self-discipline he instilled in his followers. Like a god, he was inaccessible, shrouded in mystery and worshipped unquestioningly by devoted warriors who were willing to martyr themselves at the altar of his ideals. By the 1980s, he had united thousands of angry, disillusioned, bitter Tamils irrespective of caste, age and gender under his leadership.

Taarun stopped the tuk-tuk in the shade of a frangipani tree in the middle of the village. The streets were sandy and empty, except for a couple of policemen who were chatting with the shopkeepers sitting on the pavement. As I walked past they began muttering 'Prabhakaran', as they suggested to each other that maybe I had come in search of the house where the Sun God had been born. Why else, they wondered, would anyone travel to this deserted hamlet at the forgotten end of the island? Intrigued as I had been to see the place that had produced such a mysterious and notorious being, I doubted whether the four walls of his house would offer much insight and I declined their offers of directions.

Tennent had visited Valvedditturai to meet the local shipbuilders, who were reputed to be the most skilful on the island. It was hard to imagine this sleepy little village as the industrious and enterprising place he described. But what struck him most during the night he spent there was the captivating sight of the local women drawing water from a well at sunset under a grove of tamarind trees. He particularly admired their figure and carriage, which was shown to advantage in their singularly graceful and classical costume, consisting of a fold of cloth, enveloping the body below the waist, and brought tastefully over the left shoulder, leaving the right arm and bosom free.

This together with the custom of carrying vases of water and other burdens on their heads, gives them an erect and stately gait, and disposes their limbs in attitudes so graceful as to render them, when young and finely featured, the most unadorned models for a sculptor.

Had he spoken to these women, I wondered, or simply admired their beauty from a distance, in long shadows of the setting sun?

When Tennent had finished exploring the Jaffna Peninsula he travelled by boat through the small cluster of islands that lie in the Palk Strait and curve south-westerly between the Gulf of Mannar and the Bay of Bengal towards India. The farthest of the inhabited islands was named Delft by the Dutch colonisers in the seventeenth century and I wanted to try to sail there the next day. When I got back to Jaffna I asked in the town about boats to Delft and got a variety of answers.

'There is one boat every day and it leaves at 8 a.m.'

'There are two boats every day: one at 8.30 a.m. and one at 10 a.m.'

'Boats leave every hour from 7 a.m.'

The boat, or boats, whatever time they departed, did not leave from Jaffna, but from a small islet called Punkudutivu, 30 km off the mainland, reached by a series of causeways connecting it with other islands and the peninsula.

Taarun collected me early the next morning, and we drove out of the city and onto the narrow causeway that ran out into the sea. The sun had not yet broken through the early-morning clouds and the still, unbroken shallows either side of the causeway were glassy and grey. Fishermen and their young sons were swimming between prawn traps, which were made from small wooden stakes stuck into the seabed and draped with fine fishing nets. Taarun told me that some of the traps belonged to his family, and he and his son had collected 2 kg of prawns earlier that morning. A few fishermen were sitting by the roadside, sifting through the grey sludgy mass they had lifted from their traps, picking out the prawns that would be sold in the market later that day. On the far end of the causeway the pale rocky land slowly reappeared, covered with dark green humpy bushes that looked like heads of broccoli, and skirted the shoreline of the next island, Kayts.

Kayts was sandy and barren, home to a few small settlements and herds of cows. A couple of women in cobalt-blue saris stood by a well in the distance, the only specks of colour on the sun-bleached landscape. We crossed a second causeway over to the smaller island of Punkudutivu and were stopped by two soldiers manning a corrugated-iron hut. Taarun was asked to leave the tuk-tuk and present his identity papers and I handed over my passport for inspection. Whilst the tuk-tuk was being looked over, a small child appeared and tried to sell us plastic bags of wilting frangipani flowers he had picked from the side of the road.

The sun had burned away the morning clouds by the time we arrived and, although it was not yet 8 a.m., the dry heat was already oppressive. The port was just a small shelter on the edge of the land, which housed a few concrete benches, and a couple of peeling, patched-up boats that were moored to a small landing platform. There were no signs to indicate when the boats would depart and there didn't seem to be anywhere to buy tickets. I asked a young man whether the boat to Delft had left yet, and he shook his head and waved me over to the shelter, where a handful of elderly women wearing yellow, sequined saris were slumped with their eyes closed. After I had been waiting in the shelter for half an hour, a motorbike appeared carrying two middle-aged men, one middle-aged woman and a child of about nine. The bike stopped just outside the shelter and the precariously balanced family clambered off the back, brushing the dust from their clothes and wiping it from their eyes. The mother, who was carrying a full shopping bag of food and a 2-litre bottle of water, sat down next to me in the shelter and grunted, 'Delft?' I nodded and she waved the rest of the family over to join her. She looked me up and down, and frowned at my small rucksack which clearly did not contain any food.

'Breakfast?' she asked, accusingly.

'I have already had breakfast – in Jaffna,' I replied feebly. She frowned at me again.

'You are American?'

'No, English.'

She seemed disappointed.

'Christian?'

I felt it was too early and too hot to get into a discussion of what faith I may or may not have, so I just gave an affirmative mumble. She narrowed her eyes. 'You know Jehovah?'

The family had travelled to Jaffna that morning from a village on the peninsula, and were off to Delft for a day trip and a swim in the sea. They were all Jehovah's Witnesses but the mother, Tilika, was by far the most zealous. Whilst we sat in the shelter waiting for the boat to arrive she tried her best to convert me.

'You know the Bible? First it was written in the beautiful Hebrew language, then Greek, then Latin then in the American language. It says all people must know Jehovah! Then there will be great paradise after this life. In this life, we must be mindful of Satan. You know Satan?'

She was interrupted in her stride by the chugging of a boat engine, and the people in the shelter roused themselves and began to move towards the water. The boat had no real deck and we all piled into a small room below, which was filled with hard, wooden benches. Ancient foamy lifejackets, no longer carrying their zips or clips, were stuffed under the benches. Although it seemed unlikely that they would provide any kind of buoyancy, I copied the passengers who were diligently pulling them over their heads and wrapping them around their torsos. The other passengers all seemed to be islanders, returning to Delft with shopping bags of provisions they had bought on the mainland. They were mostly frail, elderly women with sun-blackened skin still stretched tightly over their thin cheeks, dented gold jewellery and greasy, greying hair pulled away from their faces with plastic children's hair clips.

As the boat pulled out into the open sea, the passengers promptly removed their lifejackets, stuffed them back under the seats and started to wander up and down the steps onto the narrow deck. Tilika was sitting on the top step, looking out over the sea, and patted to a small space beside her. From where we were sitting we could see the vegetation that fringed the surrounding islands and the haze of the horizon, beyond which lay the east coast of India.

'In the Bible it says the Jehovah is the creator of all!' she proclaimed, as she waved her hand over the view. 'He created all this – the plants, the animals, the people. The first was a very beautiful man, so beautiful he was, named Adam. What else, other than Jehovah could have created all this?' she demanded with a glare.

'What about evolution?' I asked, without much hope. She frowned and looked at her knees for a moment. 'I think I have heard this word before,' she said, straining to remember. 'It is like with dogs, yes? Dogs breathing in and out, in and out, using oxygen?'

We looked at each other in mutual confusion for a few moments and silently agreed to abandon the conversation.

The boat landed at Delft's small pier an hour later and the islanders scrambled over their discarded lifejackets and clambered onto the land. The island has been home to a large naval base for many years, its vulnerable position so close to India making it an easy landing point for smugglers and human traffickers. A few naval officers in bright-blue shirts and white leather belts stood on the pier, and watched the islanders as they hurried past and disappeared along the shoreline. I had expected to see a bus stand or even a shack selling bananas, but other than a small building that housed the seamstresses and juddering sewing machines of the navy sponsored 'Sewing Centre', there was nothing. I looked around and wondered how I was going to explore the island. It was roughly 15 km from end to end, but with the intense heat and lack of shade I did not really want to attempt a trek on foot.

The family of Jehovah's Witnesses were in negotiation with a couple of men who, the mother explained, had vehicles, and they asked me if I would like to join them for the day. I was not particularly relishing several more hours of attempted conversion but, judging by the lack of transport, it was not an offer I was in a position to refuse. A few minutes later a tuk-tuk drove onto the pier and the family set off towards it. As there is barely enough room in the back of a tuk-tuk for three people, let alone five, I foolishly assumed that there would be another one on its way. I was wrong. The two men (Tilika's husband and brother) and Tilika sat on the back seat, I was pulled by Tilika onto her lap and her son perched on the front seat with the driver. It was 35°C in the shade, we were all sweating profusely, we now appeared to be sharing body heat, and I was tempted to abandon the whole thing and jump into the sea to swim after the departing boat.

Delft had been drained of life and colour from the beginning of time by the relentless, blinding sun. The straw-coloured land was divided into empty plots, walled by porous, dry-stone walls built from chunks of fossilised sea creatures. The few palmyra trees provided only short shadows in the midday sun and almost nothing grew in the thirsty earth, except for thorny bushes and a rash of pink-fleshed aloe vera. We stopped outside the island's small hospital, which was a collection of empty rooms and a single outside shower. A couple of nurses dressed in twee, white uniforms were tiptoeing along a cloister-like, open corridor, lined with dark rooms that contained piles of cooking pots, but no apparent medical equipment. The only visible patient was a heavily pregnant woman, who was propped up on a chair under a faded poster of venomous snakes. It wasn't until we emerged into the garden behind the hospital, where the ruins of a Dutch castle were lying in the grass, that I understood why we were there. Tilika's son climbed up the few surviving walls whilst the rest of the family posed for endless rounds of photographs in front of the ruins, watched by the silent nurses in the empty hospital.

We piled back into the tuk-tuk, which soon turned off the paved road and onto a sandy track across sparse grassland towards the cerulean sea. Wild ponies with brown coats, descendants of the creatures brought to the island by the Dutch, still roamed through the fields and trotted by the side of the tuk-tuk. Elderly men and women, who looked like products of the ossified landscape, stood in the fields using ropes to draw water from large concrete wells, which they then decanted into plastic jerry cans that could be strapped to the back of a bicycle. Emaciated old ladies in frayed saris stood on the scorching earth in bare feet, lugging the buckets out of the wells, whilst their bow-legged husbands, with rags tied around their heads to protect them from the sun, pushed the heavily laden bicycles over the rocky ground towards their distant houses.

We stopped at a patch of grey, cracked earth to inspect a metre-long impression in the ground that was apparently another of Adam's footprints. 'This is not footprint of Adam,' Tilika whispered indignantly, 'Adam was most beautiful man and this is very giant, ugly footprint. More likely, it belongs to Satan,' she concluded.

We passed tree-like sculptures formed from ancient melted rocks, from which the villagers had hung candle-lit lanterns. We posed in front of a fat baobab tree left behind by Arab seafarers, which had been surrounded by a barbed-wire fence to prevent the adolescent islanders from engraving their names on its trunk. When Tilika announced that the family was going in search of a kingdom hall, the Jehovah's Witnesses' place of worship, that she believed to lie somewhere in the interior of the island, I decided it was time to say goodbye and walk the short distance back to the pier.

The boat was not due to leave for another hour and I joined a couple of naval officers who were standing on the pier watching a military speedboat disappear into the distance. The island did not receive many foreign visitors and they were keen to talk, admitting that any distraction was welcome on this deserted, far-flung island. As we spoke, the pier began to fill up with islanders coming to catch the afternoon boat over to the mainland. They were comfortable with the officers, greeting them warmly and discussing matters that the navy were helping them with on the island. Several of the island-dwelling young men were sitting with small plastic bags in their laps, which seemed to wriggle from time to time and emitted high-pitched squeaking noises. I asked one of the men what was inside and he opened up his bag to show me an emerald green, baby parakeet that he was taking over to the mainland to sell.

When the pier was almost full, a little old man with stick-thin bow legs marched down and sat on a bench next to one of the naval officers who was reading a newspaper. Immediately, to the amusement of the other islanders, the old man demanded that the officer hand over his paper. The man seemed to be the island's resident eccentric, and the officer smiled and resigned himself to the loss of his paper. The little old man grabbed the newspaper, opened it at random and proceeded to read it aloud to himself. As the boat to Punkudutivu was spotted on its way into the harbour, the old man flung the paper to the ground and picked up a lifejacket that was lying on the bench next to him. Rejecting the help of the naval officer with flapping hands, he thrust his head urgently through the arm hole of the jacket and began to wind its tapes around his neck. Not seeming to mind his semi-strangled state, he calmly joined the line of people who were heading towards the boat.

When Tennent had finished exploring Delft, he was able to sail to Rameswaram, a small town that sits on an isthmus of India jutting out into the Palk Strait, leaving only about 30 km of sea between the Indian and Sri Lankan coastlines. Rameswaram was, and still is, home to a spectacular Hindu temple and, although Tennent grudgingly accepted its magnificence as a piece of architecture, he was generally unimpressed by the Hindu devotees he encountered.

We found the vicinity of the Pagoda surrounded by thousands of pilgrims from all parts of India; mingled with whom were fakirs of the most hideous aspect, exhibiting their limbs in inconceivably repulsive attitudes. Gaudy vehicles, covered with gilding and velvet, and drawn by cream coloured oxen, carried ladies of distinction, who had crossed in pilgrimage from the opposite coast... We were met by a band of nautch girls, who presented us with flowers, and performed before us one of their melancholy and spiritless movements, which is less a dance than a series of postures, wherein the absence of grace is sought to be compensated by abrupt gestures, stamping the feet and wringing the arms, to extract

an inharmonious accompaniment from the jingling of
bangles and anklets.

As the two countries were under British rule at the time,
Tennent had no problem in simply boarding a boat in
Ceylon and drifting out of its waters and into those of India.
Nowadays, even with an Indian visa, it is not possible to
sail from Delft to Rameswaram without a naval escort, so
I decided to skip Rameswaram and pick up Tennent's route
from the point where he landed back on the Sri Lankan
coast. When Tennent left Rameswaram, he sailed through the
chain of sandbanks known as Adam's Bridge, which form a
perforated causeway between the tip of India and Mannar,
Sri Lanka's largest island which lies just off the north-west
coast. Before the civil war it was possible to board a ferry
in Rameswaram for the short voyage to Mannar, where
you could then catch a train running over a causeway from
Mannar, directly across the mainland to Colombo. During
the war, however, all the railway lines to the north of the
island had been destroyed; when I arrived in Sri Lanka they
had not yet been rebuilt and the ferry link to India was still
suspended. To get to Mannar I would have to take to the
road again and travel from Jaffna by bus south to Vavuniya, a
large town that sits on the invisible border between the Tamil
north and the Sinhalese south, and hope that I could pick up
a bus heading west, over the causeway to Mannar.

I left Jaffna early, reached Vavuniya at noon and changed
buses for one that was going to Mannar. Grandly declared the
'Gateway to the North' by the road sign, Vavuniya seemed
an unmemorable town, dilapidated and drab. I bought a

bottle of water and some bananas from Food City, the town supermarket, which had a dirty floor and smelled of rotting fish. As I sat on the half-empty bus, waiting for it to fill up with passengers, I counted ten white Land Rovers, each belonging to a different UN subdivision or one of the international aid agencies, many of whom had their headquarters in the town. 'I was only there for a few weeks and it nearly drove me mad,' said an aid worker who had escaped to Colombo to drown his sorrows by the sea before returning home. 'There's nothing to do and only one place that serves edible food. I don't know how the long-haulers cope with the place.'

The road to Mannar ran across a flat landscape of bald grassland and yellowed, thorny bushes. Forests of palmyra trees rose up in the distance and the foreground was dotted with small huts made entirely of woven palm thatch, with windowless walls and roofs that sloped so low they almost touched the cracked earth. Elderly women were collecting firewood by the roadside, working in groups and helping each other to balance their bundles of sticks on small cushions on the tops of their heads, before they swayed along the roadside together back to their huts. A couple of waifs played on the wreckage of an old motorcycle in the shade of a contorted tree; alone together, miles from anywhere, oblivious to their isolation on the hard, unforgiving land. As we neared Mannar, I saw that the old railway line that had once connected the island to the mainland was being rebuilt by groups of sun-blackened women who were shovelling piles of gravel around the newly laid sleepers. The stretches of cloth they had wrapped around their heads, their yellowed, glaring eyes and their sharpened teeth gave them the menacing appearance of roadside bandits, as they looked up from their work and stared at the bus as it moved towards the horizon.

Set back from the road in Cheddikulam were the sprawling corrugated-iron roofs of Menik Farm, one of the island's largest refugee camps. Many families who had been displaced from the north-east had ended up in this camp three years ago and various reports claimed that 6,000 people were still waiting to return home. Children ran around outside the huts, which were made entirely out of corrugated-iron sheeting, and ducked under the lines of raggedy washing strung limply between the neighbouring roofs. A few teenage girls with pigtails stood in the doorways, biting their nails and looking silently out at the road. Only a few weeks earlier a cyclone had hit the camp, ripping off roofs, toppling the surrounding trees and power cables, destroying many of the huts and electrocuting some of the inhabitants. At the centre of the camp stood a square of white wooden crosses, driven into the bare earth and surrounding a lone, central cross, facing the road. Whether they were graves or a desperate symbol of faith was impossible to tell.

As we neared the causeway, the scrubland gave way to bare sand and then to the calm, shallow waters of the Gulf of Mannar. On the other side of the smooth, tarmac road that rose out of the sea, was the long, flat coastline of the island. The shore was studded with wind-lacerated palm trees and lines of green fishing boats moored below what looked like the ruined walls of a colonial fort. Unlike the pretty, picture-book boats that bobbed around the coastline of the rest of the island, these were larger, rougher boats that had been eroded and abused by harsher currents. The causeway led into the centre of the island's main town, and along the sandy, low-rise streets into the bus stand. At the centre of the town stood a pasty faced Virgin Mary, wearing a crown and a blue cape, and standing in a glass case that was raised high into the air on large stilts. A few soldiers in camouflage rode slowly on steel bicycles and, in front of the line of closed-up, iron-roofed huts, a few elderly men in sarongs talked quietly and nodded at each other with half-closed eyes.

Walking around these sun-drained, desiccated towns was exhausting. There was no shade and the dry air and burning sun had started to blur my vision, producing a disorienting headache that made me feel stunned and nauseous. I could see why nobody in the town seemed to be in a hurry to do anything. I wandered slowly through the streets, past a small open-fronted cafe, where a group of men were drinking tea on plastic stools that may have been upturned buckets. One of the men was larger and more well-built than the others, and was wearing trousers rather than the floor-length sarongs of his companions. Spotting me, he jumped to his feet and asked if I needed a vehicle. I wanted to travel across the island, a distance of about 20 km, to Talaimannar, the port at the far end of the island that used to connect Sri Lanka with India. 'You come with me,' he said, pointing to a battered white minibus, 'I have A/C vehicle, very little cost.' As most of the tuk-tuks that were parked out in the street were already loaded with boxes of fruit and vegetables, gas canisters and various other pieces of hardware that needed transporting over the island, I agreed and asked him to take me to Talaimannar. As we got into the minibus, he told me that his name was Nimesh and he was from Anuradhapura, the sacred Buddhist town further south on the mainland. He had been to Mannar several times, but had not visited Talaimannar since the war had started, thirty years ago.

Tennent visited the Gulf of Mannar to speak with the local pearl divers – who had been scouring the floor of the ocean for generations – to investigate the mysterious disappearance of the oysters a few years earlier, reducing the income from the colony. Explorers and historians had been fascinated by the young boys who flung themselves gracefully to the depths of the sea and were reputed to have superhuman lung capacities that allowed them to swim along the ocean bed for long periods of time. In the ninth century, the Arabian geographer Al-Masudi gave a strange account of the pearl divers of the Persian Gulf, who apparently compressed their nostrils with pieces of tortoise shell and breathed through their ears instead. Tennent observed a group of Ceylonese pearl divers at a pearl bank at Aripo and quickly dismissed any superhuman respiration levels, recording that even the most experienced of the divers could not manage more than a full minute below the surface of the water.

> The pieces of apparatus employed to assist the diver in his operations are exceedingly simple in their character; they consist merely of a stone, about thirty pounds weight, to accelerate the rapidity of his descent, this is suspended over the side of the boat, with a loop attached to it for receiving the foot; and of a net-work basket, which he takes down to the bottom and fills with the oysters as he collects them.

Diving for pearls in the nineteenth century would seem to be a fairly risky activity, as the Gulf of Mannar was home to a large number of sharks, but Tennent recorded that since the island had been a British colony, there had been only one recorded incident of a pearl diver falling prey to one of the creatures. Tennent suggested that this was due to the noise of the boats and the falling stones, which would scare the sharks away, but the local divers attributed their safety to the powers of the local shark charmer, who they employed to exorcise the sea each time they went fishing. The power of the shark charmer was believed to be hereditary and independent of any particular faith – at the time of Tennent's visit he recorded that the current shark charmer was also a practising Roman Catholic. Tennent tried to arrange a meeting with the shark charmer, to discuss the source of his grand and mysterious secret. Unfortunately the charmer was unwell at the time and instead sent along a friend, who claimed that although he himself was ignorant of the shark charmer's secret, simply being connected with the charmer would afford him the respect of the sharks, if a quick exorcism was required.

Another sea creature that still swims in the Gulf of Mannar is the dugong, a large, whale-like mammal otherwise known as a sea cow, which is now approaching extinction. A few months earlier, the navy had seized a couple of dugong carcasses and arrested a group of fishermen, who were believed to have killed them in an illegal dynamite blast used to catch large quantities of fish. It was also rumoured that some of the islanders hunted the dugongs and consumed their meat in secret – as its flesh was prized for its taste and aphrodisiac properties. Greek and Arab seafarers, who had seen the large, soft bodies of the dugong in the shallows, suckling its young by holding it to its breast with a flipper, saw what looked like a woman's body with the tail of a fish and believed they had discovered mermaids on the island. The Portuguese, too, believed that the island was home to these mythical creatures and in 1560 they sent the body of a 'mermaid' to their colony in Goa, where it was dissected by the viceroy's physician, Demas Bosquez, who reached the dubious conclusion that their internal structure was identical to that of a human.

The road ran across expanses of pan-flat, bare earth, which looked as if they may once have been part of a long-evaporated riverbed, and over mounds of white sand that had been blown into peaked dunes by the wind. Palm trees and large xerophytic bushes, with leaves so small and fine that they merged into a grey-green haze, were all that grew in the sandy earth, which soon dwindled into a wide silver lagoon. Herds of goats, cattle and small fluffy donkeys roamed along the roadside, tugging at the stubbly ground. The banks of the lagoon were dotted with more donkeys, some drinking placidly at the water's edge, whilst others thrashed violently around on the ground, rolling in the sand and kicking clouds of dust into the air. As the vegetation reappeared, so did the people, and clusters of iron-roofed huts formed small settlements beneath the palm trees. Outside a plastered building, a group of young girls dressed in yellow saris were twirling in the sand as an elderly lady taught them the traditional twisting, flowing movements of the local dances.

As we neared the end of the island, a large white barrier came into view, which turned out to be the gates of a navy compound. Two large black four-wheel drives were waiting outside whilst a young navy officer made a telephone call from a wooden booth, gesturing to the vehicles. After a few minutes, the gates opened and the black four-wheel drives were ushered through. The officer peered at me through the window and, to my surprise, ushered us through too. Inside the compound were a petrol pump, a few large buildings and big groups of naval officers jogging through the grounds in sports clothes. Any traces of the old town had obviously disappeared during the war and all that remained was an old pier that looked over the waters of the Gulf of Mannar towards India.

I had rung ahead several days earlier to book a room in the island's only small guesthouse, and Nimesh dropped me at its entrance on Station Road, which in the absence of a railway line was now just a dirt track off the main road. Cast-iron sections of track were stacked up in the thorny undergrowth. I was met at the gates by the owner of the guesthouse, an elderly Tamil man with bright, gentle eyes and a soft smile. The only other guest was a laconic butterfly enthusiast from the Netherlands, who had spent the morning trying to find and photograph a Large Salmon Arab to illustrate a book about tropical butterflies. My room was dark and bare, furnished only with a small iron-framed bed, covered with a single sheet. The toilet had been sterilised with so much disinfectant that when I flushed the chain, the foam it produced began to bubble out of the toilet bowl and floated onto the concrete floor. I spent the afternoon sitting in the reception area on a velour sofa that was still covered in plastic, drinking small glass bottles of sickly yellow cream soda and making notes. The owner wandered in and out, and asked me whether I was working for an NGO. 'No foreign people really come here except for naturalists,' he explained, nodding his head in the direction of the butterfly man's room, 'and NGO workers.' I got out Tennent's book to explain what I was doing in Mannar and, as I was starting to explain who Tennent was, he grabbed it out of my hand and looked at it excitedly.

'Yes, I know this man!' he said, nodding his head with interest, 'he was here some years ago.'

'That's right!' I replied enthusiastically. Although many of the people I knew in Colombo were familiar with *Ceylon*, I had not found many people in the provinces who were aware of the book. 'Yes, I remember him very well,' said the owner, squinting at the cover of the book in the darkness, 'he stayed here for several days and gave me his business card.'

Chapter Nine

THE ANCIENT CITIES

In 1848, as a wave of revolutions was sweeping across Europe, Tennent embarked on the final leg of his travels around the island. Although Ceylon lay thousands of miles away from the political upheavals of Europe, the news that the French monarchy had been overthrown filtered through to the islanders via the Tamils in the French settlement of Pondicherry in South India. The news was received with great excitement by the Kandyan chiefs in the hill country, who had still not given up hope of regaining their independence from the British. The disaffection of the Kandyans and members of other communities in the region had been deepened by the government's recent decision to impose a new set of taxes on the islanders. A tax had been placed on dogs, in an attempt to reduce the huge number of stray animals that the villagers had resorted to slaughtering in the streets. Firearms were also taxed as a result of government paranoia about the number of 'improper persons' who owned them, and each adult male was required to spend six days per year labouring on the new roads that were being built throughout the island. As unrest began to spread, Tennent was sent to the central regions of the island to try to placate assemblies of discontented townspeople.

The tropical woodlands and hillsides of the North Central Province shelter the ruined cities and religious monuments of the island's ancient civilisations. The Cultural Triangle, as it is now known, is one of the main tourist attractions of the island; access is now simple and the tickets expensive. But when Tennent visited the ruined cities in 1848 they had only been discovered by explorers a few years earlier and were still buried deep in the woodlands, crumbling in the heat and inhabited by snakes. His trail through the ancient cities started in Kandy, heading north to the Buddhist caves in Dambulla and Sigiriya, to the ruined cities of Polonnaruwa and Anuradhapura, and back to Colombo via the Catholic belt of the north-western coast. Following his trail by road would have been very simple, but having spent more hours on Sri Lankan buses than I cared to remember, I decided I would travel by train instead and start the journey in Polonnaruwa.

I had been watching Mr De Silva for some time before I finally spoke to him, whilst we were both waiting for the train to Polonnaruwa in the Fort Station in Colombo. In the cool morning air the station had the smell of the damp stonework, cold metal and stale air which lingers around the footbridges and waiting rooms of railway stations all over the world. Tired women wearing pastel-coloured, polyester saris were wedged together on the narrow wooden benches, with children asleep in their laps, whilst the younger generation, who were commuting to work, fiddled with the name badges pinned to their sari jackets and clicked on their mobile phones.

Mr De Sliva was a short, slight man, with a carefully trimmed, greying moustache and sparse black hair, which had been heavily oiled and scraped over his head. Sitting on his lap was an open laptop case, which had never carried a laptop, but contained instead a Tupperware box of rice and curry, and a polished red apple. His thumb was flicking impatiently through the pages of a small, spiral-bound notebook and he gave the impression he was waiting for something more than the Polonnaruwa train. As we were waiting, a long train drew in to the platform behind us and, as the people on the platform ran towards it in a frenzy, to hurl first their bags and then themselves into the oversold carriages, he left his laptop bag at my feet, meeting my eyes with an urgent nod of 'You won't let anyone steal my lunch, will you?' before disappearing into the crowd. He returned five minutes later, seeming less agitated, and opened up the little notebook he had been nervously thumbing. He turned through the pages, on which lines of letters and numbers were written in a sloping, cursive hand. He took a small gold pen from his shirt pocket, squinting at it as he rotated it to expose the nib and, after printing the date in large letters, wrote 'Class M4 MLW Alco Bombardier Locomotive'. Seeming relieved, he closed his case, put his pen back in his pocket and strolled over to a revolving book stand to look at the multi-coloured puzzle books on display.

The train lines in Sri Lanka were not built until almost a decade after Tennent had returned to England, and the first tracks were laid between Colombo and the coffee plantations in the hill country, to speed up the time it took to transport the coffee beans to the harbour. The villagers who lived along the proposed route of the railway line objected to the *Anguru Kaka Wathura Bibi Duwana Yakada Yaka* ('the coal-eating, water-drinking, sprinting, metal yaks') that would run through their land, but the colonial government ignored their objections and construction of the new railway began in 1858. It took six years for the first section of line to be completed and it was finally opened just before Christmas in 1864 by the heir to the Belgian throne, the Duke of Brabant, who happened to be on holiday in Ceylon at the time.

As the train retreated from the city out into jungle, the sun burned away the morning haze and coloured the muted, grey sky. The people who lived in the precarious, one-roomed brick houses with corrugated-iron roofs alongside the railway line stood by the train tracks, brushing their teeth and dousing their sinewy bodies with water from plastic buckets as the train went by. Solitary monks were sweeping the courtyards of small temples that lurked in the shade of the trees and smiling shrines of the Buddha, wrapped in strings of electric fairy lights, twinkled by the train tracks on the outskirts of villages. When you travel by road, the settlements that have crammed themselves along the roadside and the constant tangle of traffic make Sri Lanka feel like a crowded and overpopulated country. But when the suburbs of Colombo are left behind and you follow the train line as it snakes its way through the open grassland, towards the wooded hills that rise above the paddy fields, the island feels vast and empty.

The train stopped at a small station and six women selling steamed corn on the cob from plastic washing-up bowls jumped onto the train and ran up and down the carriages. As I was looking out of the window at a couple of Buddhist monks in orange robes who were sitting on the platform reading the newspaper, I spotted Mr De Silva, who must have taken a seat in another carriage, buying a plastic cup of milky tea from a man with a large aluminium kettle. As he was rummaging in his pocket for some money, the train started to pull out of the station, and in a panic he ran towards it and jumped into the nearest carriage. He paced up and down the moving train, looking for a spare seat and eventually took one of the few empty spaces opposite me. After looking at me for a few minutes and recognising me from the platform in Colombo, he leaned towards me and asked, 'British?'

I nodded and asked him how long he had been interested in trains.

'I have been riding these railway lines since I was a young boy,' he said, looking out of the window. 'My father worked for the British on the railways and our whole family, three brothers and two sisters, were able to travel for free.'

I had not met many Sri Lankans who were old enough to remember much about the days of the British Empire and I was interested to find out how the British had been regarded. I asked Mr De Silva what his parents' generation, who worked for and alongside the British for many years, had felt about their colonial neighbours.

'Oh my parents loved the British,' said Mr De Silva, with a laugh, 'my father was a very dark man, almost jet black, but he wanted desperately to be an English gentleman. He refused to wear a sarong and always wore a full suit with a little bow tie. He became slightly obsessed by England in general, as a matter of fact, and it caused my mother all sorts of problems.'

'What do you mean?' I asked.

'Well he loved to talk to the British plantation owners about their lives back in their home country and he was fascinated by the British way of life. After years of hearing stories about life in London, he decided he had to go. When we were all still very young children, he sold our family house to a neighbour without telling my mother and left for England on a steamliner in the night. I can't remember anything about it, but he must have been away for over a year. He came back, of course, but I don't think my mother ever forgave him.'

'Presumably your mother wasn't very fond of the British then?'

'Oh no, she was even worse than him. But with her it was the royal family. Her prize possession was a brass tray commemorating the Queen's coronation; it had a picture of a young Queen Elizabeth riding a horse etched on to the surface, and she used to polish it every day.' He looked out of the window and laughed drily. 'They both had such a romantic view of the British. For years they were only exposed to the planters' families who ran the tea plantations and drove around the town in their Bentleys. After independence though, the planters began to leave and the island became the end of the "hippy trail". All these skinny, dirty hippies with long hair, smoking marijuana, used to sail over from India and take the train over to the beaches of the east coast. One day my mother saw a group of them in the town post office and she was distraught. She couldn't believe that the British could sink to such levels of degradation. "They can't be the real British people," she kept saying.'

I asked him whether his parents' regard for the British had been a common thing, or whether most people simply wished the British would leave them to it.

'We weren't like India you must remember,' he pointed out, 'there was no mass popular movement for independence. It was just a few middle-class intellectuals. We didn't really demand it, it was more given to us by the British at the same time that they were getting rid of India. When you look back at it all now, of course, it seems wrong, but at the time, no one knew any better.' He laughed as he looked out of the window at the rural villages flying by. 'The British just thought they were doing us a favour by trying to make us more civilised. Who knows what else we are all doing today that will seem inhumane tomorrow?'

I left the train at Polonnaruwa station, which seemed to have been ignored by the twentieth century. The stationmaster's room was filled with dark wooden furniture, leather-bound ledgers and weighing scales, balanced with hexagonal iron weights, which were still being used to estimate the weight of the parcels that were being wheeled along the platform in wooden barrows. I picked up a tuk-tuk on the road and asked to be taken to one of the town's largest hotels, which lay on the banks of the wide Topa Wewa tank that had once irrigated the town.

When I arrived the place was in chaos. The driveway was being repaved, every window was being cleaned and groups of agitated hotel staff were running frantically around the large dining room, trying to rearrange the hundreds of chairs and tables simultaneously. The receptionists, swaddled tightly in pleated silk saris, were also looking on edge, smiling unconvincingly through their clenched teeth, and as I was handed my key by the manager, he mumbled something apologetic about an impending visit from the president.

When I left my room to go down to breakfast the next morning, I bumped into a moody looking soldier with a rifle across his chest standing in the hallway outside my door. Outside the dining-room windows it was a grey, windy day and the waters of the Topa Wewa tank, which had been calm and still the evening before, were being whipped into white-tipped waves by the strong breeze. Bouncing around on the waves, a small motor boat carrying more military men was making its way across the tank towards the hotel. 'The president and some of the government ministers are going to be arriving very soon,' the receptionist murmured, as he turned from the windows, frowning at the dining-room staff who were busily folding a large pile of napkins into origami shapes, to decorate the rows of tables that had been hastily rearranged the evening before.

'What is the president here for?' I asked.

'I think he's opening a hotel next door and then visiting some development projects in the district,' the receptionist explained. 'Our manager is the brother of one of the government ministers so the president always stays here whenever he is visiting the area. We see him every few months,' he finished flatly, as he looked wearily out at the tank.

I sat down to breakfast in the dining room, which in spite of its careful arrangement and decoration was still swarming with fat black flies, and looked out at the tank, wondering whether I would get a glimpse of the infamous man. The news that the president was arriving had obviously spread to the nearby villages, and families were starting to emerge from the woodland and settle themselves in groups on the grass. The armed soldiers turned away from the tank and positioned themselves several metres away from the villagers, watching them closely, pointing their rifles towards them. The villagers seemed unfazed and continued to chatter to each other and look up at the sky expectantly, ignoring the firearms pointing in their direction.

I was on the way back to my room when I heard a loud juddering in the sky, as two sleek, black helicopters landed on the water's edge outside the restaurant doors. An unfortunate young bride and groom, who had come to the hotel to have their wedding photos taken on the shores of the tank, huddled together as the choppers whipped the air around them and their photographer abandoned them, to try to get a shot of the president. As the helicopter doors opened, the soldiers marched into formation around the portly, moustachioed men who were clambering fatly down from the helicopter and moving across the lawn. I ran back towards the restaurant, but was only just in time to see the back of what looked like the sturdy figure of Mahinda Rajapaksa, with his shock of jet-black hair, strolling into the conference room.

That afternoon I paid my $20 at the entrance to the acres of dry forest that sheltered the scattered remains of Polonnaruwa.

The ancient city was initially established by the Chola dynasty from South India who had ruled the island since the tenth century. When the Sinhalese King, Vijayabahu I, finally chased the Cholas back to the subcontinent in the eleventh century, he kept it as his royal capital, and he and his descendants built a grand city and religious centre that drew traders and devotees from all over the island. I spent the afternoon wandering around the tank, between the weathered pillars engraved with lotus flowers, elephants and mystical dwarves, and the stone Buddhas that had once stood in the ancient temples and palaces. Out of the brittle woodland that surrounded the ruins, broad brick domes topped with tapering spires rose into the sky. These were the dagobas – great mounds of solid masonry which were built to house relics of the Buddha. No scene can be conceived more impressive than this beautiful city must have been in its pristine splendour, wrote Tennent, its stately buildings stretching along the shore of the lake, their guided cupolas reflected on its still expanse and embowered in the dense foliage of the surrounding forests. A group of friendly Buddhist monks from Thailand photographed the ancient stone Buddhas through the lenses of their digital cameras that their vows of poverty had somehow allowed them to acquire. I was followed round the ruins by several hundred local secondary school children, who piled on and off a convoy of buses that drove them through the forest between the sights. The girls were shy and sweet, and strolled hand in hand around the dagobas, dressed in identical white pleated dresses, their long black plaits tied with blue satin ribbons, whilst the cocky young boys jumped over the walls of the ruins and chased each other through the dry grassland. The children had also brought along a small orchestra of musical instruments and, when they had been shepherded back onto the buses by their weary teachers, the convoy disappeared into the trees in a clattering of percussion instruments and squealing of trumpets.

I left Polonnaruwa that afternoon on a filthy government bus travelling west towards Dambulla, a town famous for its cave temples and international cricket stadium. The road ran across wide, flat plains covered with prickly undergrowth and stumpy bushes. Men were working by the side of the road, spreading out ears of grain on woven mats to dry in the sunshine, as they looked up at the shifting clouds, calculating the probability of rain. A heavily pregnant woman, carrying a swollen bump on her spindly frame, clambered onto the bus and sat down next to me, streaming with perspiration and whimpering softly each time the bus lurched over a pothole in the road. Halfway to Dambulla, the road skirted the edge of calm grey expanse of the large tank at Minneriya. It was late afternoon and, as the sun started to drain from the sky, a solitary elephant emerged from the forest trees to drink from the still waters in the cool afternoon air. A couple of kilometres farther along the road, two mahouts straddled a pair of tamed creatures, driving them along the grass verge with bamboo canes.

For most Europeans there is something almost magical and strangely satisfying about the appearance of an elephant in the wild. Tennent, too, developed something of a fascination with Sri Lanka's elephants, and dedicated over a hundred pages of his book to descriptions of the animals' habits and uses on the island, or, in his words, 'their structure and function'. The interest of most of the colonial government men extended only to shooting the wild elephants for sport, and vast numbers of the creatures were killed each year by various majors and captains in an attempt to prove their masculinity. One officer, Major Roberts, according to Tennent's records, killed 1,400 elephants during his time on the island and Major Skinner, who was responsible for building many of the island's roads, killed over 700. As Tennent pointed out, rather scathingly, it required very little skill as a marksman to perforate such a large target and it was mainly due to the help of the fearless Sinhalese men, who acted as beaters and were able to track down the elephants, that the British hunters were so successful.

It came as something of a surprise to the Victorians that the Sinhalese were so fearless when it came to hunting elephants, as it contradicted the (rather dubious) research of George Combe, the father of phrenology, which was circulating at the time. Combe had studied nineteen skulls from Ceylon as part of his new branch of research into the relationship between brain shape and racial traits. The Sinhalese, he deduced, had well filled-up heads in the regions of the brain that he believed to be responsible for benevolence and veneration which, he concluded, explained their devotion to the Buddhist faith. In addition, however, he found that they had over-developed organs of cautiousness and were deficient in the organ of destructiveness which, although it explained their fear of anything to do with demons and devils, did not account for their bravery when it came to elephants.

What particularly irked Tennent about his colleagues' slaughter of these creatures was not just the wanton cruelty and glorification of the whole exercise, but also the wastage of the enormous carcasses, which were left to decompose on the forest floor. In protest, Tennent sampled elephant meat to see if it could be put to good use and reported that, whilst the steak was coarse and tough, the elephant tongue was as delicate as that of an ox, and elephant foot made a palatable soup. Although the trend for elephant meat didn't catch on in the colonial dining rooms of Colombo and Kandy, other people on the island were quick to make use of every part of the elephant's anatomy. The Kaffirs who were attached to the pioneer corps in Kandy would cut out the heart of any elephant that was shot in their vicinity and apparently eat it, as was customary in Africa. The bones were ground and used as manure on the coffee estates, the hair of the tail was made into bracelets and the teeth were crafted into knife handles and ornaments by the Muslims in the south.

However, the live animals were far more important to both the islanders and the British in everyday life. Long before any Europeans set foot in Sri Lanka, the islanders had captured and tamed the elephants for use in the royal pageants of the ancient civilisations, and in the sacred processions of the Buddhist festivals. Even today the peraheras that mark the major events in the Buddhist calendar are led by troops of decorated elephants, and during the rest of the year the unemployed animals are chained up by the ankle in the courtyards of the temples. The islanders had developed a separate caste system for the elephants, according to their physical appearance and character, and only the elephants of the highest caste were attached to the temples. There was even a Sinhalese manual about elephant breeding and management called the *Hastisilpe*, which identified these high-caste elephants as those with 'softness of skin, the red colour of mouth and tongue, the forehead expanded and hollow, the ears large and rectangular, the trunk broad at the root and blotched with pink in front, the eyes bright and kindly... and five nails on each foot, all smooth, polished and round.'

When the Europeans arrived on the island, and began clearing the land for cultivation and building roads and bridges, they too employed the creatures for their strength and intelligence. Having no idea of how to go about catching an elephant, the Europeans were dependent on the skills of the Panickeas – the skilled elephant catchers who lived in the Muslim villages in the north and north-east of the island. These men spent hours creeping through the forests unarmed, tracking the elephants with their sense of smell, and following trails of broken twigs and chewed leaves. When they eventually found one of the animals resting, they would steal up and slip a noose made from buffalo hide around one of its hind legs. Once caught, the elephants were usually trained by Arabs and some of these tamed creatures were then bought by the rajas of India, who sent their vakeels to Ceylon, charged with the difficult task of getting an elephant onto a boat and bringing it home.

As the demand of the Europeans and the Indians for the elephants grew, catching one elephant at a time was not enough and whole herds needed to be caught at once. The Portuguese and the Dutch introduced large-scale elephant hunts that took place several times a year, in which hundreds of villagers were employed to chase herds of elephants into large pens called *corrals*. The technique of capturing a whole herd became known to the British as an 'elephant corral' and Tennent went along to take part in one of these great hunts in 1847. It had been organised by the Department of Civil Engineering, which was running out of elephants at the time, and had chosen a spot for the corral in the central forests of the island on the banks of a river. After several days of travelling on foot with a trail of porters, Tennent, along with various family members of the government officers who had come along to see the spectacle, arrived at the spot where the corral was to take place. During the preceding months, crowds of Sinhalese beaters had been waiting in the jungle, slowly but surely herding the elephants from miles around towards the site of their capture.

Two months had been spent in these preparations, and they had been thus far completed, on the day we arrived and took our places on the stage erected for us, overlooking the entrance to the corral. Close beneath us a group of tame elephants, sent by the temples and chiefs to assist in securing the wild ones, were picketed in the shade, and lazily fanning themselves with leaves... Not a sound was permitted to be made, each person spoke to his neighbour in whispers, and such was the silence observed by the multitude of watchers at their posts, that occasionally we could hear the rustling of the branches as some elephants stripped off their leaves.

Suddenly the signal was made, and the stillness of the forest was broken by the shouts of the guard, the rolling of the drums and tom-toms, the discharge of muskets; and beginning at the most distant side of the area, the elephants were urged forward towards the entrance to the corral... The tumult increased as the terrified rout drew near, swelling now on one side now on the other as the herd in their panic dashed from point to point in their endeavours to force the line, but were instantly driven back by screams, guns, and drums.

Tennent became increasingly fixated with the island's elephants after watching the corral and, in his usual obsessive way, began documenting details of their habits, and collecting reports of their physiology and diagrams of their dissected organs. He was particularly interested in the knee joints of the elephant as for thousands of years there had been a worldwide misconception that the elephant was unable to bend its knees. The Ancient Greek physician and historian Ctesias was apparently responsible for the physiological error, which lies buried somewhere in the work on India he produced in the fifth century BC, and references to the curious knee-less legs of the elephant continued to crop up in works of biology and literature for hundreds of years. Shakespeare mentioned it in *Troilus and Cressida*:

'The elephant hath joints; but none for courtesy:
His legs are legs for necessity, not for flexure.'
As did Donne in his poem *Progress of the Soul*:
'Nature's great masterpiece, an Elephant;
The only harmless great thing...
Yet Nature hath given him no knees to bend:
Himself he up-props, on himself relies...'

When Tennent watched the corral, he noticed that two baby elephants had been captured with the rest of the herd, and ordered that one of the youngsters should be rescued and sent to his house in the capital. His servants became very fond of the little animal and a small shed was erected as its own private quarters, in the grounds of the house.

But his favourite resort was the kitchen, where he received his daily allowance of milk and plantains and picked up several other delicacies besides. He was innocent and playful in the extreme, and when walking in the grounds would trot up to me and twine his little trunk around my arm and coax me to take him to the fruit trees. In the evening, the grass-cutters would now and then indulge him by permitting him to carry home a load of fodder for the horses, on which occasions he assumed an air of gravity that was highly amusing, showing that he was deeply impressed with the importance of the service entrusted to him. Being sometimes permitted to enter the dining-room, and helped to fruit at dessert, he at last learned his way to the side-board; and on more than one occasion having stolen in in the absence of the servants, he made a clear sweep of the wine-glasses and china in his endeavours to reach a basket of oranges. For these and similar pranks we were at last forced to put him away. He was sent as a Government stud, where he was affectionately received and adopted by Siribeddi, and now he takes his turn of public duty in the department of the Commissioner of Roads.

Dambulla had hit the national and international headlines a few weeks earlier, following an incident at one of the local mosques. The mosque had been fire-bombed during the night and 2,000 hard-line Buddhists and Buddhist monks had descended on the mosque, forcing its evacuation and demanding its demolition. The Buddhist mob claimed that the mosque, which had existed since the 1960s, had been built on sacred Buddhist land and was one of seventy-two structures belonging to other religions that they wished to be destroyed, or at least dismantled and relocated to another part of the town. It was not the first time the two religions had clashed; several months earlier, another Buddhist monk had led a group of fanatics to destroy a Muslim shrine in the sacred Buddhist city Anuradhapura, a few kilometres up the road. To the surprise of the international media and the outrage of both the Muslims and the non-lunatic-fringe Buddhists of the country, the Sri Lankan government suggested that it would be best if the Muslims did take their mosque elsewhere.

In the increasingly atheist west, Buddhism is regarded by many as being the most sane and acceptable of the major world religions. There is no requirement to believe in the existence of an omnipotent being with a life story that defies the fundamental laws of biology and physics; meditation is regarded as trendier than prayer; and the serene statues of the smiling Buddha are far less disturbing than images of hell and crucifixion. And there is also a general perception that the enlightened Buddhist monks, who pad barefoot along the pavements of Asia swathed in saffron robes, are never drawn into acts of religious violence like their jihadist or crusader counterparts. It is difficult to see how the Four Noble Truths and the Noble Eightfold Path of the Buddha's teachings could be used as instruments of violence and hatred; but a strange turn of events in the island's history led to the development of a less-than-tolerant form of the religion that still exists in certain communities on the island today.

The Buddhist faith was first introduced to Sri Lanka from India in 246 BC, when the Indian emperor and Buddhist convert

Ashoka sent his son over to the island to convert the Sinhalese. Over the following centuries the island's kings planted bodhi trees, built magnificent temples and supported vast monasteries of *bhikkhus*, who dedicated their time to studying and translating the Buddhist scriptures. By the time European colonisers had spent almost half a millennium seducing the islanders with various forms of Christianity, however, many of the Buddhist shrines had been subsumed by the jungle and most of the *bhikkhus* had abandoned the monasteries and followed the path of the laypeople.

The great revival of Buddhism did not initially come from within the island, but began thousands of miles away in America. Henry Steel Olcott, an American civil war veteran, and Helena Blavatsky, a European aristocrat, were the founding members of the Theosophist Society, an organisation devoted to investigating the occult and the exotic spiritualities and philosophies of the East. The Theosophists were broadly against the teachings and dominance of Christianity and, as far as they were concerned, Ceylon, with its empty temples and alien rituals that had been suppressed by Christian rulers, was ripe for revival. After Olcott had spent several years travelling round the island by ox cart, delivering anti-Christian sermons to the villagers and agitating for Buddhist rights to practise their religion freely, he gained a band of devoted followers, including a young man named Don David Hewavitarne, the son of a wealthy Sinhalese merchant.

Hewavitarne met Olcott when he was sixteen and promptly joined his Buddhist revival movement. He changed his name to Anagarika Dharmapala, meaning 'homeless one', and left his comfortable life with his family to travel with Olcott as his assistant and translator. Unlike Olcott, however, he came to regard the island as the intended home of a pure Sinhalese race, the protectors of Buddhism, who had been polluted over the years by foreigners of Hindu, Muslim and Christian faith. Dharmapala began preaching fiery sermons to spellbound audiences, but his Buddhism was a political, nationalist movement, which cited the ancient Sinhalese legends as evidence that Sri Lanka was the sacred land of the chosen Sinhalese Buddhists. Any other faith, in his opinion, was an unwelcome contamination. Unfortunately Dharmapala became a celebrity and his new form of Buddhism became instilled in the mindset of much of the island's population. Even today, Sri Lanka has a nationalist political party that was founded and led by what a UN spokesman referred to as a group of 'xenophobic monks', who campaign for a Sinhalese, Buddhist state and have made no secret of their hatred of Muslims and Christians. The Sri Lankan president often appears on television and in newspaper photographs flanked by Buddhist monks, and frequently refers to himself as the promoter and protector of the island's Buddhist community. It is also not unheard of for Buddhist monks to endorse medical products and make comments in the media about national affairs.

I spent the evening sitting in the bar of a hotel in Dambulla with a fat family of pasty French tourists who had come to visit the caves, and a solitary Japanese businessman who sat alone at his table, nursing a small bottle of Lion Lager. The teenage boys who were supposed to be running the bar spent most of their time huddled around a television screen, mesmerised by the fuzzy picture of two spandex-clad female wrestlers cage fighting, which was being shown on an American TV channel.

I was reading through some newspaper articles about the incident that had taken place at the mosque, when the manager walked in and, after shooing the boys away from the television set, looked around at the guests apologetically. On his way out of the bar, the manager saw the collection of articles spread out on my table and began to look worried.

'Madam, please let me reassure you that Dambulla is a very safe place for tourists. That demonstration was a freak event, caused by only a few very bad people. You will find most people in Dambulla very friendly, please do not be concerned. Have you visited the caves yet?'

I said that I would probably go to the caves the next day and asked him how most people in Dambulla felt about the incident at the mosque.

'Well you must understand that Dambulla is a place of pilgrimage for Buddhists and some monks feel threatened by other religions. But that is not true Buddhism. I am a Buddhist and I was very upset by what happened there.' The manager sat down on the chair next to me and lowered his voice. 'Sometimes I wonder whether some of these monks actually really understand Buddhism at all. Buddhism is very tolerant of other religions and also teaches that we must not become excessively attached to anything, including pieces of land we believe to be sacred. Some of these monks joined the monasteries as young boys because their parents couldn't afford to feed them and they never received any real education. I think that many of the people who joined the monks in these attacks were just looking for an excuse to be violent. Do you have a laptop with you?' he asked.

'Not with me, why?'

'I wanted to show you a petition on the Internet that Buddhists all over the country are signing to say that we do not support the actions of monks in Dambulla. Buddhists and Muslims have lived in communities all over the island for generations and we want to show them our support. My wife's father was a Tamil and many of her family are Tamils, so we have always found this idea that Sri Lanka is a purely Buddhist land very upsetting.'

He shook his head at the pile of newspapers on the table and peered over my shoulder at the notes I had been taking in my notebook.

'But these are only the bad things about Dambulla that you are reading,' he said brightly, as he picked up my glass. 'You must go to our caves and see the beautiful Dambulla tomorrow.'

The next morning I joined a busload of European tourists and a handful of local Buddhists at the famous cave temples, which were carved into a sloping rock face high above the town. A Sinhalese king had taken refuge in the caves two millennia ago, after he had been driven from his throne in the ancient capital, Anuradhapura, by seven Tamil princes from South India. When his army finally managed to drive the princes back to their homeland, he commemorated his place of refuge by carving the interior of the caves into dark, cold temples. Later kings ordered the walls of the temples to be painted with images of the Buddha, and filled the gloomy caverns with jewelled and gilded statues of the Buddha and the odd Hindu deity. In the past few years the temples have turned into one of the island's most visited tourist attractions, and enormous kitschy statues of the Buddha and plastic figurines of Buddhist monks have been unsympathetically grafted onto the foot of the caves. I sat in the shade of a long-eared gold Buddha who looked over the car park, feeling slightly voyeuristic as I slowly found myself surrounded by local teenagers who had come to nuzzle each other under their umbrellas.

Back at the hotel, the Japanese businessman and the pale French tourists had checked out, and the only other guest beside myself was a middle-aged English sci-fi enthusiast, who spent the afternoon sitting in the shady garden, wearing a Panama hat and reading *The Fountains of Paradise* by Arthur C. Clarke. The book was not an entirely obscure choice, as its setting was based on the Sigiriya rock, a several-hundred-foot-high boulder that had once formed an inaccessible fort, built by a fifth-century king who had obtained the throne by murdering his father.

When Tennent visited the Sigiriya rock in 1848, his party stumbled upon a group of professional devil dancers performing a ceremony to try to cure a local patient who was dying nearby. His sketch of the dancers showed black figures, naked except for a loincloth, with knee-length braids of hair that swung about their dancing bodies. 'It is difficult to imagine anything more demoniac than the aspect, movements and noises of these wild creatures; their faces distorted with exertion and excitement; and their hair in tangled ropes, tossed in all directions as they swung round in mad contortions,' he wrote.

The sun was lowering itself down onto the horizon as the bus dropped me outside the Sacred City at the centre of Anuradhapura. The road had narrowed to little more than a lane, which meandered through grassy parkland strewn with the stumps of crumbling pillars. The domes and spires of the enormous, white-and-red-brick dagobas of the ancient city cast long shadows in late-afternoon sunshine, their darkening forms looking like large, upside down handbells planted amongst the trees. Early evening was always my favourite time in these ruins, when the crowds of devotees and hawkers had departed, and the gentle calm of the twilight surrounded the mystical monuments. Sturdy and placid, they had watched centuries of invaders come and go, reassuring symbols of resilience on a landscape that had witnessed so much change.

Tennent had been fascinated by the structure of the dagobas, the largest in Anuradhapura being 110 m in diameter and 76 m in height.

Even with the facilities which modern invention supplies for economising labour, the building of such a mass would at present occupy five hundred brick layers from six to seven years, and would involve an expenditure of at least a million sterling. The materials are sufficient to raise eight thousand houses, each with twenty feet frontage, and these would form thirty streets half-a-mile in length. They would construct a town the size of Ipswich or Coventry; they would line an ordinary railway tunnel twenty miles long, or form a wall one foot in thickness and ten feet in height, reaching from London to Edinburgh.

Anuradhapura was the capital of the ancient Sinhalese kingdom of Rajarata from 377 BC, a commercial centre whose trade extended to Rome, and was the home of some of the greatest engineers and Buddhist scholars of its time. The Indian emperor Ashoka sent his daughter to Anuradhapura with a sapling from the bodhi tree in Bodh Gaya, under which the Buddha was enlightened, to be planted at the heart of the city amongst its many monasteries. The engineers of Anuradhapura constructed the enormous tanks, whose still bodies of water dotted the dry landscape and irrigated the ancient kingdom. I followed the lane around the edge of the vast, unmoving surface of the Tissa Wewa tank. Leading down to the water's edge was a wide flight of stone steps, similar to those that descend to the ghats in Varanasi in northern India. A group of children were sitting at the foot of the steps, watching their fathers standing in the shallows, with their sarongs pulled up over their knees, scrubbing their shining torsos in the murky water. I had visited Anuradhapura a year earlier and had quickly fallen in love with the tranquil atmosphere that pervaded the ancient city, created by its still expanses of water and the gentle curves of its weathered monuments. Happy as I was to be back, my legs and back were sore from the hours I had spent squashed into the corner of the crowded bus, and I was desperate to get into a shower, to wash away the grime and sweat from the journey. Luckily, near to the banks of the tank was an old colonial rest house that I had discovered on my first trip. I hadn't made a booking but when I inquired whether there was a room available the tiny man behind the reception desk beamed. 'You are very lucky, madam. Only one room left. But

I think you have been here! It is same room! You are teacher, no?' I had visited the hotel six months earlier and, judging from the reaction of the selection of young male staff who were wandering around in white shirts and white sarongs, repeat visits were very rare. A waiter who had been loitering in the shade of the dining room rushed out and pumped my hand enthusiastically. 'Great to see you once again, madam!' The place was stuck in a musty colonial time warp of frayed velvet furniture and mildewed sepia photographs showing the ancient monuments in years gone by. A threadbare red chaise longue and heavy ebony desks sat in the reception hall, and various items from the turn of the century, including a gramophone, an early-twentieth-century telephone with a long stand and small conical mouthpiece, and a two-wheeled carriage lacking a horse, cluttered up the dark dining room.

'You have the same room again, madam! Come!' giggled a teenage boy who was wearing a pair of circular, owlish glasses, which began to slide down his nose, as he ignored the straps of my rucksack and hugged it enthusiastically to his chest as he led me to my room.

It was a small room under the eaves of the sloping terracotta veranda roof, which looked out over the hotel's sparse, circular lawn. After a long shower, during which a small frog crawled out of the plughole and hopped about in the bottom of bathtub, I sat under the veranda and watched the other guests, who were all taking part in a Sri Lankan wedding and spent most of the evening posing for photographs in front of the pieces of colonial memorabilia. A large, milky moon hung low in the sky and bathed the waters of the tank in a cool, silver light.

I had timed my visit to Anuradhapura to coincide with the full moon that was scheduled to illuminate the city the following night. The day of the full moon is sacred to Buddhists, as it was under a full moon that the Buddha was allegedly born, renounced the world, became enlightened and also reached Nirvana. These sacred days are known in Sri Lanka as Poya days, during which the local Buddhists are encouraged to fast, abstain from consuming alcohol or meat, and take offerings to the village temple. A few weeks earlier I had bought a small, leather-bound book in Colombo, which was simply entitled *Poya Days* and had been written in 1924 by a lady called Marie Musaeus Higgins. Higgins had lived in Ceylon with her husband for several decades, and over the years she devoted a significant amount of her time to the study of the Buddhist philosophy and practices on the island. Nowadays, every village has one, if not several, Buddhist temples, and there is a plethora of Buddhist literature and Buddhist education centres in the island's Sinhalese towns. When Higgins lived in Ceylon, however, she became concerned that the island's young population, many of whom were being educated in the colonial, English-speaking, Christian schools, had very little knowledge or understanding of their Buddhist heritage. The old, foggy photograph of Higgins showed a plump, round-faced lady in her fifties sitting in an armchair, wearing a long-sleeved, lace-cuffed blouse with a wide lace collar and white, wispy hair, piled up on the top of her head. It was hard to imagine her anywhere other than a European drawing room, let alone conversing with the Buddhist monks and scholars, who she claimed she consulted at length, to write her little volume that was dedicated to 'the Buddhist youth in the East and West', and which she hoped would satiate a long-felt want, and reach those educated in English and not much acquainted with their religion and its history.

On the night of the Poya, Higgins explained, 'The four Deva guardians from the four corners of the earth, journey over the earth searching for people who are practising merits and demerits. These four Deva guardians record these merits in their golden book and the demerits in their black book. Later in the same day, the guardians meet with the king of the Devas and read out the names that have been recorded in the black and golden books. The Devas assembled bow assent to the meritorious deeds and their faces become sad when the demerits are read from the black book.'

The next day was the April Poya day, known as Bak Poya, which commemorates the second visit of the Buddha to Sri Lanka. According to the Sri Lankan chronicle, the *Dipavamsa*, there once existed in Sri Lanka three kingdoms of Nagas – magical beings more powerful than men, who could take the form of either a king cobra or a human. Two of these kingdoms lived on the island whereas the third kingdom of Nagas lived below the sea, where they glided through gardens of coral and sea anemones. On the new moon of April, in the fifth year of his Buddhahood, the Buddha looked across the ocean from his home in India and saw that a great war was brewing between two of the Naga kingdoms. With the aid of a divine parasol, formed from the branches of the tree under which he was wont to meditate, the Buddha appeared in the air over the Nagas and dazzled them with colourful rays of light. Next, he produced a torrential thunderstorm, which reduced the warring Nagas to a gibbering wreck as they dropped their weapons to the ground.

When the darkness had cleared and the Buddha shone upon them once again, the Nagas lifted their eyes to the Buddha and began to worship him.

I was woken early the next morning by a high-pitched squawking outside the door of my bedroom and the sound of something moving the heavy wooden furniture about on the veranda. When I cautiously opened the shutters and looked outside, a large monkey was standing upright on its back legs, baring its teeth at a few smaller monkeys who were cowering behind a wooden chair. The owner of the hotel had admonished me the previous afternoon for carelessly leaving my cardigan and sandals on my chair whilst I left the veranda to fetch something from my room. 'The monkeys here are very bad monkeys, madam. They will be stealing your things from your chair. If you leave your bedroom door open they will just walk in and take anything. Last week, one lady was being very sad because they stole her camera and smashed it on the steps,' he finished, giving the monkeys who were jumping around on the grass a murderous look.

After breakfast, I walked along the narrow winding road from the hotel towards the Sacred City at the heart of Anuradhapura. The quiet lanes and ruined monuments that had been so peaceful in the mellow evening light had been transformed into a brightly coloured chaos of people and vehicles, burning under the bright morning sun. The grass verges of the lanes had disappeared under a tangled jam of parked tuk-tuks, vans and the battered intercity buses that had carried pilgrims through the night from distant parts of the island to observe the Poya under the city's ancient bodhi tree. The pilgrims were all dressed in white; the women swathed in white saris, the little girls in frilly white frocks, and the men in white shirts and plain white cotton sarongs. Some of the pilgrims were already weaving their way towards the temples through the vehicles, whilst others sat in groups on picnic rugs under the trees. As far as I could see in every direction the landscape was dotted with moving white figures, all heading towards the broad white dome of the Ruwanweli Dagoba, which dominated the horizon. I joined the throngs of pilgrims and together we fought our way through the crowds of hawkers, who were haranguing and pestering anyone and everyone with small wooden elephants, corn on the cob, ice cream, soft drinks and plastic whistles, to the 'Sacred Precinct'. A number of the pilgrims had decided to take a shortcut and little old ladies were trying to throw themselves over the wall that surrounded the dagoba, whilst others tried to squeeze their frail bodies through impossibly small gaps between the iron girders of the closed gates.

I took my shoes off and, pushed along by a wave of white-clad devotees, moved through the entrance and up a flight of stone steps, to the sprawling stone platform from which the large white dome rose into the cloudless blue sky. Men and women sat together on blankets in groups with their eyes collectively raised to its spire. Some were holding small leaflets and chanting gently in unison whilst others were sitting in silent contemplation. The dagoba was about 300 m in circumference and dotted around its base were small stone shrines holding statues of the Buddha. Smaller statues of the Buddha sat in little glass cases, smiling down at the devotees. The pilgrims circled the dome, carrying baskets of fruit and bunches of purple lotus flowers, which they placed at the feet of the Buddha, before putting their palms together and touching their hands to their foreheads.

I sat down in the shade and watched the stream of pilgrims come and go. A group of Buddhist monks in orange robes climbed up the steps and started to weave their way through the groups of pilgrims, who dropped to the ground at their feet and touched their heads to the floor, like Muslims facing Mecca. Further around the dome, a man in brick-red cotton pyjamas, with a ponytail of grey, matted hair, was giving an impassioned sermon to a group of wizened old ladies, who gazed passively through him into the distance.

I left and joined the long procession of pilgrims moving along the paved walkway to the city's sacred bodhi tree. They were barefoot, with their shoes tucked under their arms, the families walking hand in hand, smiling and chattering happily. I fell into step alongside a dumpy Sri Lankan girl, who had a long plait of fuzzy black hair that hung down over her round bottom and swung against the backs of her thighs as she walked. Like me she was on her own and was looking for someone to talk to. She was a local Buddhist girl called Inoka and her large, sad eyes, were so dark that they were almost black. 'Aren't you lonely?' she asked me, when I told her that I was travelling alone without a husband. 'Aren't you scared?'

Her husband worked in Trincomalee on the east coast and was often away. She didn't feel safe on her own. 'The men here, they are bad,' she said. 'I don't like being on my own. They look at you and sometimes they shout and follow you.' I knew exactly what she meant; I was often stared and shouted at by Sri Lankan men on the streets, but had always assumed that I was particularly targeted because of my pale skin.

The ancient bodhi tree, with its sprawling, gnarled branches and golden, heart-shaped leaves, stood at the centre of a courtyard, surrounded by a white wall topped with gold railings, which had been draped with bunting made from pieces of striped red, blue, yellow, white and orange silk, in the design of the Buddhist flag. The pilgrims were sitting under the branches of the tree, looking up at the sky through the fragile leaves. Inoka and I had both bought bunches of purple lotus flowers from one of the stalls on the road and she showed me how to snap off the stems before we placed them on an altar under the braches. The flowers would soon fade, she said, and this represented the impermanence of all worldly things. We sat down with the pilgrims in the sunny courtyard, and Inoka closed her eyes and gently began to murmur. She ran her hands through the sandy ground and slowly sifted the grains of sand through her fingers. She turned her palms over and showed me the sand that was caught under her fingernails. According to an old Buddhist parable, the grains of sand caught under one's fingernails represent the few lucky beings who are reincarnated as humans, whereas all the grains of sand in the rest of the world represent the beings who are reincarnated as lower forms of life. An old lady came and sat down next to us and, removing a prosthetic leg, laid it in front of her and started to massage her swollen amputated limb.

The sun was high in the sky when we left the Sacred Precinct and Inoka insisted on buying us both a king coconut from one of the hawkers. We sat on the grass under a tree and she continued to tell me about her life. She was much older than I had thought, her soft pudgy features showing almost no signs of her forty years, and, unusually for a married woman of her age, she didn't have any children. She spoke about her husband, who she proudly said does not drink and spend all their money on alcohol like many of her friends' husbands. He spent many months away from home, however, and she often felt lonely. She made what little money she could by teaching traditional Sinhalese dancing to children at a local dance school, but was desperate to leave Sri Lanka. Like many Sri Lankans I had spoken to, she was convinced that the world beyond the island was a utopia that had the capacity to make her infinitely happier. When she was young her mother had spent many years away from home, working as a maid for an English family in Dubai. 'Can you get me a visa for England?' she asked. 'I could come and work as a maid in your father's house.' I tried to explain that we didn't have maids any more in England and, unfortunately for her, the British government was doing everything it could to keep foreigners out of the country. I could see that she thought I was lying. We talked for the rest of the afternoon and, as the sun fell from the sky, her loneliness became more palpable. Her father had died from diabetes, the most common disease in Sri Lanka, and her brother had been shut away in a psychiatric hospital far away in Unawatuna, a small coastal town on the south-west coast. She had a sister, who lived close by, but her brother-in-law was an abusive drunk and Inoka tried to avoid spending much time with them. She asked me whether husbands in England were all drunks and whether they beat their wives, as she claimed many did on the island. She had a low opinion of men, but it was fatalistic and disappointed, not the angered bitterness I would have expected. We left the ruins together at dusk and said goodbye at a parting of two narrow lanes. When she asked for my phone number, she began to cry. Sometimes I still get phone calls from Inoka, late at night, asking if I am going to go back to Anuradhapura.

Early the next afternoon at the hotel, I met a middle-aged English couple, Jack and Marion, as they were trying to move the heavy wooden furniture on the veranda out of the sunshine. They wore the middle-class-in-the-tropics uniform of matching hiking sandals, lightweight, crease-proof, drip-dry shirts and knee-length beige shorts with detachable trouser bottoms. The triangles of skin exposed at the necks of their shirts had turned pink in spite of their factor-40 Soltan suncream (two-for-one on offer from Boots) and their ankles were dotted with puffy red mosquito bites, in spite of the '50 per cent-DEET insect repellent'. They sank into the rush-bottomed chairs, and looked around with frowns of fraying tolerance and repressed frustration for a waiter who was nowhere to be seen.

'I've had enough,' said Jack, closing his eyes and dropping David Starkey's *Crown and Country: A History of England Through the Monarchy* to the floor. 'I told you that you should have had more for lunch,' he said wearily to Marion.

Marion sighed lightly, with the acceptance that comes with a marriage that has made it through the silver wedding anniversary, and went in search of a waiter.

She returned a few minutes later with a leaflet, perched on the armrest of her chair, and tapped Jack on the arm.

'The waiter says they can make us an egg sandwich, which shouldn't upset your stomach, and he has told us he can arrange for a tuk-tuk to take us to Mihintale this evening.'

Jack looked slightly pained at the thought.

Mihintale was a small village a few kilometres away where, according to the Sri Lankan legend, Buddhism was first introduced to the island in the third century BC by Mahinda, the son of the devoted Indian emperor Ashoka, who sent him to Sri Lanka to convert the island's population. Mahinda is said to have preached to the island's king, Devanampiya Tissa, on a hilltop which became known as Mihintale, meaning 'Mahinda's Hill', whereupon the king was promptly converted and went on to encourage the conversion of the rest of the population. Tennent had visited Mihintale on his way to Anuradhapura in 1848, so I introduced myself to Marion and asked her whether she had been told how long the journey would take.

'Why don't you come with me?' she suggested brightly, 'and we can leave Jack here. He has had the most terrible diarrhoea ever since we arrived and may be too weak to climb the hill. I don't think he is very interested anyway,' she said with a sigh, as she gazed at her husband, who had slumped into the seat of his chair.

At the mention of his feebleness, Jack suddenly woke up and spluttered that he was feeling fine and the three of us would go to Mihintale together, as long as the egg sandwich, which was yet to appear, did not vex his troubled gut.

Tennent compared the 12-km road between Anuradhapura and Mihintale to the Appian Way between Rome and Brindisi, 'the Via Sacra of the Buddhist hierarchy, along which they conducted processions led by their sovereigns'. Jack, Marion and I travelled along the road together in a tuk-tuk, but it was not an enjoyable experience. Parts of the road were being resurfaced and we spent long periods of time stationary, sitting in the grit and dust being thrown into the air by teenage boys driving large industrial diggers. Jack developed stomach cramps almost as soon as we left the hotel and spent the journey contorting his body in an attempt to find comfortable relief. Marion tried to read the guidebook, but soon began to feel sick from the bumps in the road, quietly slipped it back into her bag and turned her attention to a diligent routine of hydration, in which Jack stubbornly refused to join her, in spite of her gentle, repeated warnings about the dangers of dehydration.

We were greeted at Mihintale by a corpulent guide wearing a gold chain and rubber flip-flops, who was sitting on the sprawling roots of an ancient tree, making patterns in the fallen leaves with the sharp end of a red golf umbrella. He led us through the red-brick ruins of the monastery, which bore tenth-century inscriptions of the rules the monks had to abide by, and through a series of natural caves in the hillside, where the monks would have slept and meditated. He had an obsessive recall of facts and figures relating to the specific age and dimensions of each section of the ruins, and his relentless commentary drained the place of much of its beauty and mystery. Marion keenly absorbed the facts, cross-referencing them with those printed in the pages of her Lonely Planet guidebook. A long flight of stone steps led up towards a white dagoba and we joined the trails of Sri Lankan pilgrims who were clambering their way to the top. At the top of the stone steps was a large clearing of bare, red earth shaded by slender palm trees. Three further flights of stone stairs led higher; one up to a large white, seated Buddha, the second up to the dagoba and the third spiralled up the rock face of an enormous boulder to a vantage point at the summit.

'Very beautiful view, madam,' said our guide, pointing to the group of people who had assembled at the top and were taking photographs of the surrounding plain.

Marion looked uncertainly at her hiking sandals and wistfully up at the rock. She lowered her eyes and looked slowly round to Jack.

'Absolutely not, no way,' he said with a hint of panic. 'Look at them, they're going to break their necks,' he snorted, pointing to a group of pilgrims who were sliding their way over the boulder's polished surface, back down to the ground.

'Will you come with me?' asked Marion shyly.

We followed a few pilgrims who were climbing up in their bare feet, clinging to the rock with their toes as they hauled themselves up a single metal hand rail. When a group going up met a group coming down, one group had to press themselves against the hand rail and help the others as they skidded past. Frail, toothless old ladies clambered up and down the rock face, the liberal ones hitching their saris up above their knees, whilst the more modest ladies battled with restrictive skirts which kept getting tangled around their ankles. European health-and-safety inspectors would have shut the place down. Marion pulled herself up the final few steps and helped me up to the platform at the top of the boulder. Panting and laughing, we looked out at the horizon, over the patchwork of paddy fields. Jack waved up to us from the foot of the large white seated Buddha on the red earth below and, seeming to have recovered some good humour, waggled his camera at us and took a photograph. As the pilgrims came and went, dusk began to fall over the gentle hillocks, and the large ancient tanks, choked with lotus flowers, darkened in the twilight, merging with the deep-green checkerboard of the land.

Chapter Ten

ALONG THE CATHOLIC BELT AND BACK TO COLOMBO

I had passed through Puttalam a number of times in the previous year and it had quickly become my least-favourite town on the island. This was probably unfair as it was no different from any of the other dusty towns that sit by the sea on the edge of the dry zone. But then, that was part of the problem. The place was so generic and I had been travelling for such a long time that all the unexceptional Sri Lankan towns were starting to merge into one. It was now late April and, as the heat and humidity were reaching their yearly peak, the long uncomfortable journeys on crowded buses had begun to lose the allure of adventure and had become draining. As my energy and motivation were at an all-time low, I had stopped noticing their differences and was sensitive only to their common, charmless features. I saw the lopsided buses and filth-excreting trucks, the street stalls of lurid plastic toys and fake Diesel rucksacks, the peeling plaster, the cracked windows, the knots of electric cable, the red dust, and the pock-marked Muslim women sweltering in the heat under their black hijab whilst their husbands strolled along in shorts and sandals. My last trip to Puttalam had been pretty grim too and that didn't help either. It had been hard to find anywhere to stay, and I had asked for directions to a guesthouse from a tuk-tuk driver who had decided to follow me and spent the rest of the night hanging around outside the hotel, throwing stones at my window and making lewd propositions. Going to a tuk-tuk driver for directions had been asking for it, said the owner of the guesthouse snootily, when he had finally chased the boy away at midnight. What he had to be snooty about I was not quite sure, as there had been bloodstains on the sheets, cigarette butts in the sink and the stale rice had tasted of wet dog. I was not happy to be back.

Luckily, all I had to do in Puttalam was change buses and I was able to get straight onto one heading for Kalpitiya, the small town at the end of a narrow spit of land surrounded by a lagoon. As I sat waiting for the bus to depart, a long-haired beggar with legs so limp and withered from polio that he had given up on them and thrown them over his shoulders, pulled himself up the steps of the bus with his arms. With his feet sticking up behind his head, he had been moving his way through the bus station on his bottom, walking himself along on his hands. He settled himself halfway along the aisle of the bus and, cocking his head to one side, began to sing softly to the passengers in a deep, melodic voice. When he had finished, he swung his upper body up and down the aisle of the bus, reaching up to the passengers to collect money in his cupped hand. As he came to leave the bus, the driver and his mate lifted him down onto the ground. They exchanged a few jokey words with the beggar, who laughed and waved to them as the bus drove off, leaving him sitting alone on the tarmac.

It was market day in Puttalam and, as the bus made its way southwards along the coastal road, women jumped on from the roadside clutching rubber baskets of fruit, vegetables and rice. Puttalam produces most of the island's salt and the salt flats – large, square pools of grey water bordered by raised ridges of earth – were smooth and glassy in the sunshine. When Tennent passed through Puttalam, salt purification was already taking place and, according to the Moorish historian and traveller Ibn Battuta, it had been the main source of employment when he visited Puttalam in the early fourteenth century.

The bus turned off the main road heading towards Kalpitiya, passing more salt pans and a few stationary wind turbines. The isthmus was a narrow spit of land jutting out into the sea, surrounded by the lagoon and coconut trees. A few palm-thatched huts perched on the edge of the land, in amongst the palms, their owners leaning against the wooden-slatted walls and staring out over the lilac water of the lagoon that gently lapped at their land. Men were dozing by the roadside under the wide brims of straw hats, next to piles of bulbous, orange king coconuts. Elderly men on bicycles cycled slowly along the road with large piles of dried coconut fronds stacked up behind their saddles, to sell to the people of the isthmus for fire wood. As the bus left the mainland behind, it felt as if we were driving towards some distant point isolated in the middle of the ocean.

When the Portuguese colonised the island in the sixteenth century they were particularly successful in converting the inhabitants of Kalpitiya and the north-west region of the mainland to Catholicism. The white statues of the Buddha had now disappeared again and, instead, large glass cases stood by the side of the road holding pastel-coloured statues of the Virgin Mary and brown-robed saints, holding the baby Jesus. There were also several curiously effeminate statues of the crucified Christ, who had somehow escaped from his cross and was standing on the roadside, pulling open his shirt and provocatively thrusting forward his chest to the passing vehicles to expose gaping wounds, dripping with cerise blood. Although there didn't seem to be many people living on the isthmus, huge neo-baroque catholic churches with twin bell towers and pale-pink and butter-yellow facades towered over the tiny, flimsy settlements.

I got off the bus halfway along the peninsula at a small village and waited by the side of the road for a tuk-tuk to drive past. I was on my way to one of the newly opened boutique hotels that had recently sprung up on the isthmus. Although their websites made them all look equally appealing, I had selected the one that was rumoured to be owned by Glen Terry, a blues guitarist, whose concerts in Colombo drew large crowds every year. I sat on my backpack by the road and watched the old, bow-legged men cycling their bundles of firewood between the houses. I was picked up a while later by a green tuk-tuk, which drove me along a track in the sand that wound through a small collection of huts. Old women were hunched under twisted frangipani trees, which were somehow managing to grow in drifts of golden sand, washing their pots and pans by scraping at the metal with their fingers and splashing them with a few precious drops of water, whilst their husbands sat by on their haunches, staring out to sea. A little beyond the settlement, the tuk-tuk swung round a bend and into the grounds of a large, white villa, set a few metres back from the beach, next to a turquoise infinity pool. As I got out, I heard footsteps behind me and a plummy English male voice said, 'You must be Cherry. It's so nice to meet you darling! Welcome.'

Born in Mysore in India, to Indian, anglophile parents called Daphne and Basil, Glen Terry spoke with an accent and had mannerisms as English as his name, yet I discovered later, to my surprise, he had never lived in the UK. After escaping from the Indian army by being confined to a psychiatric hospital – 'nothing serious, just neurosis' – he crossed the border into Nepal with a few rupees in his pocket and lived by the monkey temple in Kathmandu, where he played Bob Marley numbers on his guitar to entertain the resident sadhus. Somehow this led to a marriage to an Australian diplomat, a music career, a divorce and the decision to settle in this remote part of the island in a collection of architect-designed villas on the beach. He was short and slight, with the careful, self-possessed movements of someone who had never struggled with an adolescent growth spurt. He had a polished, closely shaved head and bright, dark eyes that asserted confidently that you knew what he was talking about.

A servant led me to one of the spacious, whitewashed rooms in the villa that had a deep, sunken bathtub at its centre and was decorated with large, abstract canvases and antique furniture. The room was cool and smelled of damp concrete, so I opened the wooden shutters to let in the late afternoon sunshine and the salty sea breeze. Through the window I could see Glen, sitting on a wooden swing that he had suspended from the branches of a sturdy frangipani tree, swinging gently back and forth with his ankles neatly crossed, as he clicked on his BlackBerry. He wore a pink polo shirt, knee-length checked shorts and the kind of sports socks that are carefully designed to be only just visible above the top of your trainers. As I walked out of my room, Glen bounced onto his toes from the swing and walked towards me through the sand.

'Darling, there's going to be a glorious sunset,' he oozed, pointing to the beach that lay beyond the gardens of the villa. 'You must watch it and then you should come to my villa for cocktails. I have friends arriving from Colombo any minute now!'

A single fisherman was far out on the waves, in a small, flat-topped canoe, which he balanced and steered with a long bamboo pole. A few fishermen with larger boats were sitting in the late-afternoon sunshine mending their nets, whilst their children splashed around at the water's edge. It was a Saturday evening and some of the families from the village had come down to the beach to sit together on the sand and watch the sun set over the sea. Small crabs were skittering on the areas of flat, hard sand that had been smoothed and compressed by the rhythm of the waves. They had dug little burrows, deep into the damp sand, which formed pores that fizzed and bubbled when the waves receded back down the shore. Glen wandered out onto the beach, talking into a laptop, which he turned to the horizon so the person he was Skyping could see the orange ball of the sun falling from the violet sky.

When I emerged from my aesthetically pleasing room later that evening, after soaking in my sunken bathtub, a party of people had assembled around a table outside Glen's villa. A beautiful, willowy French girl in her twenties, called Pauline, with long, brown, L'Oreal hair and pale skin, was perched on the knee of a good-looking Sri Lankan man called Canishka, who looked about thirty but, it transpired, was in fact forty-five. Sitting next to them was a sturdy Spanish woman called Sylvia, who was in her thirties and wore heavy silver jewellery and a lot of smudgy black eye make-up that made her look like she was suffering from sleep deprivation. Glen was reclining on a cushioned banquette in the corner of the veranda, smoking idly from a Turkish hokum, with a glass of neat vodka in his hand. The two girls were both working for travel companies, organising package holidays in the island's resorts, and lived very near to my house in Colombo. When I asked Canishka what he did for a living, he answered, in a soft, Australian drawl, that he 'came over regularly to do business'.

'You all need drinks,' announced Glen sleepily from his reclining position in the corner. 'Somebody throw me the horn.' Sitting on the table was an old-fashioned bicycle horn with a steel trumpet, which Glen held above his head and proceeded to honk repeatedly by pumping its black rubber air-filled ball. A curly-haired young man in T-shirt and shorts hurled himself out of a small outhouse in the corner of the garden, where Glen's house staff lived, and came running over. When Glen had ordered the boy to squeeze a jugful of lime juice, and find some bottles of gin and rum, the boy turned around and ran off into the darkness towards the kitchen. Sylvia rolled a fat cigarette and began to drag on it lazily, looking up into the night sky. When she realised she did not have an ashtray, the horn was honked again and this time a young girl hurried from the outhouse and arrived, panting on the veranda, to be sent in search of a suitable ash depository.

We sat around the table making awkwardly polite small talk until the drinks arrived and lubricated the conversation. Canishka started to tell me about his latest business project in Sri Lanka – a bid for his engineering company to complete the final stretch of the Southern Expressway; the famous alternative to the Galle Road that was supposedly lurking inland, deep in the jungle, still waiting to be unveiled any day now. The final stretch, which was yet to be started, would run south of Galle, deep into the Sinhalese heartland to Hambantota, the birthplace of president Mahinda Rajapaksa. 'It's not been an easy bid for us,' Canishka explained, as he waved away Sylvia's offer of a cigarette and reached across the table to pour more lime juice into an angular, blue glass of rum. 'I'm having to compete with companies that are owned by the relatives of government ministers and, against them, I just don't have a chance.' He sighed and shrugged his shoulders. 'My engineers are really experienced, really skilled at this kind of thing, but that's just how it is here – family comes first.'

Whilst Canishka continued to talk about his investment plans in Sri Lanka, Pauline, not feeling that she was receiving enough attention, began to provocatively remove her clothes until she revealed a small bikini. Swaying her hips, she walked slowly away from the table, over to Glen's swimming pool and slid her toned body carefully into the water. She returned a few minutes later in her wet, clinging bikini, with her bottom half wrapped in a towel, and perched herself on Canishka's lap. Canishka continued the conversation he was having with Sylvia about a mutual friend of theirs in Colombo, absent-mindedly toying with the strings of Pauline's bikini and lightly flicking her wet hair. As Pauline continued to drink she became more and more unstable, wrapping her arms around Canishka's neck and pulling his face to her chest as she tried to steady herself. I was surprised when Canishka casually mentioned that he had four children, which he clarified by glancing nonchalantly at Pauline and explaining, 'Not with her, of course, with my wife who's back at home with them in Melbourne.'

As the evening wore on, Glen seemed to wake up and got off his banquette to join us at the table. He was a warm and generous host, attentive to the needs of his guests and, as he reclined in his chair with his arms folded behind his head, he began reciting stories from the more bizarre episodes of his unusual life. He drifted into his villa, returning with his guitar, and started to strum a boogie-woogie rhythm over which he sang lyrics of his life in India and how he came to be thrown out of his parents' home, before he joined the army. His playing was as relaxed as it was skilful and he sang his moving lyrics in a smooth, mellow voice. 'You know Cherry,' he exclaimed through the applause as he put his guitar down, 'you should stop writing about Sri Lanka and write my story instead. It would blow your mind!'

We were still listening to Glen's strumming at midnight, when there was a screech of brakes and the garden was briefly illuminated by the headlights of a Land Rover. Inside the Land Rover were Ravi and Chubby, friends of Glen's from Colombo, who had driven up the coast to drink and smoke the night away with Glen at his villa. Ravi was in his fifties and had a head of thick, dark, curly hair that was flecked with grey. Although his body looked lean and healthy, the whites of his eyes were yellowed and bloodshot, and his pupils had the frozen diameter of someone who needed a profound change of lifestyle. Chubby was slightly younger and, with his round, boyish face and soft snub nose, it was a name that suited him. After Glen had pumped his horn several times and sent his house staff running over the grounds to fetch more food and drink, Chubby, who had taken a seat at the table and drained a glass of whisky, launched into a tale about his daughter, who had just come home to Sri Lanka after finishing her master's degree in law in America.

'So, get this, my daughter comes back and she says, "Dad, I'm really worried about you, I really think you need to find someone to look after you." It's cute – she's worried that I can't cope on my own now that I have left her mum.'

'And did you show her the picture of your new girlfriend?' Ravi asked him as he pulled up a chair for himself.

'Of course!' Chubby replied with a smirk. An explosion of laugher erupted round the table. Canishka leaned over to me and whispered that Chubby's new girlfriend was twenty years old – thirty years younger than Chubby.

'But she is OK with it,' said Chubby sincerely as he looked with wide eyes into the faces of his drunk friends around the table. 'She says, "Daddy, if you are happy so am I." She's cool with the fact that her stepmum could be younger than her. She really is.' He genuinely seemed to believe it.

Canishka leaned over to me again. 'He's OK really, but you should have met him ten years ago. He used to own all the casinos in Colombo, and man, people were scared of this guy. If you messed with him then, whoa… But he's softened up now. He sold the casinos and he's gone into hotels, haven't you?'

'Yeah,' said Chubby vaguely, 'I'm building one in Trincomalee, one on Delft, the one down south is going to open soon and I think... I'm sure I've bought some more land somewhere else,' he said frowning, trying to remember where it was.

The night turned into the early morning, the conversation became incoherent and, as the guests all honked away on the horn, the house staff began to look limp and exhausted. A sound system was set up under the stars and they began to stagger around to Bob Marley. I slipped away to bed. Walking towards my room, past the outhouse, I saw one of the young Sri Lankan boys waiting outside its back door, slumped in a plastic chair, asleep, with one ear cocked to the veranda, waiting for the honk of the bicycle horn.

When I left the villa early the next morning, Glen's other guests, in spite of their hangovers, had actually risen earlier than me and gone out in a fishing boat to try to spot some blue whales. They had invited me to go with them but, tempting as it had been, I was in a rush to get back to Colombo for the Vesak celebrations, the most important Poya of the island's calendar, which would be starting in a few days' time. I debated spending the morning by Glen's infinity pool and heading straight back to the mainland that afternoon, but I was curious to follow Tennent's route to the end of the peninsula to pay a quick visit to Kalpitiya, the small town at its northernmost point that looked out into the Gulf of Mannar.

The quiet peninsula road headed further into the sea past herds of dwarfishly small goats with long, silky brown ears, trotting along the side of the road. Each goat had three pieces of wood nailed together in a triangle around its neck to prevent it from squeezing through the fences of the plantations that teetered on the edge of the land by the lagoon. Peculiar-looking miniature donkeys, with mottled coats and large tufts of fur in between their ears like heavy fringes, were also standing in the road, tugging at the grass that grew in the sand. Stuck out in the ocean, isolated from the mainland, the Kalpitiya donkeys had presumably become inbred over the centuries and morphed into this strange phenotype. As the peninsula ran out into the sea, the land seemed to disintegrate into a marshy patchwork of swamps and lagoons, on which small islands of land and little thatched huts floated. Narrow raised causeways ran between each patch of land, just wide enough for the old men in their floppy straw hats to cycle their bicycles along.

When Tennent came to Kalpitiya in 1848, it was famous for the shark fins, which the local fishermen caught and sold to Chinese traders, and for the turtles that he saw being caught in small penned enclosures in the shallows. Tennent also commented on the abundance of dried fish in Kalpitiya and, as my tuk-tuk drove down the narrow streets of the ramshackle town, many shop owners were still drying small silver fish on the pavements in front of their doors. When the Dutch had managed to capture the bay and evicted the Portuguese in the seventeenth century, they built a small fort, and the ramparts were still standing in the middle of the town, where they had been commandeered by the Sri Lankan army during the war. The remains were a grim reminder of the violence that had subsided only a year before; coils of razor wire and daubs of khaki paint adorned the walls, and soldiers in military uniform were still sitting in small watchtowers, monitoring the waters of the harbour.

Neither Tennent nor I seemed to find very much in Kalpitiya, so I headed to the bus station – a small piece of bare land on which a couple of old rusting buses stood, with handwritten, Sinhala, cardboard signs taped to the top of their cracked windscreens. A few old men wearing ragged shirts and rubber sandals lay in the shade of a tree on a pile of old bus tyres, smoking and looking up at the sky. The bus back to the mainland was already half-full and, as I settled myself by a window, everyone already sitting on the bus turned around to stare at me for a few moments, before simply ignoring me again and turning back to look vacantly out of the windows. I don't know how long we waited, but the bus eventually trundled its way back along the peninsula road and onto the mainland. It was a slow journey, punctuated by stops for small groups of women who were standing by the side of the road, their saris fluttering about them in the sea breeze as they leaned out into the road, waggling their arms to flag down the bus.

I changed buses at the junction with the main road and boarded an almost empty bus that was heading for the fishing town of Chilaw, 54 km south along the coast towards Colombo. Tennent had passed through Chilaw on his way back to Colombo from the ancient cities, but had not stayed there for long and simply passed it off as 'a place of no great antiquity'. However, I was intrigued by a newspaper article I'd read about the large Hindu temple just outside the town in the small village of Munneswaram.

The Munneswaram temple had been the source of controversy for several years, because the swamis continued to sacrifice animals at the altar of the Hindu goddess Kali – who is believed to have landed at the site when she came to the island from India. Every September, for many years, a large festival took place in the temple, during which over 1,000 chickens and goats were sacrificed at the altar of the fearsome black goddess. The Sri Lankan newspaper, *The Sunday Times*, sent an undercover reporter, who was told by a resident swami that, although it was not widely known, animals were also sacrificed to Kali throughout the year; you could either bring along your own animal or buy a goat for $15 from the temple swamis, or if you weren't feeling quite so flush, $2 for a chicken. The temple would retain the head of the animal and the rest of the flesh could be returned to the person who had ordered the sacrifice, to be eaten when they returned home.

The temple had hit the headlines again during the September festival in 2011, when one of the country's most notorious government ministers, Mervyn Silva, stormed in during the ceremony, and proceeded to round up any animals he could find and load them into a truck, announcing that the temple was in violation of the country's animal rights laws. Silva had frequently appeared in the headlines whilst I lived in Sri Lanka, usually for various bouts of bizarre and thuggish behaviour. A year earlier, he had tied a government official to a mango tree in public as a punishment for not attending a dengue fever workshop and had then invited the press along to witness the official's humiliation. He also liked to harass journalists, and a few years earlier had stormed into the offices of Sri Lanka's national television network and assaulted the news director. When he was later appointed the deputy minister of mass media and information, the organisation Reporters Without

Borders commented that it was like asking 'an arsonist to put out fires'.

When the bus drew into the bus station in Chilaw it was late afternoon and a tropical storm had begun to unfurl over the ocean. Dark clouds hung heavily over the town, and men and women huddled together under umbrellas and hopped between the potholes in the tarmac that had turned into large puddles in the downpour. The hawkers were trying to hitch their floor-length sarongs above their knees, whilst balancing their baskets of lentil wadis on their heads, and the packs of mangy dogs looked even more miserable than usual as they tried to shelter under the stationary buses. I made a dash for a line of tuk-tuks waiting on the side of the road and asked to be taken to the Munneswaram temple. I sat myself in the middle of the back seat, to try to avoid the water that was splashing up from puddles in the road, and we set off down a narrow country lane that wound through pale-green, sodden fields.

In comparison with the calm, open spaces and the simple elegance of the white Buddhist dagobas, the Hindu temples in Sri Lanka are dark, enigmatic and forbidding. Much of the Buddhist's devotion takes place under the branches of the bodhi tree in the courtyards and the doors to the temples are thrown open to the outside world; the acts of devotion are soothing and peaceful, and the smiling figure of the meditating Buddha exudes an aura of serenity. The Hindu temples, however, are hidden behind high, red-and-white striped walls and all that can be seen from the outside is the pyramidal roof that rises into the sky, covered in hundreds of brightly coloured carvings of the Hindu gods, who seem to be fighting each other for space. All that can be seen of the dark interiors are the flames and smoke of a ceremonial fire, burning somewhere deep inside.

Outside the Munneswaram temple a few cows were standing despondently in the puddles, licking the mud and looking sadly at the cold grey sky. I took off my shoes and tucked them under my arm as I walked through the high doorway. Before I could get inside and out of the rain, an emaciated man with ash smeared on his forehead ran at me brandishing a stick and started to shout at me in Tamil. Realising that it was the shoes under my arm that were upsetting him, I took them back outside and placed them on a rock to get soaked in the rain.

The inside of the temple was warm and the air smelled of incense. The evening puja was taking place and a fat shirtless musician in a sarong was playing a long reed instrument that looked like a large oboe. He was seated on the floor on a cushion, his thick legs barely managing to cross in front of the rolls of his torso on which his instrument rested. Another musician was seated on the floor next to him beating an eastern rhythm on a drum. The music was amplified through speakers hidden around the temple, and the reedy wailing and fast drumbeats reverberated around the stone walls. I followed a group of women dressed in brightly coloured Indian silk saris, carrying the usual baskets of fruit and incense sticks, which they placed in front of small dark statues of the Hindu gods, housed inside deep stone cases built into the temple walls. Small pieces of embroidered silk that looked like they had been torn from the borders of saris had been tied around the necks and limbs of the figures. In between these small shrines sat huge plaster statues of the Hindu deities, several feet taller than a man. Although they were made of the same plasterwork, and painted in the same gaudy high-gloss paint as many of the Sri Lankan Buddhas, these gods were not smiling placidly, but were engaged in violent, aggressive activities. A bright-blue Vishnu in the form of the lion-headed Narasimha sat with his hands buried in the entrails of the demon Hiranyakashipu. An eight-armed Kali rode a lion as she thrust a spear into a buffalo, whilst another avatar of Vishnu reclined on a bed of hooded cobras.

In the middle of the temple, enclosed by walls on three sides, was the small inner shrine to Shiva. A small bell began to ring and the devotees all started to push their way in. I had never felt completely comfortable intruding on other people's worship and already felt a bit like an unwelcome spectator. I hung around in the shadows outside the inner shrine and watched whilst five bare-chested swamis in long sarongs began to perform the puja. One elderly swami was sitting cross-legged on the floor, chanting from a small book that rested on his lap. A large oil lamp was lit by the other swamis, who waved it in a circular motion around a lingam of Shiva that stood on a small stage, framed by velvet curtains. The swamis placed garlands of flowers around Shiva's neck and started to wash the statue by pouring water over it from above. Suddenly the velvet curtains were drawn, shielding the swamis and Shiva from the view of the devotees, and all that could be seen through the chink in the fabric was the circular movement of the swamis and clouds of smoke.

I spent the night in a small hotel far away from the town, in a little fishing village, surrounded by miles of empty sand. Thorny xerophytic plants and small clumps of prickly pear grew along the beach, where the village children played fully clothed in the surf. The fishermen lived in small, one-roomed houses that had been painted in bright shades of blue and pink, and the older generation were sitting outside their open doors on plastic chairs, talking to their neighbours as they looked out to sea. As peaceful as it was, the little village, so far away from the capital and so far off the tourist trail, seemed like a strange place to build a hotel. The place was owned by a Swedish couple in their sixties, who had been development workers on the island for over a decade. The husband, Ingemar, was tall and broad, with white hair and a gentle, slightly troubled face. Although he had lived in the tropics for decades, he still chose to wear black suit trousers and closed, leather shoes, which looked absurdly out of place as he stood on the edge of the hotel's small swimming pool, inspecting the clarity of the water. I was the only guest and I asked him why he had chosen to build his hotel so out of the way.

'I have travelled all over the island,' he explained, as he turned his back to the pool and sat down on a sun lounger, 'but Chilaw is the only town I have found where the Buddhists, the Hindus, the Muslims and the Christians all live happily together without any kind of tension.' He pointed along the coastline, north, to where the centre of the town lay. 'The town has also started to develop a lot in the past few years. Many families from Chilaw sent their children to work in Italy and now all the money they earned is flowing back into the town. It has its problems too though,' he said with a sigh, looking beyond the garden towards the children playing on the beach.

'Such as?' I asked.

'Well, when you drove down the track by the sea this afternoon, how many children did you see playing in the trees?' he asked.

'Lots,' I said, 'but they all seemed quite happy.'

'Yes, but they weren't at school,' he replied. He led me to the wire fence that bordered his garden and looked out with a furrowed brow over the beach were the village children were playing. 'One of the men who lives in a house farther along the beach is the local priest,' he said. 'He's also the headmaster of the village school. He says that he has difficulty persuading the parents to send their children to school as they would rather send them out to work and earn money for the household. It's especially bad for the girls.' It was a familiar story in many developing countries. As Ingemar continued to look out at the sea, he talked about the years he had spent on the island, most of which had been during the war, trying to help the islanders to develop economically. He spoke of the Sri Lankans he had worked with, with the familiar tension of respectful sympathy coupled with utter frustration that I had seen in many of the long-term expats, who seemed willingly but hopelessly marooned on the island. I asked him if he thought he and his wife would stay in their hotel by the sea for the rest of their lives, but he shook his head as he looked along the beach to the elderly men slumped on their plastic chairs outside their wooden houses. 'This is not a good place to grow old.'

The next morning I boarded a bus for the last time and stood by the open doorway as it followed the coastal road back to Colombo. It was a Sunday and the doors of the baby-pink catholic churches were thrown open to the congregations who were spilling out onto the front steps. Prim old ladies sat in the pews wearing white lace veils, which hung down over their shoulders, whilst the latecomers, anticipating that the pews would already be full, carried kitchen chairs and pieces of garden furniture through the gates, to set up at the back of the church. On my lap sat Tennent's book, which had been my travelling companion for almost a year. The pages were now thumbed and dog-eared, and the once-white borders that framed the wonky type set were covered in ballpoint scrawling. Even after a year of reading his words almost every day, as I looked through the last few paragraphs of the book I was still in awe of his attention to detail and persistent desire to understand and record every aspect of the island.

From Chilaw to Negombo the road passes through almost continuous coco-nut plantations; and in the shade of the palms one hears the creaking of primitive mills, which, from time immemorial, have been used by the natives for expressing oil. Under a large banyan tree on the side of the highway, near the village of Madampe, is an altar to Tannavilla Abhaya, a chief who, in the fourteenth century, ruled over the district, under the title of King of Madampe. He died by his own hand; but, in gratitude for his services, his subjects celebrated his apotheosis, and the people now worship him as a tutelary deity of the place.

But how had he found all this out? For me, gaining factual information had not been too difficult. I had access to comprehensive history books written by prominent Sri Lankan historians, articles and studies by contemporary anthropologists and Sri Lankan friends and colleagues, who spoke (as many Sri Lankans do) fluent English and had shared their stories with me. When Tennent arrived on Ceylon in 1845, as he stated in his introduction, very little had been written about the island for hundreds of years. How did he have the patience and perseverance to trawl through the ancient and classical texts to unearth 1,094 pages of lost historic minutiae and find the chapters of facts and figures about Ceylon's botany and geology?

But when I read his last pages again I could see why. For Tennent, his work had been nothing less than a labour of love. From his first description of the view from the ship, to his final description of the road back to Colombo, his deep affection for the island and his admiration of Ceylon's natural beauty and fascinating society was undiminished.

For me, my journey had also deepened my love and respect for the island and, I hoped, my understanding. Two years after my arrival in Sri Lanka, its simplistic image as a former warzone and a tropical paradise remains. Tourists are now arriving in droves to soak up the sun in the growing number of hotels in the reopened coastal resorts, whilst the UN continues to investigate the final stages of the war, and an increasing number of books and documentaries about human rights abuses on the island are released – and rightly so. But what had fascinated me most about Sri Lanka was the stories, which rarely make the dismal, pessimistic headlines of the international media, of the staggering resilience of the survivors and witnesses of the civil war and the tsunami, who had experienced life in a way I could not comprehend, yet had picked themselves up and learnt to live and even love life again.

Like Tennent, I too had been fascinated by the spirituality that pervaded the island and surprised by the grip that the mystics held. Whilst, I had to admit, I still wondered if faith in the prediction of astrologers encouraged people to relinquish responsibility for their own decisions and was partly responsible for the slow development of the island, my encounter with the ola readers had given me some sympathy for the security and relief these predictions could bring. I also shared with Tennent his captivation by Sri Lanka's diverse and natural beauty, and in my new home in a different continent thousands of miles away, I wake up every morning and miss the frangipani flowers from the streets of Cinnamon Gardens and the eternal sunshine of the blue Sri Lankan sky.

Tennent's trip to Negombo, and in fact his whole book, came to an abrupt end on 30 July 1848 when an orderly from the government intercepted him in Negombo with the news that a rebellion had broken out in the central provinces. A king had been crowned in the temple at Dambulla and was on a march towards Kandy with an armed force of supporters. Tennent ordered his horses to be saddled immediately and left for Colombo early the next morning to meet with the governor.

To Tennent's surprise and sadness, he then left Ceylon for good in the winter of 1849. He was asked to sail to London by the governor of Ceylon, Lord Torrington, to give evidence at a parliamentary enquiry into the conduct of the colonial administration on the island. During the course of the enquiry, it came to light that James Emerson Tennent had been bullied and persecuted from the moment he had arrived on the island by the jealous civil servants who had resented his appointment as the colonial secretary. Over the four years that he worked in Ceylon, attempts were made to damage his character, to discredit him professionally, and it seemed that his abusers were determined to run him out of the country at any cost. When the enquiry was over, Tennent was assured that parliament held him in high esteem and that his conduct on the island had been applauded. It was suggested however, that 'for his own comfort', given the enemies he had in the colony, it would be best if he did not return to Ceylon.

My journey finished where it had begun, in the bus station at the heart of the Pettah in Colombo. As the tuk-tuk drove me back to my house in Cinnamon Gardens, we passed a group of men putting the finishing touches to a rotating pavement display of wooden Buddhist monks, which had been constructed to celebrate Vesak, the biggest Poya of the year, commemorating the day of the full moon in May on which the Buddha was born, enlightened and died. The preparations continued for the rest of the week, as Buddhists all over the island set up food stalls and displays in the streets, and hung paper lanterns along the roadsides and outside their doors. The night of Vesak was clear and still as the people of Colombo gathered on the pavements under the light of a pale, milky moon to watch the perahera organised by the local temple. Sinewy young men in white billowing trousers led the procession, cracking long whips along the pavements to clear the way. Shirtless boys, dripping in perspiration, staggered behind them carrying flaming coconut-oil lanterns. Elephants followed, dressed in capes of gilded, sequined fabric and studded with fairy lights, powered by electrical generators, which were pushed along behind them in wheelbarrows. The new and innovative Budget Taxi tuk-tuk company, which had caused a recent stir by introducing regulated meters in their three-wheelers, had entered a convoy of their newest vehicles, with large plastic lotus flowers fixed to their roofs. A small baby elephant, not yet trained in the discipline of the perahera, got overexcited and scampered off-piste, charging head first towards a lamppost. The people watching from the pavement screamed, ran out of the way and collapsed into laughter as the elephant was rescued and pushed back into the procession. I laughed too and looked up at the moon hanging silently above the city, as two small specks of light from the wings of an aircraft leaving the international airport began to make their way across the dark sky. My time on the island was drawing to a close too and, as I began to contemplate my imminent departure, I realised that at the end of my travels, Sri Lanka now felt like home.

I flew back to the UK only a matter of weeks after having completed Tennent's journey, and as I was loading my suitcases into a taxi outside my house in Colombo, Ajith raced around the corner in his tuk-tuk to say goodbye. He no longer drove his tuk-tuk during the day and had been offered an office job in the city whilst he waited for his music career to take off. He presented me with a copy of his first CD, which had a picture of his beaming face on the cover, Photoshopped to look about twenty years younger. Several of the tracks had been played on the local radio stations and he told me that it was also possible to download one of his songs as a ringtone.

When my Sri Lankan landlord and his wife were standing in my kitchen, going through the house inventory before my departure, they spotted the bottle of Pranajeewa Miracle Oil that I had not persevered with, gathering dust on my windowsill. 'Have you been taking it?' my landlord enquired with surprise. 'Who prescribed it to you?

'Oh that woman wasn't the doctor,' explained his wife, when I described the odd exchange I had had with the lady in the purple spandex top. 'I thought she was just an assistant and I'm surprised she is giving prescriptions. The real doctor is an older gentleman, who is very highly qualified. You should have persevered with the Pranajeewa oil, I took it three years ago when I had severe problems with my liver and I have never had any trouble since.'

Writing this from my new home in Bogotá, Colombia, I can confirm the predictions of the ola readers that I would have the opportunity to travel to many countries around the globe, but as I am not forecast to enter the auspicious period for my marriage for another couple of years, the predictions relating to my future spouse remain to be tested. If, however, your name is Stanley, you were born in 1981, you are a PhD scientist and you live near to a stream or a prominent religious place, please do give me a call.

FURTHER READING

Books

Alexander, Denis R.; Number, Roland L. *Biology and Ideology from Descartes to Darwin* (2010, University of Chicago Press)

Bond, George D. *The Buddhist Revival in Sri Lanka: Religious Tradition, Reinterpretation and Response* (1992, Motilal Banarsidass)

Gunaratne, Herman *The Plantation Raj* (2012, Sri Serendipity Publishing House)

Gunaratne, Herman *The Suicide Club* (2010, Sri Serendipity Publishing House)

> These works by Herman Gunaratne gave me an invaluable insight into both life on the tea estates and their nationalisation. They were also the source of much of the information about the politics of the tea industry in Chapter 5.

Hussein, Asiff *The Lion and the Sword: An Ethnological Study of Sri Lanka* (2005, A J Prints)

Hussein, Asiff *Zeylanica: A Study of the Peoples and Languages of Sri Lanka* (2009, Neptune Publications)

Knox, Robert *An Historical Relation of the Island of Ceylon in the East Indies* (1681, Royal Society; reprint 2011, Echo Library)

Lynch, Caitrin *Juki Girls, Good Girls: Gender and Cultural Politics in Sri Lanka's Global Garment Industry* (2007, ILR Press)

Masaeus-Higgins, Marie *Poya Days* (1925, Maha-Jana Press, Colombo; reprint 2000, Asian Educational Services)

Roberts, Norah *Galle: As Quiet As Asleep* (1993, Vijitha Yapa Publications)

Seligmann, C. G.; Seligmann B. Z *The Veddas* (1911, Cambridge University Press)

Skeen, William *Adam's Peak: Legendary traditional and historical notices of the Samanala and Sri-Páda with a descriptive account of the pilgrims' route from Colombo to the sacred foot-print* (1870, W. L. H Skeen & Co; reprint 1997, Asian Educational Services)

Tambiah, S. J. *Polyandry in Ceylon with Special Reference to the Laggala Region* (2011, Social Sciences Association)

Tennent, Sir James Emerson *Ceylon: An Account of the Island, Physical, Historical and Topographical* (1860, Longman, Green, Longman and Roberts)

Thera, Mahanama *The Mahavamsa: The Great Chronicle of Sri Lanka* (2005, Vijitha Yapa Publications)

Weatherstone, John *The Pioneers: Early British Tea and Coffee planters and their way of Life, 1825-1900* (1986, Quiller Press)

Weiss, Gordon *The Cage: The Fight for Sri Lanka and the Last Days of the Tamil Tigers* (2011, Bodley Head)

This work by UN spokesperson, Gordon Weiss, was the source of much of the information in Chapter 6 relating to the history of the Sri Lankan conflict, its final stages, and the role of Dharmapala and Olcott in the evolution of Buddhism on the island.

Yogasundram, Nath *A Comprehensive History of Sri Lanka from Prehistoric Times to the Present* (2010, Vijitha Yapa Publications)

Papers and Articles

Emerson Tennent Papers, Public Record Office of Northern Ireland (www.proni.gov.uk)

Mervyn ties man to tree (3 August 2010, www.dailymirror.lk)

Mervyn storms Munneswaram festival, stops 'sacrifice' ritual (18 September 2011, www.sundaytimes.lk)

Outlook (9 February 2012, BBC World Service) – a section of this programme followed the journey of a BBC reporter who spent time with the Veddas of Sri Lanka in 2012

Planetary changes driving political leaders overseas (10 June 2012, www.sundaytimes.lk)

Prabhakaran (21 May 2009, *The Economist*)

Report of the Secretary-General's Panel of Experts on Accountability in Sri Lanka, Executive Summary (www.un.org)

Sri Lankan mosque forced to abandon prayers by protesters (20 April 2012, www.bbc.co.uk)

Sri Lankan Muslims Strike over Dambulla mosque (26 April 2012, www.bbc.co.uk)

Have you enjoyed this book?
If so, why not write a review on your favourite website?

If you're interested in finding out more about our books,
find us on Facebook at **Summersdale Publishers** and
follow us on Twitter at **@Summersdale**.

Thanks very much for buying this Summersdale book.

www.summersdale.com